Contents

*

CAMBRIDGE TEXTS IN MODERN POLITICS

Tokugawa political writings

The modern political consciousness of Japan cannot be understood without reference to the history of the Tokugawa period, the era between 1600 and 1868 that preceded Japan's modern transformation. In this volume Tetsuo Najita introduces the ideas of the leading political thinker of the period, Ogyū Sorai (1666–1728), a pivotal figure in laying the conceptual foundations of Japan's modernization. Two of Sorai's texts are provided here in translation – the *Bendō* and the *Benmei* (as well as a short piece by one of his students) – presenting Sorai's basic thoughts about history and the ethical purposes of politics and revealing the richness of the philosophical legacy of eighteenth-century Japan, a legacy which cannot be seen through the perspective of "Westernization." His ideas reveal a vision of human diversity and individual virtue which can be viewed in comparative perspective, as well as an insight into the history and politics of Japan. The texts are accompanied by a chronology of Sorai's life, a glossary, a guide to persons mentioned in the text, and a guide to further reading, as well as Professor Najita's introduction, which puts Sorai's work into philosophical and historical context.

TETSUO NAJITA is Robert S. Ingersoll Distinguished Service Professor of Japanese History at the University of Chicago. His books include *Hara Kei in the Politics of Compromise*, *The Intellectual Foundations of Modern Japanese Politics*, and *Visions of Virtue in Tokugawa Japan*.

CAMBRIDGE TEXTS IN MODERN POLITICS

EDITORS

John Dunn

King's College, Cambridge

Geoffrey Hawthorn

Faculty of Social and Political Science, University of Cambridge

Political aspirations in the twentieth century are usually expressed in the political languages of Western Europe and North America. In Latin America, Africa and Asia, however, in the movements of "national liberation" from colonial rule, in the justification of new states, and in the opposition to such states, these aspirations have also drawn on other traditions, and invented new ones. Outside the West, the languages of modern politics and the ideas these languages embody are nowhere simple, and almost nowhere derivatively Western. But for students and scholars access to the relevant texts is not easy.

Cambridge Texts in Modern Politics are intended to remedy this by providing editions in English (often for the first time) of texts which have been important in the politics of Latin America, Africa and Asia in the later nineteenth century and twentieth century, and which will continue in importance into the twenty-first. The editions will be authoritative and accessible, and can be used with confidence by students and teachers as a source. Each text will be edited by a specialist in the history and politics of the area concerned, whose introduction will explain its context, provenance and significance. Readers will also be provided with a chronology of events, brief biographies of relevant individuals, and guides to further reading.

Preface

*

An understanding of modern political consciousness in Japan is inconceivable without reference to the intellectual history of the Tokugawa period, the era between 1600 and 1868 that preceded Japan's modern transformation. Even as they revolted against their feudal past, modern intellectuals were inextricably drawn to Tokugawa Confucian thought, a conceptual construct that defies simple and stylized characterization.

One of the pivotal referent figures in this history is Ogyū Sorai (1666–1728). Sorai's historicism claimed that all sure knowledge must be sought and discovered not in accordance with cosmological norms but within history itself, and, most importantly, in the "beginnings" of history when the rationale for social organization was first articulated. For Sorai, the original purpose was to distribute justice in an orderly and precise manner and to nourish diverse human virtues. This intent, therefore, ought to inform political analysis and reform over the course of all subsequent history. Two of Sorai's texts are provided here in translation: One is the *Bendō* that focuses on the meaning of the Way; the other, the *Benmei* on names. A short piece by Sorai's student, Dazai Shundai (1680–1747), has been added to suggest the influence of Sorai's thinking. My introductory essay will serve to situate Sorai as a thinker and as a significant intellectual resource for modern and contemporary Japan.

To maintain some "distance" for Sorai's Tokugawa texts from contemporary East Asian civilizations, I have used the "old-fashioned" Wade-Giles system of romanizing Chinese names and terms.

The reader should not expect these texts to be expositions of the history of Chinese thought. They are not that at all. They are about whether truthful knowledge could be controlled in order to govern the Tokugawa realm. They are, in short, about a discourse on knowledge and epistemology in the context of the non-centralized Baku-Han system of governance in eighteenth-century Japan and not about the actualities of centralized imperial regimes on the Asian continent. Historical consciousness in this respect has less to do with empirical verification of the evolution of Chinese thought than it does with the selective use of the Chinese past for polemical purposes in the Tokugawa present. In this regard, I might call the reader's attention to the macro-chronology that Sorai has in mind in the introductory passages of the *Benmei*. Readers curious about the development of political and ethical thought within the context of Chinese history itself may wish to consult some of the works listed in the guide to further reading.

By Sorai's time, the Tokugawa regime had already been in place for 100 years. The Tokugawa Bakufu was located in the central, eastern region, anchored by Edo (today's Tokyo), a city then of over one million people. The Bakufu, in turn, was joined by charters of reciprocal obligations to some 250 regional centers or domains called han, each with its own castle town with populations ranging between 10,000 and 100,000, comprised of aristocratic samurai and merchant townsmen in roughly equal proportions. While the charters were weighted in favor of the Tokugawa Bakufu to insure its hegemonic authority, they also allowed the regional domains considerable autonomy in administering such matters as taxation and education. The long journeys taken by the aristocratic retinues to and from Edo, to confirm their pledges of loyalty to the Bakufu, fueled a commercial revolution that reached a high tide in what is called the Genroku period (1688–1704). Rice collected as tax was converted to silver in Osaka and gold in Edo to finance this enforced movement of the aristocracy. Domainal governments became indebted to merchant houses and the rice taxes were harsh on the peasantry, causing hardships that Sorai himself witnessed first hand. Famines and rebellions recurred periodically in the countryside. These took an especially severe turn during the Kyōhō period (1716–35), at about the time that Sorai and his student Dazai Shundai were composing their treatises; and they recurred thereafter in the Tenmei (1781–89), Tenpō (1830–44), and Keio (1865–68). The year 1868 marked the revolutionary Meiji Ishin that brought the

Tokugawa regime to its end with its military defeat at the hands of rebellious regional domains in western Japan. The construction of the modern industrial order followed thereafter.

In this troubled history, Sorai may be seen as the first "crisis thinker." Through textual criticism he called into question and then discredited the claim made by philosophers of the time that the Tokugawa Baku-Han order was fixed into place by cosmological reference and hence could be projected into the future as a continuing reality. This for him was to believe in a fantasy, no different from relying on religious faith, for no political system was sacrosanct and guaranteed by a metaphysical identity. The promise by the Tokugawa regime to provide "The Great Peace Under Heaven" – Tenka Taihei – had to be realized by addressing concrete social ills in the present with policies guided by the original political ethic of benevolence and the epistemology of righteousness, which involved the accurate and measurable exercise of political economy. To Sorai this would mean, for example, returning the aristocracy to the soil as agricultural labor; and to Shundai, increasing monetary wealth for the polity through trade. Both prescriptions were potentially corrosive to the order, and were deeply entwined with the historicity of crisis and a reflective sense of uncertainty about the competency of the regime.

Sorai was born in Edo into a family of physicians. His father Hōan was a personal physician to one of the Tokugawas, Tsunayoshi. Sorai himself studied as a youth to become a physician, but finding this unsuitable to his "virtue," turned to a career as a Confucian scholar. He first immersed himself in the study of Neo-Confucian philosophy and steadily developed a skepticism toward it because of its speculative cosmological reasoning which reminded him of Buddhist theology. Around 1690, Sorai began reading the works of Itō Jinsai which confirmed his view that Neo-Confucian philosophy was unreliable. In 1704, Sorai wrote to Jinsai to begin a scholarly dialogue. Although Jinsai, already in poor health, did not reply, Sorai maintained the view that Jinsai's thinking was flawed. Sorai believed Jinsai focused his attention on the moral practices of all human beings as an inevitable extension of individual natural energy and potential. To Sorai this was no different from the view that argued that all human beings were alike, and basically good, which failed to address the issue as to why there was governance, why some governed others within a large grouping of disparate individuals. Scattered throughout the translations, therefore, are comments by Sorai directed against Jinsai, to whom he owed a great deal, but whose thinking he believed to be inadequate.

Sorai's ambition was to advise the Tokugawa regime and he served briefly between 1696 and 1709 as an adviser to one of the shogunal ministers, Yanagisawa Yoshiyasu; but devoted the rest of his life primarily to teaching and writing at his personal academy in Edo, the Ken'en. He gained enormous fame during his day, and he attracted outstanding students to his academy. By all accounts of friend and foe alike, the intellectual world was never the same after Sorai. His ideas continue to reverberate in the discourse on politics in modern Japan.

Acknowledgements

*

The primary intent of this volume is to render and make accessible the ideas of Ogyū Sorai to non-specialists in East Asian studies, and to students and scholars of intellectual history and political thought to whom questions of comparative and theoretical interest may be raised by a reading of him. Accordingly, the translations have not been accompanied by scholarly glosses that might otherwise be expected.

The task of translating Sorai is a formidable one, often involving something of an intellectual brawl in reading and translation seminars and workshops. These translations are the products of such sessions and hence are results of the teaching and training process; and, while I assume responsibility for them, they are not mine alone. Indeed, I was often at the receiving end of the instructional process. I am deeply grateful to Shigeki Niiyama who first introduced me to reading Ogyū Sorai, and the *Bendō* in particular, in the late 1970s. In more recent years, I have benefited from the readings made by Jan Furlong and Kazuhisa Yoshida, and, in preparing the *Benmei* in the final stages, the contributions on meaning and expression made by Michael Eastwood, Katsuya Hirano, and Yasuko Sato. Yuen-ching Lee provided valuable assistance on Chinese terms and names. Elinor Najita supplied editorial interventions at strategic turns. I am grateful to each of these individuals.

In the pages that follow, I have relied on the convention utilized in Tokugawa times of referring to thinkers by their adopted scholarly, rather than family, names. Thus, for example, Sorai and Jinsai, rather than Ogyū and Itō.

These were names that identified them as independent scholars and teachers of note and, out of respect, no other scholar used them.

Interpreting the historicism
of Ogyū Sorai

*

What doubt, or any other cognitive activity, always ... brings us back to is
the realization that some sort of probably pretty rich and complicated
thing is being cognized. We never in cognition can sink lower than that.[1]

These words seem appropriate when seeking to cognize the conceptual
properties of Ogyū Sorai's historicism. A complex scholar of Tokugawa
political ethics, Sorai presents us with texts that are "pretty rich and
complicated," and whose full significances have yet to be determined.
Although there may be, in the conceptual characterization that follows,
historical similarity, analogy, significant resemblance, and sympathetic
perspectives with historicist theorists in other societies, it is not my purpose here to show that Sorai along with other historicists thought similar
thoughts, reached identical conclusions, followed the same logic of
reason. My main purpose is to uncover Sorai's analytical "preoccupa-
tion," problem solving and explanatory activities, which, in the wording
of Sheldon Wolin in his provocative work on "politics and vision," are
also "creative" and "radical." This means looking for significant intellectual repetitions, arrangements and epistemological constructions with
which Sorai perceived, analyzed, and understood things and somehow
grasping through these structures of reasoning a comprehensive intellectual pattern and order in his thinking.[2]

Largely through the famous essays of Masao Maruyama that he wrote
in the early 1940s and which have been translated into English as *Studies*

---

1 Stephen C. Pepper, *World Hypothesis* (Berkeley: University of California Press, 1970),
  p. 319.
2 Sheldon S. Wolin, *Politics and Vision* (Boston: Little, Brown and Company, 1960).

xiv * *Editor's introduction*

in the Intellectual History of Tokugawa Japan, Sorai is recognized as a pivotal figure in the shaping of Japan's modern political consciousness and, especially, as one who provides the conceptual handle with which to understand the modernization of Japan. This historical process is widely viewed in Japan as an extension of the political philosophy of Ogyū Sorai.[3] Maruyama emphasized in Sorai the ideas of absolute agency, and of history being rendered separate from nature as a moral order and thus being artificial and fabricated. Maruyama's construction was enormously influential in Japan's post-war reconceptualization of its modernization and of the potential in creating or "fabricating" a democratic future. Despite Maruyama's powerfully conceived argument, however, the full significance of Sorai's vision of society and history remains implicit and is not likely to have a conclusive resolution. While the translations presented in this volume are not intended to displace Maruyama's construction, they suggest an alternative reading of Sorai's texts.

A controversial thinker in his own day and throughout the Tokugawa period, Sorai was the object of much polemical debate, and he continues to retain a controversial and vital place in the ongoing discussions and debates on political philosophy in modern Japan.[4]

Sorai's thought abounds with intellectual riches and is not easily given to narrow reductions. Articulated best in such concise treaties as *Bendō*,

3 Masao Maruyama, *Studies in the Intellectual History of Tokugawa Japan* (Tokyo: Tokyo University Press, 1974) trans. Mikiso Hane from *Nihon seiji shisōshi kenkyū* (Tokyo: Tokyo daigaku shuppankai, 1952).

4 Besides Maruyama's work, other works in English include: Kojiro Yoshikawa, *Jinsai, Sorai, Norinaga* (Tokyo: Toho Gakkai, 1983); J. R. McEwan, *The Political Writings of Ogyū Sorai* (Cambridge: Cambridge University Press, 1962); Naoki Sakai, *Voices of the Past. The Status of Language in Eighteenth-Century Japanese Discourse* (Ithaca: Cornell University Press, 1991); and my *Visions of Virtue in Tokugawa Japan* 1987; (Honolulu: University of Hawaii Press, 1977). Other translations include: Olof G. Lidin, *Ogyū Sorai, Distinguishing the Way* (Tokyo: Sophia University, 1970); Richard Minear, "Ogyū Sorai's Instructions for Students: A Translation and Commentary", *Harvard Journal of Asiatic Studies* (7:1977), pp. 5–81); and more recently, Sorai's *Tōmonsho*, an explanation of his ideas in a letter, by Samuel Hideo Yamashita, *Master Sorai's Responsals* (Honolulu: University of Hawaii Press, 1994). For a recent critique of Maruyama and the "event" based on Sorai, see Koyasu Nobukuni, *Jiken to shite no Soraigaku* (Tokyo: Seido sha, 1990).

"A Discourse on the Way," *Gakusoku*, "Principles of Learning," and, more fully, in *Benmei*," A Clarification of Names," *Tōmonsho*, "A Collection of Questions and Answers," and *Seidan*, "Prescriptions on Political Economy", Sorai left an intellectual legacy often rendered in deliberately difficult and complex language and allusions that seem at times to resemble a conceptual puzzle. One might well approach this puzzle, somewhat in the manner suggested by Harry Wolfson in searching for the keys into Spinoza's universe of reason, which is to read and pull the texts apart and rearrange them piece by piece by their relationship to each other.[5]

Ogyū Sorai's political philosophy was directed against a theory widely held among political thinkers that just or "righteous" action (*gi*) was the inevitable extension of inner virtue. This virtue was theorized to be innate and universal among human beings and its potential could be realized through disciplined introspection (*kei*). Sorai believed this theory of action was idealistic and fundamentally flawed because it was subjective and speculative. Empirical observation revealed inner virtue to be variable and diverse among human beings and, therefore, logically unreliable as a basis for trustworthy action in the public realm. Sorai's historicism constitutes a relentless polemic to establish an alternative basis for political action, one that would give human diversity its necessary due, and which would also establish firm ethical norms identified with history when it was first created, and thus outside of the immediate historical and social context. Sorai believed the original intent of historical creation needed to be clarified before proposing solutions to social ills through precise and righteous action. His rejection of human identity and similitude in terms of virtue, and of the metaphysics that sustained this view, informs the entirety of his elaborate historicism and political ethics.

Sorai's philosophy is framed within a polarity, with Heaven's Way, or simply Heaven, as a "transphenomenal imperative" (*Tenmei*) on the one

5 Harry Austryn Wolfson, *The Philosophy of Spinoza. Unfolding the Latent Processes of His Reasoning* (Cambridge MA: Harvard University Press, 1934).

hand and, on the other, as the many concrete and immediately perceiv-able social things including artifacts and utensils (*mono*) first created and ordered in the Way of the Ancient Kings (*Sen'Ō no Michi*). Out of this essen-tially non-dialectical polarity emerges Sorai's comprehension of ethical "norm," bequeathed by the Ancient Kings at the beginning of historical time, as being at once vast and concrete. This framework is then used to project an open-ended vision of historical continuity, an expansive view of the future that theoretically allows no closure. Closely intertwined with this general view of history is a theory of language or, more properly speaking, of ancient philology, designed to provide empirical verification for his radical historicism.

Connecting the transphenomenal and the concrete, as noted, are the Ancient Kings who perceived the principle of "sociality" as an ethical imperative to provide order and well-being, and to foster mutual trust among human beings all of whom are endowed by Heaven with concrete and separate virtues, a theme whose importance will become evident as my essay proceeds. This framework allowed for structured political regu-larity but not at the exclusion or at the expense of the other human activ-ities. In characterizing the Ancient Kings as providing decisive and creative mediation for humankind with reference to an ethical impera-tive of sociality, Sorai's philosophy contained a decidedly "ethical" rather than a "legalistic" dimension for which critics in his day and schol-ars subsequently have not given him his due. The Ancient Kings, Sorai consistently observed, mediated to make the great Mandate of Heaven concrete, and, in so doing, left a theoretical legacy in which the compre-hensive Way would permanently serve as the limitless, open-ended norm that would integrate the tangible world of social history with its many differing human virtues.

The first important clue to reconstructing Sorai's overall conceptual design appears in the enigmatic opening lines of the *Bendō*.[6] The Way is a truly great and limitless thing – *dai naru mono* – he observes, beyond the scope of human description. Social and political artifacts, on the other

6 Yoshikawa Kojiro, Maruyama Masao et al. eds., *Nihon shisoshi taikei: Ogyū Sorai* (Tokyo: Iwanami Shoten, 1973), *Bendō*, #1, pp. 10–12.

hand, are readily detailed since they are based on clear and explicit "norms" (*jun;kyoku*) that render them internally coherent. Thus, while the Way as an abstraction cannot fully be fathomed, or controlled, since it is a limitless principle, nonetheless it is a concrete reality in human history, easily comprehensible, and never arbitrary. This allows human beings to make conscious and responsible ethical choices.

In a passage brilliantly insightful, if punishingly difficult to read, Sorai discussed this problem of "choice" as it related to the concept of the "mean." Sorai rejected the idea that the *Doctrine of the Mean* presented a convincing case that a "mean" could serve as a fixed and stable norm in the manner that the Way was thought of as being absolute. The "mean" was simply one among several prescriptions for *action* each of which contained debatable positions. What made it a "mean" was the consistent arrangement of thought based on a prior assumption that permitted humans to "choose" (*yue ni erabu*) it as against other forms of action. Sorai observed that the *Doctrine of the Mean* was actually a polemic directed against Lao Tzu who had said that Confucian teachings were artificial (*itsuwari*), fabricated rules and regulations that violated the way of nature where these rules did not exist. To counter this criticism, the author of the *Doctrine of the Mean*, Tzu Ssu, stressed the point that the rules and regulations in Confucianism were formulated out of a complete awareness of the natural human personality (*sei*) and, therefore, were not merely "artificial." Tzu Ssu, however, did not argue that the Confucian way of rules was consistent with the natural order as later scholars claimed. Nor did he say that the natural human personality was "good"; nor that "goodness" was identical with "truthfulness" as found in nature. Indeed, at no point did Tzu Ssu deny the artificial character of the Confucian concept of the "mean."

To Sorai, then, the "mean" was not identical with the Way; nor was it an intrinsic norm unto itself. It was a prescription for consistent action, which human beings consciously chose. Lao Tzu would not exercise the power of choice at all because it was contrary to nature to do so. Tzu Ssu's teaching, therefore, was clearly socially responsible; while Lao Tzu's was reckless and arbitrary. It is well to note, however, that although Sorai firmly rejected Lao Tzu's ideal of the natural community, he nonetheless retained in his overall theory Lao Tzu's insight that Confucian ideas were artificial constructs and not extensions of the natural order. Whereas Lao Tzu denounced them for this reason, Sorai endorsed them as creative constructions of the Sages.

In this exegesis, Sorai underscored some of the main epistemological points in his system of thought. To begin with, there is no such thing as a "mean" without a "norm." The "norm" in the Confucian way is not "natural" even though it does address itself to natural human needs. External nature cannot show the normative basis of ethics; neither can introspection as a route to rational cognition and choice, for in all likelihood it is an arbitrary subjectivism based on the passionate whims of the present. The decisive intellectual task is to identify the prior assumptive norm upon which predictable ethical choice is to be made. Norm cannot be subjective and, therefore, must be external to the self, but not in nature. Sorai concluded it must be uncovered in history, in a field of language and texts disengaged from the cosmos, and more specifically, as he repeated in all of his writings, at the beginning of history, when the Way of the Ancient Kings was first constructed. Without studying the Way of the Ancient Kings Sorai asked repeatedly through all his writings, what can human beings, including rulers, rely on as stable, cognizable, norm? The norm is in historical genesis, the epochal point in time that interconnects the transphenomenal imperative and the creation of concrete human society.

For reasons that will always remain beyond the full comprehension of humans, the Ancient Kings in a distant epoch in ancient China intuited the transphenomenal imperative of Heaven to establish peace and order among humankind. They received this imperative with their great yet limited intelligence and with deep reverence for the limitlessness of Heaven. Being human, the Ancient Kings admitted their failing, and never claimed to know Heaven. In their humility is to be located the source of their deep reverence for Heaven.[7]

7 Ibid., *Benmei*, p. 123.

Now this reverence carried special meaning for Sorai. The Ancient Kings, as humans, were bound to infuse in this historical vision of Benevolence an endless potential that was consistent with infinite Heaven itself, comprehensive and expansive beyond what the human mind could foretell. It was erroneous to believe, therefore, that an individual, through his own efforts, could understand Heaven. It followed that all scholarship and efforts at governing society must proceed from this sense of limited human intelligence before Heaven. None of the Kings nor any in the school of Confucius ever hinted that they could acquire a "self-knowledge" of Heaven and become "sages," an idea popularized by later Neo-Confucian scholars. Instead, they emphasized being respectful of one's mission in life as mandated by Heaven. Thus, when Confucius observed that in his fifties he understood his mission from Heaven (*Gojūnishite Tenmei o shiru*), he did not assume that he had acquired a self-knowledge of the meaning of Heaven, but simply that he had finally become aware of his personal mission in life in terms of what Heaven had endowed him with, meaning, in this specific instance, recording and compiling, as would an editor, the Way of the Ancient Kings for the benefit of all posterity.[8]

Following Heaven's imperative, the Kings organized human society by formulating rules and rituals and an orderly hierarchy to regulate behavior. And this was documented for posterity. Human time thus came into existence. This beginning "created" by human Sage Kings, distinguishable from the flow of natural time, is one of the crucial thematical propositions in Sorai. Society is not natural, he observes frequently. While the temple is made from cedar trees and the lunchbox is fashioned out of pliant willow branches, each relying on what the natural character of the material will allow, both temple and lunchbox are no longer natural but fabricated "utensils". Sorai's ethical intent behind his distinction between nature and history was to show the mystical and grand character of historical genesis as it intertwined with the flow of nature. Historical time could be created but once. The creative beginning could

8 Ibid., pp. 124–6.

not be duplicated, so that the ethical value embedded in that beginning would always be "external" to the self. But history once begun is endless. How great, therefore, was the Virtue of the Ancient Kings in providing creative mediation and bequeathing as their gift a constant point of reference for the rest of human history.

Exercising their special power of genius (*Sen'Ō no ken*), the Ancient Kings offered to humankind the principle that human beings in society ought never again live in the world of natural violence, but in peace and regulated harmony. This act to establish the principle of society is termed Benevolence (or humaneness) and is indeed the Great Virtue of the Kings. Sorai would thus write, for example: "And so of the virtues of the Ancient Kings there is none greater than that of Benevolence [*Jin*]"; or, "Benevolence is the singular Virtue [*ichi Toku*] of the Sages"; and "Benevolence is the Great Virtue [*Taitoku*] of their human essence."[9]

Since Virtue was specifically accorded to the Ancient Kings at the beginning of history it is logically external to and not inherent in all human beings as a universal natural or moral property. More crucially, this placement outside of human beings, allowed Benevolence to be a value that everyone, high and low alike, could refer to, comprehend, and rely on (*yoru*) to make ethical choices.

This Benevolence, then, is identified only with the Great Virtue of the Ancient Kings. A closer look reveals it to be first and foremost a comprehensive principle of political and social existence and not a reductive concept of law or autonomous hierarchy. It is broad, incorporating all human activities; yet it is flexible, theoretically tolerant to actions that have yet to be conceived and thus constantly allowing for creative change – the perpetual shaping of "custom" over time. Being all inclusive, it excludes nothing; and hence it is the ultimate norm for all social formations. Rich and poor alike comprehend this principle of society and of mutual trust among human beings in a community and it therefore need not be didactically imposed on everyone systematically with laws or examinations.[10]

9 Ibid., *Bendō*, #3–5, pp. 13–16.
10 Ibid., #7, pp. 17–20.

The conclusion Sorai drew was that a king must always be a social king – *kun wa gun nari*, his every political act must be for social and not personal ends. A king treats neither human beings nor natural things with callous disregard. He does not rule by decree. He does not see people in terms of a rigid definition of good and evil. He sees evil when human beings are endangered by beasts or other men. Just as humans choose to protect grain from weeds knowing that nature favors neither grain nor weed, a king will save humans from tigers and wolves. The nourishment of people and things, he sees as "good." The King's fundamental duty is always to protect the comprehensive and benevolent Way of social existence.[11]

This idea was interpreted by Sorai to mean that the Ancient Kings identified themselves with the imperative of community existence, and that this meant the benevolent nourishment of individual virtues. The Way of the social king, therefore, was also to be called the way of human nourishment – *Yashinai no Michi*. To realize this ethical goal, the Ancient Kings immersed themselves in creating concrete ways to nourish social existence, gained strength from it, mastered it, internalized its spirit, enjoyed it and, having realized their special Virtue, allowed themselves to rest. In cultivating their Virtue in this manner, these Kings established, and all subsequent kings and ruling princes were obliged to sustain, the principle of society as a broad and comprehensive way of human nourishment.

As can be readily ascertained, Sorai wished to set aside monolithic definitions of "good" and "evil" from his system of thought, because each was oppressive and legalistic. The idealist conception of "good" espoused by Sung philosophers and the materialistic view of "evil" by ancient Chinese Legalist scholars, in his view, were similar modes of thought that sought to reduce and coerce men into being what they were not and could not be. Good and evil in this regard resembled the religious problem of Heaven and Hell, convenient extremes with which to intimidate the human mind but unrelated to the problem of human ethics in society.[12]

11 Ibid., p. 17
12 Ibid., #5–6, pp. 15–16.

Removing the absolute standards of good and evil from his epistemology allowed Sorai to conceptualize society in highly diverse terms. Human beings cannot be reduced to a single principle of either good or evil. Instead, they possess "virtues." As stated earlier, Sorai argued that Benevolence was a Virtue specific to the Ancient Kings and must be external to humans as a social ethic and not inherent in them as a moral norm, as proposed in Neo-Confucianism. Each person, however, possessed a virtue that was specific to the self. Sorai called this a "little virtue" in contrast to the "Great Virtue" of the Ancient Kings, and he understood this as heavenly endowed, as the intellectual propensity and special potential one received at birth. Now the accumulation of these "little virtues" cannot add up to the King's Great Virtue since they are generically different. Nor can an individual through intense personal cultivation fundamentally alter his virtue from one thing to another. A person's identification with his heaven-given nature remains throughout his life. No King or teacher can intervene to alter this fact, however skillful his "technique."

Sorai cited the example of firing gypsum and aconite substances. Gypsum is a mineral substance that produces great coldness and can be used to reduce fever; aconite is a plant that can generate warmth. The Ancient Kings would not have been able to govern society without relying on the specific character of each thing. Moreover, gypsum is prepared in fire and aconite is baked in ashes, reminiscent of the reliance on specific rules as in rites and music for human beings. Yet, while gypsum is fired, its essential character of producing coldness is not lost; and although aconite is buried in hot ashes, its inherent capacity to generate heat is not lessened. Possessing different natural characters one becomes a medicine to reduce fever – the other was used to provide warmth to the body. The "rules" to fire the substances were strictly controlled and hence may be viewed as the "system"; but the actual transformations were plural and determined by the particular virtue of each, which neither the system nor the individual monarch could change.[13]

13 Ibid., #24, pp. 24–5.

To Sorai, therefore, the belief that all human beings could achieve, through diligent observation, study, and meditation, the goodness epitomized by the sages was completely misguided. The argument that all human beings were essentially alike and the accompanying ambition to make human beings aspire to sageliness were to him nothing other than reductive "legalism" deceptively clothed with idealistic ethical language.

It was the Way of the Ancient Kings to tolerate variety, and to allow the littlest virtue to flourish. The Ancient Kings ruled by relying on the wide variety of virtues available in society. Indeed, by establishing the Way as a clear principle of society, they permitted all to move to and fro on their own. The small people, in his wording, will realize their goals on their own accord. To use another of Sorai's precious examples, not all men can carve the image of a monkey on a rose thorn, nor a mulberry leaf out of jade; but those who can and desire to do these things should be allowed to do so and not coerced into doing something unsuited to the virtues they possessed. Virtue, in short, was not a unified ideal of goodness but a dynamic process of achievement, or perhaps more accurately, the potential to realize the ideal implicit in one's virtue, which is undoubtedly the sense of Sorai's terse phrase: "virtue means achievement [*toku wa toku nari*]." Clearly, the little virtues of men were not vulgar and demeaning as one might gather from a quick glance at Sorai's language. They were basic to his overall system of thought, and they underscore the limitless potential of the Way of the Ancient Kings to incorporate the myriad and untold virtues of humankind. No virtue could ever exceed the expansive and flexible limits of the Way of the Ancient Kings.[14]

This being the case, then, what reflection might there be on the competence of the king should the little virtues fall within the gracious bounds of his way? Sorai offered an important interpretative twist that needs to be underscored. The king is definitely not endowed by Heaven with omnicompetence, superior skills in every way. He is not a totally independent agent. His virtue is particular and limited, although it is the highest

---

14 Ibid., #7, pp. 17–19, # 11–12, p. 22.

virtue because it represents the principle of social benevolence. However, because this virtue is limited, the king is not at liberty to do with the kingdom as he wishes with absolute and arbitrary abandon. In other words, he is not free to mold humans in any way he pleases according to a single principle of law or ethics, or ideology; he does not endow individuals with their virtues; and, being neither a substitute or representative of nature nor a son of heaven, he cannot intervene to fundamentally alter them. The king is limited by the workings of Heaven in distributing virtues, which is a process beyond the comprehension of any human being, and beyond his political control. Instead, therefore, he nourishes his subjects and allows them to follow their proper course to their own specifically virtuous conclusions. The Ancient Kings accepted this special and limited character of their Virtue, and, thus, relied on the myriad talents of the people to realize their goal of social peace and well being.[15]

No king, however powerful and severe his rule, could govern alone, and had to appreciate the supportive strength of society. Sorai's language on this point is clear and unequivocal: The task of bringing peace and well being to the people cannot be achieved through the efforts of a single person. The strength of the people at large must necessarily be called upon. Thus, the smallest talents of society are not to be wasted; and, as in the ancient era of Yao and Shun, all under the king shall be as lords (not so much "officials" as sometimes claimed), each possessing a dignity that comes from having achieved his own virtue and thus having also contributed to social wellbeing.[16]

A major problem remains as to the manner in which a king actually governs, the theme Maruyama drew heavily on in his essays. How does a king translate Imperative into concrete "thing" – *mono*? A king governs through an organized system – *seido* – with internally consistent norms strictly measured and hence non-arbitrary, much akin to the carefully scaled construction of a temple or any other artifact. Being a fabrication, the system is neither an extension of nature nor of human personality. It is an instrument and hence "external" to humans. Seen in this stark

15 Ibid., #7, pp. 17–19.
16 Ibid., #7 and 11, pp. 17, 22.

light, Maruyama envisioned the "amoral" king who might use the system as a completely independent agent to protect his power and to preserve the kingdom as his personal possession. As already suggested, his reading appears to be somewhat extreme.

Sorai also viewed the concrete system to be neither an extension of nature nor of kingly personality, but as an embodiment of the ethical imperative traceable to the Ancient Kings at the genesis of history itself to always nourish human virtues under conditions of order and peace. All systems must contain this ethical principle of social benevolence. Thus, while systems differ with age and culture they must all foster the growth of life and things – as does the "gentle breeze" in nature. A system that destroys "evil" in accordance with a simplified concept of the "good," but which cares not for the littlest human virtue is to be deemed ineffectual – *mujustu* – and, by implication, ought not be allowed to continue.

The Ancient Kings made their vast Way concrete and through the concrete, the normative potential of their Virtue became the all-inclusive Way of human history. Now seen in this light, the ethical intent of the "thing" becomes evident. It is to make concrete and clear the Great Virtue as a continuing social norm in history, encouraging all to concentrate on their specific gift or calling from Heaven. The Ancient Kings, however, did not specify all the details as to how structures should appear or how human beings ought to behave in all times and places. They did leave the legacy that through the concrete, human beings in all their myriad variety could be nourished into the future, which is definitely the sense of Sorai's language describing the infinite when explaining the Way of Sages: "[The Way of the Sages] therefore, is intertwined with nature, actively, continuously and endlessly developing both human and natural things into the vast and infinite future."[17]

Sorai's expansive vision of the future should not be confused with an idea of progress. The image one gets from Sorai is not linear history so much as it is ever widening circles moving over time and defining epochs. The governing concept is the broadening range of sociality, not

17 Ibid., #20, p. 29.

predictable development in a causal pattern. Indeed, there is no "pattern" in Sorai's vision of the future, for the future is not yet known, and this is consistent with his view of the Way as limitless and beyond the descriptive power of existing language. Instead of a causally linked sequence of development there is a perception of history as continuously inclusive of human activities as they fashion custom in time. Thus, while Sorai's historical vision is not "progressive," neither is it a narrow one in which legally fixed structures regulate closely the lives of the little people; it tends instead to emphasize the broadly inclusive character of the Way in the historical process. This would seem to be a key critical perspective in Sorai's moral historicism; the proper understanding of the Way ought to lead to the receptivity of new forms of knowledge and actions and to exclude no virtue, however insignificant it might seem.

A related point implicit in Sorai needs elaboration. History, as noted, is to be distinguished from nature. Nature follows a causal pattern over time and space so that, although its precise workings can never be fully comprehended, humans know the seasons will run through their cycles endlessly. History, on the other hand, begins with a single moral cause, the creative establishment of the Way as a concrete thing by the Ancient Kings. The effect of this, however, is not causally repetitive as is nature, but rather is manifold and ceaselessly worked out in dynamic ways that cannot be fully grasped from the standpoint of the present. The important point, however, is that while history is obviously unlike nature, it is also *like* nature in its being infinite, and hence, ultimately a mystery beyond human explanations. Seen in this frame of reference, history is not "liberated" from nature and hence from timeless morality, suggesting a dialectical process often imputed in the Western experience, and emphasized by Maruyama as well. History is placed conceptually on an equal footing with nature in constant and continuous interaction with it. By creating history, the Ancient Kings separated society from nature and made it, unlike nature, moral, but like nature, also unending and hence immortal. Sorai's reverence for the creative beginning is traceable to this optimistic perception of natural and social immortality.[18]

18 *Bendō*, #7, p. 17.

Sorai proceeded to outline the analytical method with which to penetrate and reconstruct the Way of the Ancient Kings, which he presented in is "Principles of Learning" – *Gakusoku*.[19] Written for his students, the *Gakusoku* states Sorai's theory of philology, the precise study of ancient language in terms of its historical context, a philological approach Sorai called *kobunjigaku*. Sorai, whose appetite for the Ancients had been whetted by Itō Jinsai's writings, was decisively steered in the direction of ancient philology around the year 1705 by a reading of Li P'an-lung, a Ming scholar of ancient poetics, who emphasized that language changed and that "modern" vocabulary could not be relied upon to comprehend the ancient world. Sorai combined this approach with his historicism about the creative beginnings of political and social history.

History began in ancient China, Sorai observed, and nowhere else (certainly not Japan), a fact documented in the Books of Songs, History, Rites, Music, Spring and Autumn Annals and Changes. But these six classical Books and other ancient writings are not extant in their complete original form. Histories were written based on documents that no longer existed in the original. And where, for example, there were no elephants (as in China and Japan) descriptions were inaccurate. Inevitably as ideas and images were transferred over time and space, language changed and distortions became common.

And so it was with the transference of the Way of the Ancient Kings to Japan. Kibi no Makibi created a system of linguistic accommodation called *kanbun*, which involved reading Chinese according to Japanese sounds and sentence patterns, inserting verbal endings (*okurigana*) and reversal marks (*kaeriten*) that to Sorai resembled catfish whiskers, toads with tails, and insects attracted to light at dusk. This to him was analogous to confusing the thorny orange shrub with the aristocratic mandarin orange; or – in an even more pungently colourful witticism – similar to the mudwasp's distorted hope, as in ancient folklore, that in time its image would be transformed together with that of the silkworm. Language transference creates illusions. Yet the Japanese, like the wasps, believed they could embellish their language with deceptive designs.

19 Ibid., *Gakusoku*, pp. 187–97.

Sorai's contemptuous language belied his real theoretical argument. Because language transported over time and space leads invariably to distortions, and because language reflects the human experiences of a particular historical context it must be understood in relation to that context and not according to later interpretive conveniences. If this principle is understood, the Way can be comprehended; there should be no reason at all for "sages" to be restricted to China or to any one culture or era. The Way of the Ancient Kings is indeed universal, and this is the underlying principle of learning: *Kore kore gakusoku to iu*. Thus, while Kibi's objective might have been good, his method was erroneous. To achieve his goal one must avoid his method.[20]

This argument in the first section of *Gakusoku* starts out rather opaque and then becomes forceful. Why later nationalists would find this piece especially repugnant can be easily surmised. Yet Sorai's insistence on the crucial significance of language as the carrier of culture, knowledge, and social self-awareness, remains theoretically provocative.

Language changes over time (*u*) and space (*chū*) – the modern-day ideographic compound in Japanese for the universe. It carries with it the Way; and also obscures the Way. The Essho clan in Annam, Sorai explained, translated the Classics nine times to approximate the Chinese version of the Chou period, but the result was utter chaos. In another example, Hsuan Tsang travelled to India in the T'ang period to gain ancient Buddhist texts over 1,000 years old. Distortion was inevitable. The only tool humans have to unlock fundamental historical meaning is language. Yet language distorts. But it also lasts forever – *kuchizarumono wa bun nari*. Once written, there is in language the possibility of immortality. A written text remains unchanged; and it is this original text that must be comprehended. Through it, one comprehends the language universe, and hence the culture of an era – the Way itself when the Ancient Kings first created society.[21]

Sorai's philological method here is crucial. It intervenes decisively to broaden his approach to discovering the Way. All Confucian scholars in

20 Ibid., *Gakusoku*, #1, pp. 188–9.
21 Ibid., #2, pp. 190–1.

the seventeenth and early eighteenth centuries faced a conceptual choice that had far-reaching significance in determining the orientation of their thinking. One could follow the introspective route to search for spiritual and principled truth in the self followed by righteous action in the objective world. Yamazaki Ansai is representative of this mode. The other approach was to seek normative principles external to the self, which one sees clearly in Kaibara Ekken, a Neo-Confucian scholar, as well as in the thinkers of the Ancient Studies lineage, in which, of course, Sorai was the most powerful. Kaibara determined that the proper object of knowledge was primarily nature. Sorai rejected this and isolated history for special focus, for reasons mentioned earlier. The fundamental and normative meaning of the Way was to be found when history began, and the philological method was the tool to achieve this end. And the method dictated that the "object" of analysis must be "language."

The Way was "objective" only in so far as it could be extracted in its original meaning through language. Hence Sorai's comment that the meaning of the Way must be sought in language alone and not through diffuse speculations on the Way as an abstraction. Hence Sorai's words: "The Way is sought in language and not in the Way itself." This conclusion had provocative implications, for now all ancient documents, even scraps and traces, gained historical value, not just the Classics. While these classics were certainly the most important any ancient document that aided the historian in deepening his comprehension of the ancient world was deemed worthy of study. Whether the authorship was Moist or Taoist made no difference. All ancient language contained concrete clues with which to comprehend the "spirit" (*kokoro*) of the Way of the Ancient Kings.[22]

It was within this broad "archaeological" frame of reference that Sorai praised but also criticized the Taoist text, *Lao Tzu*, and also the classics of *Songs, History, Rites,* and *Music.* The brilliance of the philosopher, Lao Tzu, according to Sorai, was comprehending that when a utensil is reduced to

---

22 Ibid., #2.

its separate parts the utensil no longer exists; but that the "name" of it does. This is exactly what is meant by the Way in human history. It no longer exists as a functional whole, but lives as basic meaning. Sorai, however, faulted Lao Tzu for his theoretical critique that the way of human history was not the true unchanging way of nature. By identifying nature as being devoid of changeful constructs and despite the intensity of his effort to understand the potentiality of natural talent, Lao Tzu erred further by losing sight of the fundamental importance of language as the basic resource for "names."[23]

In a similar manner, Sorai surveyed the Four Classics to emphasize their distinctive importance that should not be reduced to a single ethical idea. The central meaning of *History*, for example, was that society must be organized in a predictable manner in contrast to natural chaos, which, as previously emphasized, was central to Sorai's understanding of why human history began.

It is Sorai's evaluation of the *Book of Songs*, however, that illustrates best his theoretical grasp of language. Unlike *History, Songs* had nothing to do with issues of "order," or "moral truth," and to read the *Songs* in the same manner as *History* would lead to serious distortion. Ancient aesthetic feelings would be reduced simply to moral didactics. Indeed, an unprejudiced reading of *Songs* clearly reveals that the language says nothing at all about goodness overcoming evil, contrary to scholars who traditionally made it out to be so in order to teach moral virtue. Thus, Confucian scholars throughout the ages argued that the "great introduction" contained a special moral significance, symbolizing true princely romance, while the "small introductions" are presented as being less virtuous because they were often poems about the passions of ordinary people.

Sorai rejected this moralistic view as untenable, arguing instead that the "great introduction" was simply a statement of poetic principle to the first poem in the *Book of Songs* and that the other shorter "introductions" were brief explanations added much later in the Han period from

23 Ibid., #3, pp. 191–2.

a decidedly ethical point of reference that was irrelevant to the original ancient meanings. These "glosses," in time, gained authoritative moral stature. Poetry, however, has no fixed principle but rather is elegant and suggestive language (*biji*) that includes the expressions of individuals from all segments of society, from the princely to the rustic.

Emphasizing the obvious, that true feeling was not the possession of "moral" men of high birth, Sorai went on to conclude that since poetry contained true human feelings, it was a fundamental form of data from which scholars might ascertain the concrete reality of human emotion or passion and hence also the changing universe of historical custom.

To Sorai, then, the historian should try to focus not on a preconceived principle of "truth" but on objective language itself. Through this objective linguistic mediation, cultural actualities would emerge as credible constructions. This approach allowed scholars of all ages to identify themselves with the original source of culture and to converse all through the day and evening with the ancients, as though the ancients were actually there with them in the very present.[24]

The philological method is obviously central to Sorai's moral historicism. Although sages existed only in ancient times and not in the present, philology could transport the spirit of the ancients into the culture of the Tokugawa present. Without such a reference to the ancient period, the present would simply be politically arbitrary, lacking consistent social purpose. Similarly, understanding that the present is different from the past because custom inevitably changes fosters a view of the ancient world in terms of its genetic beginnings. This leads further to the awareness that, despite constant change in history, all historical time is interconnected with an original purpose. Each age is, from Soria's perspective, both ancient and contemporary. By focusing on the beginning of society when norms were created, and holding these norms clearly as constants, one can see with unadorned lucidity the details of historical change in popular custom. This method, Sorai urged, was entirely superior to viewing all ages in terms of an unchanging and timeless metaphysical

24 Ibid., #2.

standard formulated in a particular period, meaning of course the ethical subjectivism of the Sung dynasty scholars.[25]

Sorai's view of philology was also logically consistent with his conception of society as a complex mixture of "little virtues." No student, he documented in his Gakusoku "principles of learning," could be coerced to learn the philological method. A student must possess, to begin with, a natural potential or "virtue" that orients him towards philological studies. A student who perceives this to be his "virtue" will set out to develop it until the limits of his capability bring him to an extreme point of irrepressible anger and frustration. Only then, Sorai reasoned, can a teacher step in to help the student excel and achieve the finest level of his virtue.[26]

If a student generates a powerful drive from within to realize his virtue, he cannot be stopped; but if there is not this drive, instructional efforts from outside will not help. Learning philology, like realizing any other internal virtue, is a *desire* (*hito no jō*) that underlies all human reflection and achievement in history. There is, furthermore, no single path by which humans realize their virtue. It was his disciples' different approaches to achieve their virtues that led Confucius to remark of himself as a teacher, "Is there anything special that I have done?"[27]

By the same token, the teacher, like a king, is neither omnipotent nor omnicompetent: The king cannot be at once a boat on water and a wagon on land. The teacher likewise cannot give to students a virtue they lack. Not every human being has the virtue to achieve the goodness of the sage and ought not seek to realize this goal. The same is true of historical scholarship. The teacher cannot undo what Heaven has granted to individuals. Like the king, he must rely, therefore, on the virtues that Heaven has given to his students. In accord with the Way of the Ancient Kings, the teacher nourishes, but does not seek to alter the basic virtues of humans, the specific gift of talent and potential that is their heavenly calling.

True to his theory of virtue, Sorai concludes by urging his students not to be conformists and instead to attend to their own special talents. He

25 Ibid., #4, pp. 192–3.
26 Ibid., #3.
27 Ibid., #5, pp. 193–4.

declared his own virtue to be that of a scholar whose essence, however dogmatic his ideas may appear to some, could never be confused with the idealistic and cosmological philosophers of Sung and later times – *Dōgaku sensei*.[28]

Steering away from the cosmological excesses of Neo-Confucianism, Sorai oriented his historicism to the epistemology that best evaluated the historical present, and explained why hierarchies functioned as they did in the Tokugawa order, and why the political landscape appeared so troublesome. In other words, Sorai's romantic vision was oriented to clarifying practical issues of shaping policy and structural renovation if this be necessary. Like all other major thinkers in the Tokugawa period, Sorai was engaged in the debate over the meaning, purpose and effectiveness of the administrative system at hand.

Throughout his discussion of practical matters Sorai retained the cardinal theoretical features of his historicism. The kingly virtue of Benevolence to nourish all human virtues was based on reverence for Heaven. This reverence was steeped in the awareness the Ancient Kings had of the limited intelligence of human beings in relation to the transphenomenal workings of Heaven. And, finally, the comprehensiveness of Heaven was infused as a principle of history in which human virtues would continuously be nourished over time. These themes of limited intelligence, reverence, and limitless historical potential impinged directly on Sorai's conception of "hierarchy."

The Ancient Kings, Sorai reasoned, comprehended Heaven's Mandate to organize or construct an orderly hierarchy to institute the Way of Nourishment, and detailed their approaches in the Classics containing the rites, music and formal rules of governance – *reigakukeisei*. They accepted their position at the head of the newly erected hierarchy and sought to carry out Heaven's deepest intent of harmonizing or joining together Heaven with human beings. Sorai's point was that concrete hierarchy, and the norms underlying hierarchy, must embody a pro-

28 Ibid., #7, pp. 196–7.

found "spirit," which originated in Heaven and was thus beyond the reach of the human mind. The Ancient Kings, therefore, remained consistently reverent before Heaven and, despite their intelligence and power, did not despise the lowly or see themselves as inherently superior to other men – *mizukara takashi to sezu*.[29]

For Sorai, then, the specific "techniques" – *waza, jutsu* – of governance that are associated with hierarchy must embody a spiritual or moral dimension and ought not be severed from the Way of Heaven as a transphenomenal absolute. As extensions of Heaven's Mandate, the rites, music and legal norms that were established continue into history with a potential as great and vast as Heaven's Way. Without moral spirit and purpose, Sorai insisted, "techniques" were "false technique" – *jajutsu*. Bound in particular by their own moral virtue of Benevolence, the Kings fostered the ideal of people living in peace and did not seek to make each individual into a sage nor did they view hierarchy as an amoral apparatus to be used according to their personal whim, or as their private or personal possession – *jibun no mono*.[30]

Sorai linked this idea of hierarchy directly with his understanding of human nature. As emphasized, Sorai's conception of individual human nature was curiously individualized and his view of humanity, pluralistic. Since human nature could not be explained except as a gift from Heaven, one's generic nature or being was basically "fixed," an inevitable fate that one did not choose, and it could not be altered by external authority. As he explained through his well-known analogy, a grain is always a grain, a bean a bean, and no political or ethical intervention can alter that fact of life at its beginning.[31]

Sorai held firm to this novel idea of human diversity. Individuals could not be transformed into sages, since individuals were not endowed with a certain universal essence, either good or evil, and could not, therefore, be taught to approximate a norm of external goodness. He thus limited

29 Ibid., *Benmei*, pp. 99, 127.
30 Inoue Tetsujiro ed., *Nihon rinri ihen v. 6* (Tokyo: Ikusei sha, 1901); *Tōmonsho*, pp. 146–203, esp. 170–8; see also, Yamashita, *Master Sorai's Responsals*.
31 *Benmei*, p. 124.

the scope of what hierarchies could achieve in relation to human virtues. All individuals, Sorai insisted, were born with a potential intelligence, which could be realized in varying degrees, depending on circumstances, but the actual variety of human potential could not be predicted, since the source in the end was Heaven itself. All that could be said empirically about human nature was that it was incessantly active – *katsubutsu*; desirous of things – *mina yokusuru tokoro ari*; and manifested itself as passion – *jō ni arawaru*. Princes and commoners were no different in this matter. This reading of human nature is close to his understanding of the natural human, blessed with life. "The great virtue of Heaven and earth," in his wording, "is termed Life." On occasion he used the ideograph for grace as the gift of faith in Buddhist terminology – *on* – to convey the same meaning. The Ancient Kings "enjoyed life" – *sei o konomu* – and were reverential toward nature and, like all human beings, learned from it. But the gift of life and the vision of Benevolence were not to be confused. Despite certain basic and natural similarities, no two human beings were ever the same, and in fact were qualitatively distinct from the moment of birth. Different virtues, moreover, could only be realized through consistent effort from within each individual. The objective in each person, Sorai therefore insisted, was to identify with his own heaven-given nature and work consistently toward realizing the potential within it: "And therefore each conforms to the inner nature that is close to the self, nourishes it, and realizes its virtue." The crucial implication of this theory was that the realization of one's virtue must come primarily from within the individual and not from artificial, hierarchical instruments.[32]

The Ancient Kings fully took into account the variability in human nature when they created, or "fabricated," political structures. Realizing that without a norm of social existence each individual would remain in an atomized form, unable to realize his particular virtue because of the anarchic and conflictual state of nature, the Kings shaped Benevolence into a norm of peaceful and orderly social existence. In constructing hierarchies, therefore, the Kings relied on human nature and did not treat it

32 Ibid., pp. 49, 53, 136–44.

as a hindrance to peaceful rule. Thus, Sorai observed, the Way of the Ancient Kings was simply the constructing of a hierarchical system based on the reliance of human nature.[33]

Indeed, it was a hierarchy imbued with respect and reverence for human nature in all of its variety, directly akin to the reverence the Ancient Kings had for Heaven. They believed that human nature, like Heaven, could not be created by authoritative will or whim. As Kings, they simply fostered human activities of all kinds, allowing individuals to pursue their separate wishes – *konomi ni makase soro*; they evaluated humans in terms of their virtues and not their failings and promoted the very talented (*jinzai*) to rise from lowly levels to positions of intellectual and political esteem; above all, they excluded no one from their peace, not even those at the lowest levels of society.[34]

Sorai celebrated this grand vision – *Seijin no miru tokoro* – bequeathed by the Ancient Kings to all subsequent humankind, a vision that to Sorai addressed the peace of the whole and the achievements of the particular. Once the grand frame was set in place, then the little virtues of their own accord would not be sacrificed. Hence Sorai's words: "What the Sages saw was truly grand. They excluded not even the small people. Should the large framework of things be chosen, then the small people of their own accord will not be lost.[35]

The emphasis that Sorai placed on the preservation of virtues remains impressive when seen from a modern perspective. However trivial a virtue may seem – such as in painting, sculpting and flower arranging, and in aesthetic ceremonies as well, each had a value within the confines of the kingly ideal of peace and harmony. It was in this sense that Sorai referred to each individual as potentially serving the public order. By this Sorai meant not as an administrator, as such language might be mistaken to mean today, but the fulfillment of individual desire which had a certain sacred meaning within the Way of the Ancient Kings.

Rather than an oppressive bureaucratic polity, it would appear that

---

33 Ibid., p. 140.
34 Ibid., pp. 49–54.
35 Ibid., pp. 151; 49–50.

Sorai held to a romantic and dynamic vision of people living and working together in a "human community" (*ningenkai*). Sharing a common living place, people would bring together their many different talents (*unyō ei'i no sai*) and build a flourishing society. Thus Sorai described in optimistic terms these people providing mutual assistance and nourishment in a cooperative spirit of affection for each other. The realization of small virtues in this context is clearly to promote well-being in everyday life.[36]

In Sorai's thought system, then, the vast and limitless Way of Heaven, the infinite potential of kingly Benevolence as the Virtue in all political and social history, and the distinctive virtues of individual human nature, were all interconnected in a scheme of ethical thinking, and his view of "hierarchy" should be discussed and appraised within this overall conceptual design. Sorai's frequent references to the Ancient Kings constructing politics has been often taken to mean direct "pacification" and "control" of the people in instrumentalist terms devoid of moral substance and intent. But such a reading distorts Sorai's philosophy. Rather than radically dividing "politics" from "morality," Sorai's concern may better be seen as reconciling the potentially contradictory forces of practical hierarchy or the "vertical" requirements of governance within the ethical community, to an essentially "horizontal" and communal dispersion of a wide variety of individuals with their virtues.

Although the Benevolence of the Kings, which undergirds hierarchy, and the virtues of ordinary humans, which are the actual content of community, are conceptually distinguishable, they are both anchored to a non-rational absolute, namely Heaven. Recognizing the limitations of human intelligence *vis-à-vis* this absolute, Sorai searched for a kingly "potential" of Benevolence to harmonize "hierarchy" and "human nature" within a social and historical context. In this regard, Sorai, it appears, sought to integrate "politics" and "morality" rather than render them intellectually disparate with the former taking precedence over the latter. One is left with Sorai's constant reminder that hierarchy without Benevolence is futile: *Jin ni arazumba izukunzo yoku sen*.[37]

36 Ibid., p. 54.
37 Ibid., p. 54.

Continuing on this line of thought, Sorai's apparent separation of
"public" and "private" would also seem to require reconsideration. Here
again, Sorai's intent does not seem to be to show how these distinctive
spheres were irreconcilable; clarifying their differences helped to integrate them into his overall ethical scheme. Actually, the translation of
"public" and "private" for the terms *kō* and *shi* are somewhat misleading
unless understood in relation to Sorai's general vocabulary. "Public" or
kō carried a meaning similar to his understanding of "community"
alluded to above, and suggests the idea of a people living and supporting
each other in a common space: *Shu no onajiku tomo ni suru tokoro, kore o kō*
[public] *to iu*. Opposing "public" was something entirely independent and
personal, something "private": *Onore hitori o moppara ni suru tokoro, kore o*
shi [private] *to iu*. Each person embodied both public and private aspects.
"Did not even a prince", he observed, "have a private sphere [*Kunshi to*
iedomo ani shi nakaran ya." Therefore, it was misleading to speak of the
"public" as a principle of Heaven (*Tenri*), and the "private" as individual
human passion (*jinzoku*) for it suggested the superiority of the former
over the latter and thereby denigrated private feelings within the individual and those close to him. Each individual living in a community
simultaneously enjoyed a private existence that was entwined with his
very virtue and that was also, therefore, distinct from the wider community and those who ruled.[38]

What then was the relationship between that which was "private" in a
person and his public "function" in society, his *shokubun* in Sorai's language? Theoretically, each private sphere was as valuable as the next.
There is no necessary hierarchy of virtues in human society but rather a
random dispersion of variable potentialities and virtues within a common social space. Everyone, however, lives in some sort of "functional"
and mutually supportive social group. What gives these relationships
manageable coherence are the functional classes – such as those of the
Tokugawa order. Classes were created by the Ancient Kings and are not to
be found in the natural order. Classes, however, are not fixed absolutes,

38 Ibid., pp. 105–6.

binding individuals to them from birth as if they reflected some sort of moral law. Talent and virtue, Sorai insisted, were distributed randomly throughout society, and were essentially a matter of "fate" and not a monopoly of a certain class. Drawing on classical Confucian thinking, Sorai underscored his belief that human virtues were not determined by heredity. An outstanding person born at a low status who realizes his virtue is to be called a "prince" (*kunshi*); a person born at a high level who fails to realize his virtue, in particular his duty to society appropriate to his position, is an "inferior person" (*shōjin*).

The foregoing tends to suggest that for Sorai, the "public" was not a specialized "political" sphere but a broad ethical arena that included a wide range of activities besides those that were strictly speaking "political," such as scholarly, artistic and occupational. To Sorai, the utility of political devices was that they prevented violence and destruction and in general maintained peace and material well-being of society. They were, however, limited as to what they could do inasmuch as they could neither create nor transform human nature. The essential purpose of politics, therefore, was ethical, the fundamental task being to carry out the ideal of Benevolence as in fostering "trust" (*shin*) among the members of society.

This idea of trust provides important mediation between "public" and "private" in Sorai's thinking. Trust, in one sense, means "credibility" or "trustworthiness" between individuals, allowing for communication with language supported by evidence. Rulers must also have this credibility in order to maintain the trust of the people. Most important for this discussion, each individual must have trust in a truth outside the immediate self, such as in Heaven as the source of personal virtue, or in the Way of the Ancient Kings. It does not seem to have been Sorai's intention to argue that truth resided exclusively outside the individual, although he and his students were often taken to task on this point. Rather he emphasized that trust in an external truth beyond the comprehension of men's intelligence was a necessary condition for believing in one's self: "Without trust human beings will not know their own potential to do things." And so too, scholars must proceed in their work on the basis of trust in the Ancient Sage Kings.[39]

Trust in, or reliance on, the "basic intent" (*hon'i*) of these Ancient Sage Kings was especially crucial to Sorai. Faith in their grand benevolent vision confirmed the value of one's little virtue in historical time. Stated somewhat differently, trust in the "public benevolence" of the Kings allowed one to gain conviction in his "private virtue." Thus, the "public" or "social" sphere on the one hand and the "private" and "personal" arena on the other, while clearly not identical and certainly distinctive as Sorai stressed, are reconciled through the ethical link of trust.

Trust, however, must never be based on vague and abstract principles, but on concrete reality. Thus scattered through Sorai's writings is the argument that while Benevolence informed the whole with ethical purpose, the details must always be empirical and verifiable. Hence the determination of policy, the exercise of authority in a thousand different ways, and the distribution of justice, must all be based on clear method, never on a single, mechanical, exercise of power but adaptive to the social goals at hand, and executed with precision. Ultimately, he would say, the starting point is the use of language anchored to specific evidence. Herein was the basis of trust. This entirety that combined ethical purpose with precision, Sorai summarized with the term "righteousness" – *gi*.

As just observed trust must rest on something that was credible evidence and not merely on a fabricated myth. Trust, therefore, must also be supported by the systematic and scholarly search for evidences through the historical and philological method. History encompassed a wide spectrum of data drawn from distant countries and ancient and modern periods and history specialized in the study of "prose" (*bunsho*) and "language" (*moji*) that embodied the Way in ancient "books" (*shoseki*). Therefore, Sorai held "the study of history is truly the highest form of scholarly knowledge" – *Gakumon wa rekishi ni kiwamari soro koto ni soro*.[40]

Historical scholarship interconnected the ancient with the present in a number of concrete ways, including matters of governmental policy. The

39 Ibid., pp. 87, 169.
40 *Inoue*, ed., *Nihon rinri Tōmonsho*, p. 153; Yamashita, *Master Sorai's Responsals*, p. 45.

prince gained an understanding of the Great Virtue of Benevolence on which he must "rely" or identify to nourish his own virtue and to rule his people according to the norms of culture and peace. The people were informed, in general, as to how social and political organizations came into existence to regulate the inner and outer realms of human behaviour. Scholarship affirmed the validity of individual virtue. Furthermore, it explained historical change, since it clarified the normative meaning of history that did not, or ought not, change over time. It thus provided the crucial perspective for the present, showing the character of that present and clarifying what ought to be changed in order to sustain the kingly virtue of benevolent peace. Historical scholarship, then, provided humans with the evidences to sustain their faith and trust in the present for the Ancient Kings; and that trust, in turn, clarified their grasp of the present and the practical prescriptions as to what should be done. Sorai worked out these issues of policy in great detail in the treatises *Seidan* and *Taiheisaku*.

The practical prescriptions that Sorai made for his society grew directly out of the preceding structure of thought. Some historians have tended to deemphasize the historicist theories underlying Sorai's practical prescriptions as in the case of J. R. McEwan in his otherwise excellent presentation of Sorai's "political writings," especially the *Seidan*. A reading of McEwan might lead one to believe that Sorai's treatises on the Way and Names, *Bendō* and *Benmei*, were merely pedantic exercises and unrelated to assessments of his historical present. Historians have often pointed out the inadequacy and somewhat simple-mindedness of some of Sorai's proposals such as returning to the soil the samarai and the burgeoning class of vagrant people and registering households to prevent the aimless wandering by many in society – a policy called *dochaku or hitogaeshi*. That these prescriptions were inadequate and anachronistic cannot be doubted, but they were totally consistent with a theoretical premise that was not by any means trivial.[41]

41 J. R. McEwan, *The Political Writings of Ogyū Sorai* (Cambridge: Cambridge University Press, 1962).

Sorai proceeded from the premise previously elaborated, that the moral imperative of princes, sages, and scholars in general is to promote peace among the people. Society, however, degenerates with time. This is inevitable as history amply demonstrates. No system, however idyllic it may have been in the archaic past, has continued uninterruptedly down into the present. As he put it, "there is no such thing as an unchanging system over the ages" – *bansei fueki no sei to nasu mono wa hi nari*. The Prince or King well aware of this historical fact still must seek to carry out his mandate of marshalling all the skills and talents at his disposal to prolong peace in order to nourish human virtues. His methods ought not be coercive for this reduces human beings to ignorance. Aided by scholars, the prince seeks instead to identify those social and economic causes within the system itself that if left unresolved, would spread human misery and generate "insurrections" – *ransei*. To Sorai, insurrections were always symptoms of deeper causes that, in one way or another, were traceable to flaws in the system itself. Never in his view were they due to human nature, or moral failure of ordinary individuals, or the absence of talent in society.[42]

Sorai identified the specific threat to the Tokugawa Peace as "poverty" or "economic hardship." He then proceeded to explain the actual cause of such poverty. The 100 years of Pax Tokugawa which had culminated in the period called Genroku (1688–1704) had been shaped out of the warfare of the sixteenth century in the era known as Sengoku. Society was unified and structured by leaders on horseback who were suitable to the conditions of civil war. The Tokugawa Peace continued to be ruled by men who identified with the "virtues" of that tradition. A society at peace, however, cannot be ruled by military leaders since their talents were inappropriate to practicing the Way of Benevolence. Military talent ought to be relied on in emergency situations but not during "normal" conditions of peace. In the Pax Tokugawa military leaders who founded the regime perpetuated themselves and their progeny, using the ideas of "the way of the warrior" to justify their actions. By perpetuating rule by

---

42 *Nihon shisō taikei*; Ogyū Sorai, *Benmei*, p. 54; and *Seidan*, pp. 259–445, esp. p. 303.

military talent, these leaders failed to establish government based on culture and historical scholarship that was consistent with the Way of the Ancient Kings. The unfortunate results of material and spiritual hardship throughout society could thus be traced to the basic flaws of the system itself, or in the faulty norms governing hierarchy.[43]

Foremost among these misguided norms were the artificial rules that were established to protect the special identity and status of the samurai aristocracy. Those with military "talent" were legally disengaged from the "people," thus denying the possibility of men of ability to rise from among the populace. Members of the aristocracy were assigned a special place to live – the castletowns, and they were scheduled to travel periodically to Edo and to reside there in expensive mansions. The results according to Sorai were absurd. Edo, in his famous characterization, had been transformed into a city of hotels. Times, however, had indeed changed. The samurai aristocracy was no longer the warrior class that it once was. While mouthing the virtues of a splendid military tradition, they in fact, lived a life of luxury and leisure that had little to do with that legacy. The myth of the aristocracy could be resolved only by "redesigning the laws" that favored the aristocracy. To begin with, the aristocracy should be stripped of its stipends and returned to the soil to engage in productive labor along with the peasantry. The aim here was clearly not to reunite "sword" and "land," but to separate "sword" from "privileged status," to redefine legally the samurai into commoners, register them as such, and place them in the setting from which their ancestors once rose to positions of influence and power as men of military ability.[44]

It must be emphasized that Sorai's primary aim was not to punish the aristocracy. His concern went deeper. Viewing the broad flow of history, Sorai was convinced that the Tokugawa Peace could not be maintained unless the existing "custom" of military governance was made completely subordinate to the Way of Benevolence, that is to say, rule by the "custom" of culture and scholarship, which he believed entirely

---

43 *Benmei*, p. 102; *Seidan*, pp. 303; *passim*; Inoue, ed., *Ninon rinri Tōmonsho*, pp. 183–5.
44 *Nihon shisō taikei*; *Seidan*, pp. 273 *passim*.

appropriate to a society that sought to prolong peace. Seen in this frame of reference, it is clearly evident that Sorai's recommendation that the aristocracy be returned to the land was primarily to recreate a new basis of talent that would no longer be dominated by the stipended samarai living in castle towns and in Edo.

To Sorai the survival of a peaceful order depended on discovering talent – *jinzai, saitoku* – wherever it might be found. In that regard, classes were functional designations and not fixed, hereditary, social constructs, since individual "virtue" was not hereditary. Even the descendants of the Ancient Kings were not memorable men of ability; nor the progeny of Minamoto Yoritomo, founder of the Kamakura Bakufu. Sorai believed that history showed that talent rarely came from among those born in high places but almost always from the lower classes: *Kensai no hito wa mina shimo yori idetaru.* It was among the lower classes that there was the greatest amount of suffering (*nangi*), and suffering and struggle were the most important stimulants to learning. The Tokugawa system, however, perpetuated itself instead on the anachronistic "custom" of heredity that inevitably divided society between those who ruled as against the rest of the people. It did not proceed from the premise that talent was varied and distributed widely in society. Moreover since human nature was always "dynamic" – *katsubutsu* – the issue for any government was identifying talent in society and determining whether that talent could be nourished and incorporated within the system.[45]

The movement of talent in and out of hierarchy was extremely important for Sorai, and it is linked to the idea of "faith" in his conceptual scheme. If "faith" linked the Way of the Ancient Kings with princes and scholars in the present, it was men of "talent" who brought the norms of the Way into actual practice within structures and harmonized them with the feelings of the people. It was talented men, in other words, who took the value of Benevolence to the people and united the high and low into relationships of mutual trust. In addition, talent drawn from below would convey the sufferings and passions of the people to those in high

---

45 *Seidan*, p. 367; and *Nihon rinri; Tōmonsho*, p. 470.

places, thus again contributing to the unity of high and low into a single existence (*ichizon*), in short, unifying hierarchy and community. All regimes dedicated to the ideal of peace, Sorai insisted, must allow talent "to rise" (*risshin*) from the lowest levels of society and thereby not "violate" the feelings of the people – *ninjō o yaburazu*.[46]

The Tokugawa rulers thus faced very clear choices. They must scuttle the hereditary aristocracy; renounce the norms of military rule as being no longer appropriate; and accept as their primary function the nourishment and selection of talent from among commoners. The prescriptions were entirely consistent with Sorai's general theory that the Ancient Kings, recognizing their limited knowledge before Heaven and human nature, refused to see themselves as inherently superior and treated all human virtues as valuable to the King's peace. It was time, Sorai warned, for the Tokugawa leadership to heed the teachings of the Ancient Kings. The alternative would be a deepening division between the high and the low that would result in a fundamental crisis to the order.

As poverty and hardship spread and "faith" in the leadership declined, men of talent would inevitably rise from below to lead a general uprising that would surely topple the so-called Tokugawa regime of "peace and tranquility": "When talent is lacking above, the regime approaches its end and the era of insurrections sets in. Talent from below will rise to overthrow the existing order [*Yo o kutsugaesubeshi.*]"[47]

Sorai's ambivalence about the Pax Tokugawa is obvious. Political systems are historical constructs and are not sacrosanct. It is not unusual, he thus observed, that systems should be built anew. The broad trend of history as it unfolded in the present, moreover, revealed to him an irreversible crisis. The Tokugawa adaptation from "warfare" to "peace" had been far from adequate. The regime continued to govern in the name of the "Great Peace" in accordance with norms shaped when the country was at war. Unless these laws were drastically altered the discrepancy between the maintenance of hereditary rule by a military aristocracy and

46 *Nihon shisō; Seidan*, pp. 367–8.
47 *Seidan*, pp. 366.

benevolent governance for human nourishment, would lead to wide-spread distrust and, inevitably, to revolt from among the populace.

Embedded in Sorai's skepticism is a provocative argument for histori-cal change. The fundamental dissonance between high and low, existing rulers and the norm of Benevolence, heredity and talent, military and scholarly practices, and the exercise of control rather than the promo-tion of human nourishment led Sorai to seek a theory that would clarify political economy in the present. His would avoid Neo-Confucian meta-physics which, in his view, offered, at best, a speculative and unpersua-sive view about the continuum from cosmos to history, nature to society. He would not, however, argue society and nature to be in a dialectical subject to object relationship, and, as I have argued, he actually sought to reconcile these categories as being entwined in an unending process. The guiding purpose to his moral philosophy remained the vision of peaceful social existence.

Sorai believed change was inevitable in light of this vision. To change things because they were old, he observed in *Seidan*, was absurd; but it was equally unrealistic to cling to what was old merely because it was cus-tomary. It was the central intention of the Ancient Kings to respect Heaven and human virtues, but they never insisted on the preservation of what people believed to be customary. On the contrary, customs and received laws must be altered if the populace lived in misery, and when talent languished without proper nourishment. Under these circum-stances systemic alteration was entirely in accord with the deepest intent (*oku'i*) of the Sages of ancient times.[48]

However inadequate in detail, Sorai's practical recommendations for reform were addressed directly at the deepening crisis in the Tokugawa order. Sorai believed at the end of his career that while insurrections from below were imminent, decisive reforms that immediately opened up government to talent would have a salutary effect and restore confidence in the regime. His student of political economy, Dazai Shundai, was far less sanguine.

48 *Seidan*, pp. 365–66, 455.

In Shundai's pessimistic view, systems that had deteriorated beyond a certain point could not be restored by ordinary efforts. Shundai urged an active reformism that went far beyond Sorai's views on what needed to be done. He rejected Sorai's proposal that the aristocracy be returned to the land, claiming it was not feasible and anachronistic in view of the irreversible trend of expanding commerce and trade. As land was limited and hence agricultural production also limited, and the growth of population inevitable and unlimited, Shundai argued the necessity of creating wealth through commerce and trade. Formulating a major conceptual breakthrough, Shundai, observing the hustle of tradesmen in Osaka, proposed the urgency of turning into a public good the practice of trade in generating wealth. Shundai put his thoughts in these words:

> For our degenerate world to become one with the ancients the needs of the country would have to be met with a vastly reduced supply of money. Inconveniences reduced thereby would be welcomed among the aristocrats and commoners. However, unless the political system of the entire country is reconstituted and the customary traditions of the people altered, such a goal could not be achieved. We are left with no alternative but to devise a plan to increase monetary income within each domain. The quickest way to do this is through trade. Surely within three to five years the domain would be enriched thereby.[49]

Shundai openly urged, therefore, that the domainal governments adopt the practices of merchants and engage actively in inter-domainal trade to systematically create wealth and counteract the pattern of inflation and perennial indebtedness. Shundai's main perception was that the general economic crisis of the day could not be resolved through the study of ancient texts, and that, ultimately, such resolution could be achieved only through the comprehensive reorganization of the political structure.

Indeed, Shundai went further, to speculate as to what a political critic ought to do when a system fails, when it had gone hopelessly beyond

49 Rai Tsutomu, ed., *Nihon shisō taikei 37: Sorai gakuha* (Tokyo: Iwanami Shoten, 1972), pp. 45–56.

reform and refurbishing. He argued that one should withdraw support from it and "do nothing." This prescription he claimed to be the true meaning of the idea of inaction in Taoism. It meant, according to Shundai, radical and complete disengagement from existing politics, letting go and watching the system stumble and fall. Taoism, Shundai concluded, was not about nature but politics.

The alternative to doing nothing, Shundai further reasoned, was to revolt against the system itself. In this option, the critic could shape a strategy of attacking the center directly, mainly to make a statement about righteousness and justice, without necessarily achieving immediate victory. The optional strategy was to withdraw to the regions and organize and mobilize a domain and to raise a flag of revolt that would thereby challenge the regime at the center to do battle in the regions. These strategies would be relied on 100 years later in the civil wars of the 1850s and 60s that would result in the demise of the Tokugawa order.

Shundai retreated from these more drastic prescriptions and called on the semi-autonomous regional domains to maintain their viability through trade. Shundai saw with great clarity the inadequacy of the "agrarian" response to the deepening economic crisis, and perceived that reorganizing the social basis of talent as Sorai urged must be accompanied by a substantial alteration in the economic foundation of the order.[50]

It is important to remember, however, that it was Sorai who had paved the way conceptually for Shundai to make the dramatic intellectual moves suggested above. It was Sorai, for example, who viewed merchants in strictly functional and not moral terms. Talent and virtue, after all, were to be found in all classes; hierarchy must continuously circulate new talent into it from below. Sorai had also proposed the idea of the social prince whose moral obligation was Benevolence in the special sense of nourishing human virtues in ways not yet known. Benevolent rule ought to promote peace for a community populated with distinctive

50 See my essay, "Political Economism in the Thought of Dazai Shundai (1680–1747)," *The Journal of Asian Studies* (4:1972), pp. 821–839.

and ever expanding fields of virtues and, within this moral philosophy Sorai held to the view that laws and institutions were not sacrosanct, and, indeed should be altered in the face of broad historical forces. Political systems, Sorai had argued, rise and fall as history amply documents, but the ethical intent underlying politics remained true, and systems would once again be built with this intent as the basis of guidance. These vital parts of a structure of critical thinking extended well beyond their specific uses by Shundai with regard to commerce as a public necessity and may be thought of as central concepts in the Tokugawa discourse on political economy.

A few additional interpretative themes will serve as summary comments. What we perceive behind the recurrent arrangement of often elusive language and allusions in Sorai's secular moral philosophy is a grand conceptional design. The imperative that human beings ought to live in order and peace is given concrete substance through the mediation of the Ancient Kings and documented in the great ancient classics of Songs, History, Rites and Music. It is in this moment that historical time begins and, with it, also the ethical discourse on politics. From this genesis, Heaven's Mandate became intelligible as the Way of the Ancient Kings, an all-inclusive norm for historical existence as a concrete and continuous process. Humankind thereby gained immortality in a manner akin to nature. Although nature endlessly perpetuates its cycles of life and season, in the Way of history, political structures change, as do customs and meanings in language. However, the original ethical intent of the Ancient Kings remains constant: they created politics for the purpose of nourishing diverse human virtues, not to change them or make them homogeneous. To this end, humans must live in accordance with an ethical principle of sociality that allows for trust and the relatively unencumbered movement of human beings with their virtues and talents. Structures and laws ought not to impinge on human activities in minute detail; they should only serve as concrete embodiments of the Way as human nourishment.

Reconstructed in this manner, the intellectual objective toward which

Sorai had arranged his ideas, the "intentionality" underlying his thought, takes on a coloration significantly different from the one usually painted. It does not appear to be Sorai's intent to render "politics" autonomous from "morality" or, for that matter, from "nature," thus liberating it from these categories and dialectically opposing them. Sorai's argument from the stance of moral historicism is that the concrete "things" that had emerged from centuries of political chaos contained a broad social principle for Tokugawa Japan that would survive into the future. His is an optimistic statement. There need not be a reversal to a world of barbarous war, as in the sixteenth century, but rather a fortunate world enjoying the Way of the Ancient Kings now made potentially concrete to accommodate the wide variety of virtues scattered throughout society.

Sorai's overall conceptualization is impressive and provocative. Vertical political constructs are not autonomous from morality, but must be clearly anchored to the moral principle of historical genesis. In this beginning was established a general norm for society that all classes could "rely on" and identify with ease. Political structures gained their *raison d'être* from the incorporation of this social norm, and were ethically committed to care for all subjects without waste. Hierarchy, moreover, must be informed by the practice of trust, of the use of language based on evidence, and the exercise of authority with clear method and commitment to precision or "righteousness."

For Sorai the concrete "thing" must always represent "people living together"; and it did not mean merely an external "apparatus" the "prince" had at his personal disposal to use as he wished. Indeed, every act of the prince must be "social" rather than "personal" since he was morally committed to encourage the virtues of all the people. He himself was "social" because his competence was limited and he needed to rely on the virtues of the people. Graciously nourished by the Way of the Ancient Kings the people formed a spiritual community. Within such a community humans pursued their virtues which, although never adding up to an approximation of an abstract goodness or Benevolence (which was specific to the Ancient Kings hence logically external to humans),

always pointed in complicated ways to the virtuous strength and potential of society as a whole.[51]

It was always within the context of promoting social well-being and the
sustenance of virtues in precise and trustworthy ways under conditions
of peace that Sorai conceptualized "politics," never in isolation from
these issues. Here is the optimism that prompted the brilliant social
critic of the modern, late Meiji era, Nakae Chōmin, to liken Sorai's
thought to Bentham's theory of maximum social happiness – *Bendamu no
saidai kōfuku shugi*.[52]

Sorai used the concept of sociality to cut across the vertical emphasis of
hierarchy, without negating it, and stressed the identification of all to
the ethical intent located in the Way of the Ancient Kings. Equally important, by doubting that human beings possessed a uniform potential to
realize an abstractly conceived goodness and emphasizing instead the
diversity of virtues, he had articulated an open-ended theory of social history and of human beings creating custom over time. Sorai therefore also
vehemently opposed the centralization of knowledge through an examination system (and by extension, his thinking would support the opposition to the standardized education of modern times).

Since new human virtues would continue to appear in ways that could
not be foretold, and since custom, therefore, would inevitably undergo
change over time, Sorai believed it essential that Benevolence remained
as an underlying basis of social existence. The Way of the Ancient Kings
would thus be dynamically interlinked with ongoing history as it underwent change. Sorai integrated, in this manner, "external" ethic, located
in the ancient world of historical beginning, and "potential" history.

Sorai believed that this relationship between historical beginning and
the continuing present would be readily understood by people in general.
He therefore did not advocate the rigid enforcement of punitive laws to
assure social order and cohesion. To be sure, politics must see to it that
dangerous beasts such as tigers and wolves must be removed from society
and that hence criminals must likewise by appropriately punished, but

51 *Bendō*, #16 and #24.
52 Nakai Chōmin, *Ichinen yūhan* (Tokyo: Hakabunkan, 1901), p. 103.

Sorai's ideal was that of society not intensively regulated. If the broad principle of social well-being were embraced, Sorai repeatedly argued, the exercise of legalistic authority would be unnecessary and inappropriate. He envisioned political structures remaining at a benign distance from daily life, like the worn and tattered reins (a favorite image of his) loosely guiding a spirited steed. The myriads of human beings (Sorai saw in the teeming streets of Edo) could thus come and go as they wished to pursue their passions and realize their essential virtues. In short, political systems may rise and fall, but the principle of fostering human life in a social context remains in history, which in turn serves as the basic premise from which to once again reconstruct an order. In his view of nourishment as the fundamental purpose of politics, and the distribution of authority and justice based on informed precision, Sorai reveals himself to be a romantic and optimistic thinker often denied of him by historians. We have in fact tended to view Sorai as the "Machiavelli" of modern Japan. Distrustful of human passion and greed, Sorai is seen as an advocate of harsh political control from above by an absolute prince. More specifically, in the presentation of Maruyama Masao, it was Sorai who first defined the "autonomy" of politics from cosmos, nature, and moral norms and thus also, articulated the principle of secular "fabrication" and "invention."

That modernizing impulse went awry as a result of nativist interventions – the key interlocutor being in Maruyama's analysis, Motoori Norinaga, the late eighteenth-century scholar who appropriated Sorai's concepts for National Studies. This connection too is probably overdrawn. Sorai's political ethic was based on the theory of human difference and diversity. Norinaga's National Studies pivoted on the ideal of identity and similitude of human beings, anchored to an uncontaminated native language first uttered in archaic times. Norinaga's ideas in this regard are closer in spirit to the Neo-Confucian concept of an internal moral center or mean as common to human beings and to the Buddhist idea of inner grace, both of which Sorai vehemently rejected from his particular perspective of human nature. The idea that based on a common identity everyone ought to strive toward an abstract and fixed moral or ideological goal, was also anathema to his way of thinking.

Suffice it to say that the overall interpretation that connected Sorai's historicism and political ethics with Norinaga's National Studies, has had a largely negative impact on our understanding of Sorai's ideas. It is not our main purpose in this essay, however, to criticize Maruyama's powerful interpretation of Japan's political modernization and especially of the important need to "fabricate" a new democratic future. Yet, in reading Sorai and reassembling some of the larger pieces, certain themes other than those emphasized by Maruyama emerge from the texts.

It should be kept in mind that some of Sorai's critics in the eighteenth century were deeply skeptical of his ideas and anticipated some of the concerns of modern historians. Singled out for polemical criticism was the emphasis Sorai placed on political virtue being a special talent of only a privileged few. His historicist mystification of ancient genesis at the exclusion of creative possibilities in later times also was criticized, especially as regards new insights into nature that were made after the ancient beginning and, indeed, in eras yet to come. Merchant scholars in Osaka, defensive of their status and claims to knowledge, were particularly vehement in this regard. They emphasized the value of general education for all commoners regardless of their special virtue, and prized the relative enrichment of human understanding of nature over the entire course of human history. Despite his critics it is apparent that other meanings are embedded in Sorai's political philosophy, and his romantic vision of political benevolence as nourishment of all humans is especially intriguing.[53]

In our view, Sorai's view of politics and hierarchy was neither narrow nor amoral, and the prince not the "independent" or "autonomous" agent who uses power as he wishes without reference to morality or natural life. The prince retains reverence for Heaven and human virtues, which are beyond his management, and the ethical intent of historical genesis. For Sorai, these were fundamental references outside the immediate arena of instrumental politics. The purpose of politics for him was not to replicate historical models or to mold culture through legal

53 See my *Visions of Virtue in Tokugawa Japan.*

instruments but to succor randomly scattered virtues, thereby also fostering cultural creation and historical change into the indefinite future.

We began this essay with Pepper's comment about the cognitive challenge involved in studying a creative concept. Sorai's historicism, his moral political philosophy, certainly confirms that generalization. Sorai's historical texts are truly "rich and complicated" things, and the variety of meanings contained in them remain very much a matter of interpretation and argumentation. Sorai's text in this sense should remain open and not be closed with fixed meanings. It may be well, in closing, that we recall the words of advice offered by Ernst Cassirer for the study of intellectual history:

> The history of philosophy shows us very clearly that the full determination of a concept is very rarely the work of that thinker who first introduced that concept, for a philosophical concept is, generally speaking, rather a problem than the solution of a problem – and the full significance of this problem cannot be understood as long as it is still in its implicit state.[54]

A brief note serves as a transition to Sorai's texts. The *Bendō* and *Benmei* are not essays in the way we might expect of a formal treatise. They are rather polemical statements, clearly numbered, and intended, through a pattern of repetition in the use of a consistent set of perspectives on a variety of different subjects, to relentlessly undermine the metaphysical dualism and introspective idealism of Sung Neo-Confucianism. The *Bendō*, therefore, consists of twenty-five terse statements about the meaning of the Way. The *Benmei* reveals Sorai's philological method of clarifying the meaning of key ideographic terms or "names" based on his reading of ancient texts. Again, he seeks to show how recent Neo-Confucian philosophy had drastically distorted original, ancient, meanings.

Working under conditions of failing health, as he suggests in the opening pages of the *Bendō*, Sorai completed both works between 1717 and 1720.

---

54 Ernst Cassirer, *Essay on Man* (New Haven: Yale University Press, 1944), p. 180.

Principal events in the life of
Ogyū Sorai

*

1666 Born in Edo on February 16 in a physician's family; the second son of Ogyū Hōan.

1671 Hōan becomes personal physician to Tokugawa Tsunayoshi, lord of the Tatebayashi domain and later shogun.

1672 Sorai begins studying in the Hayashi school at Shinobugaoka.

1679 Hōan incurs official displeasure and is banished to a village in Kazusa province, across the bay from Edo; Sorai accompanies his father.

1680 Sorai's mother dies in February.

1690 Sorai returns to Edo; opens a private school and teaches Confucianism by the entrance of the Zōjō Temple in Shiba.

1691 Sorai begins *Yakubun sentei* (A Guide to Translation).

1692 Tsunayoshi, now shogun, allows Hōan to return to Edo on June 2.

1695 The bakufu recoins gold and silver bullion and debases the currency to increase government funds; Sorai reads and is intrigued by Itō Jinsai's writings.

1696 On August 22 Sorai is retained by Yanagisawa Yasuaki (known as Yoshiyasu after 1704), chamberlain and confidant of Tsunayoshi and the lord of Kōfu, with a stipend sufficient to maintain fifteen people; attends Tsunayoshi's lectures on the Confucian classics at the Edo Castle; on November 10 he marries Miyake Yasumi.

1702 On December 14 forty-six of the former retainers of the lord of Akō attacks Kira Yoshinaka to avenge the wrong done to their lord.

1704 Sorai writes to Jinsai asking for instruction; Jinsai does not reply.

1705 On March 12 Jinsai dies; on October 5 Sorai's wife dies, and Sorai is left a widower with two small children; Sorai obtains two collections of verse and prose prepared by the Ming scholars, Li P'an-lung and Wang Shih-chen, which subsequently exert an enormous influence on him.

1706 In September Sorai visits the Kai regions and sees first hand the sufferings of peasants; on November 9 Sorai's father dies.

1708 The bakufu issues a large copper coin (known as Hōei currency) worth ten times any existing denomination in copper.

1709 On January 10 Sorai moves from the Yanagisawa house; he settles in Nihonbashi in Edo and establishes the Ken'en School.

1711 Dazai Shundai becomes a disciple of Sorai; "Instruction One" of *Gakusoku* (Instructions for Students) is composed; "Yakusha" (Translation Society) is organized.

1712 The first edition of *Yakubun sentei* is published.

1713 In September Sorai marries the daughter of Sassa Rikkei.

1714 A collection of his philosophical essays, *Jottings from a Miscanthus Patch* (Ken'en zuihitsu), is published; on October 24 Sorai's stipend rises to a comfortable 500 koku; on November 2 Yoshiyasu dies.

1715 On September 25 Sorai's second wife dies.

1716 The eighth shogun, Tokugawa Yoshimune introduces the Kyōhō Reforms.

1717 *Bendō (A Discourse on the Way)* is completed.

1718 Yoshimune sustains Hakuseki's monetary reform program and pursues the recoinage policy; Sorai is stricken with a serious lung illness.

1720 *The Benmei (The Clarification of Names)* and *Rongochō (Commentaries on the Analects)* are completed; the death of the last of his seven children leaves him childless, Sorai adopts his older brother's (Shunchiku) son, Sanjūrō.

1721 *Taiheisaku (A Proposal for Great Peace)* is composed.

1722 The bakufu imposes a rice levy (agemai) on daimyo with incomes of over 10,000 koku and reduces their period of residence in Edo (sankin kōtai) by half.

1727 In January *Gakosoku* is published; in May *Sorai sensei tōmonsho*

(*Master Sorai's Response to Questions*) is published; *Seidan (Discussions of Politics)* is completed.

1728 On January 19 Sorai dies at the age of sixty-three.

1729 Shundai drafts the *Keizai Roku* (Thought on the Political Economy).

1737 The *Bendō* and *Benmei* are published.

Biographical synopses

*

CH'ENG HAO 程顥 (1032–1085)

CH'ENG YI 程頤 (1033–1108)

Northern Sung Confucian scholars; the Ch'eng brothers, known as the two Ch'eng Masters; divided Neo-Confucianism into two main schools and initiated them; whereas Ch'eng Hao taught the idealism that originally there is a oneness between self and all things, Ch'eng Yi theorized the concept of the Principle.

CHOU LIEN CH'I (CHOU TUN-YI) 周濂溪（周敦頤） (1017–1073)

Northern Sung Neo-Confucian scholar; the first cosmological scholar of the Supreme Ultimate; drew his idea from the *Book of Changes* and Taoism; teacher of the Ch'eng brothers.

CHUANG TZU 莊子 (369?–286? BC)

Taoist philosopher; developed the ideas of Lao Tzu on life, death and freedom; his name is applied to the book he wrote, which is an essential part of the canon of Taoism.

CHU HSI 朱熹 (1130–1200)

Southern Sung scholar and official; unifier and synthesizer of Neo-Confucian thought; forged Neo-Confucianism into a state orthodoxy; a philosophical dualist who propounded a distinction between mind and nature; espoused the idea that the Supreme Ultimate was the supreme standard for the universe as a whole.

CONFUCIUS 孔子 (551–479 BC)

Greatest and most highly revered of all traditional Chinese philosophers; a native of the state of Lu in the Spring and Autumn period; resigned from his official position and traveled from state to state; preached that government should be based on ethics; looked back with favor upon the practices of the early Chou dynasty.

DAZAI SHUNDAI 太宰春台 (1680–1747)

Confucian scholar of the middle Edo period; one of Sorai's most distinguished students who became a teacher in his own right; in 1729 completed the treatise on political economy, *Keizai roku*.

FU HSI 伏義

First of the Three Sovereigns of the legendary period; *c.* 3000 B.C.; credited with teaching his people the basic skills of fishing, animal farming, and written language.

HAN YÜ 韓愈 (768–824)

T'ang Confucian scholar and official; prose stylist and critic of Buddhism and Taoism: a forerunner of the Neo-Confucian school of the Sung period.

HSÜAN TSANG 玄奘 (602–664)

T'ang Buddhist monk; embarked on a pilgrimage to India in 629; returned in 645 with scriptures which he spent the rest of his life translating into Chinese.

HSÜN TZU 荀子 (298–238 BC)

Warring States Confucian scholar; noted for his underlying principle that man is evil by nature; emphasized formal education, discipline, the study of the classics and proper conduct according to traditional rules and rituals; these ideas formed the basis of the Legalist School of thought.

ITŌ JINSAI 伊藤仁齋 (1627–1705)

Early Edo Confucian scholar; born into a Kyoto merchant family; established his school of ancient learning; emphasized the importance of the *Analects* and *Mencius* and commented upon them in the *Gomō jigi* (1683); taught in his private school, the *Kogidō* (The Hall of Ancient Meaning); remained independent of political patronage.

KAIBARA EKIKEN (EKKEN) 貝原益軒 (1630–1714)

Early Edo Confucian scholar; born in the domain of Kuroda in Chikuzen Province; his diverse scholarship includes writings on medicinal and food plants, health, the education of women and children, and ethics for commoners; in *Taigiroku*, refuted the Neo-Confucian cosmology for true moral action.

KAO TZU 告子 (*c.* 420–*c.* 350 BC)

  Warring States Confucian scholar; noted for his controversy with
  Mencius; held the theory that human nature is in itself neither good
  nor bad; for him, morality is something that is artificially added.

KIBI NO MAKIBI 吉備真備 (693–775)

  Nara scholar and courtier; studied in T'ang China from 717 to 735;
  introduced to Japan new elements of Chinese culture; the creation
  of the phonetic kata-kana script is attributed to him.

KUMAZAWA BANZAN 熊沢蕃山 (1619–1691)

  Early Edo Confucian scholar; born in Kyoto; studied under Nakae Tōju,
  from whom he learned the idealistic doctrines of Wang Yang-ming;
  stressed the importance of practice over theory; arrested in 1669 for
  criticizing the Shogunal administration.

LAO TZU 老子

  Author, probably mythical, of the *Lao Tzu*; Father of Taoism; sage and
  recluse; traditionally supposed to have lived some time before
  Confucius, between about 570 and 490 BC

LI P'AN-LUNG 李攀竜 (1514–1570)

  Ming man of letters; together with Wang Shih-chen, became one of the
  leading figures of the renaissance movement, or return to ancient style;
  took as a model for prose the Chi'n-Han period and as model for poetry
  the Han, Wei, and mid-T'ang period; Sorai, who still followed Sung
  Confucianism, owned one of his anthologies.

LU HSIANG-SHAN (LU CHIU-YÜAN) 陸象山（陸九淵） (1139–1193)

  Southern Sung Neo-Confucian scholar; developed the philosophy of
  Ch'eng Hao; maintained that "the mind is the Principle" and had a great
  controversy with Chu Hsi, who endorsed Ch'eng Yi's saying that "the
  nature is the Principle."

MENCIUS 孟子 (*c.* 372–289 BC)

  Confucian scholar; said to have been a pupil of the grandson of
  Confucius; during the period of the Warring States, he served several
  states as an adviser; his view that man is by nature good became one
  of the central tenets of Confucianism.

MO TZU 墨子 (*c.* 470–*c.* 391 BC)

Philosopher of the Warring States period; founder of the Mohist school; argued a utilitarian but altruistic philosophy; preached the idea of universal love as the only guarantee of peace and order.

MOTOORI NORINAGA 本居宣長 (1730–1801)

Mid-Tokugawa eminent scholar of National Studies (*kokugaku*); born in Ise; during his medical studies in Kyoto 1752–1757, introduced to the philological studies of Neo-Confucianism as well as Sorai and Keichū; advocated a re-identification with the spirit prevailing in ancient classics such as the *Kojiki* and *Tale of Genji*.

NAKAE CHŌMIN 中江兆民 (1847–1901)

Meiji political thinker and advocate of popular rights; studied in France 1871–1874 and then opened an institute for French studies in Tokyo; translated Rousseau.

SAKYAMUNI (SHAKYAMUNI) 釋迦牟尼 (*c.* 566–*c.* 486 BC)

Another name for Buddha; the founder of Buddhism.

SEVEN CREATIVE INDIVIDUALS 作者七人

Seven creator-sages who are said to have established cultural and regulative institutions, who ruled the world in ancient China between approximately 2200 and 700 BC.

EMPEROR YAO 堯

The 4th legendary emperor; model ruler; one of the Three Sages; the subject of a passage in the *Book of History*; abdicated in Shun's favor and passed over his own unworthy son.

EMPEROR SHUN 舜

5th mythical emperor; model ruler; one of the Three Sages; the subject of a passage in the *Book of History*; set an example of filial piety by living amicably with his father; passed over his own son and bequeathed the throne to one of his ministers, Yu.

YÜ OF HSIA 禹/夏

Founder of the Hsia dynasty (2205–1766 BC); one of the Three Sages; mentioned in the *Book of Songs*; credited with having spent several years in taming a great flood which afflicted China, and for this service was given the empire by his predecessor, Shun; passed the empire to his son, thereby founding the Hsia dynasty.

T'ANG OF SHANG   湯/商

First king of the Shang dynasty; a paragon in accordance with
traditional belief.

KING WEN   文/周

One of the three founders of the Chou dynasty; the King of Chou
under the last ruler of the Shang dynasty; celebrated as the epitome of
the wise and benevolent ruler; conceived the plan of overthrowing
the Shang, but it was left to his son and successor King Wu to revolt in
about 1133 BC

KING WU   武/周

One of the three founders of the Chou dynasty; the son of King Wen;
brought to completion the deposition of the Shang dynasty.

DUKE OF CHOU   周公

One of the three founders of the Chou dynasty; the illustrious son of
King Wen; the younger brother of King Wu; persuaded the Shang
people to cooperate with the new regime; acted as regent to King
Ch'eng, King Wu's successor.

SHAO YUNG   邵雍   (1011–1077)

Northern Sung Neo-Confucian scholar; cosmological philosopher;
developed his theory of the universe from the *Book of Changes*; made use
of diagrams to illustrate his theory, with "the circular diagram of the
sixty-four hexagrams," he explained the law of the evolution of things
as world cycles.

SHEN NUNG   神農

Second of the Three Sovereigns of the legendary period; reigned from
2737 to 2697 BC; credited with the introduction of agriculture.

TZU SSU   子思   (483–402 BC (?))

Confucius' grandson and second-generation disciple; allegedly author
of *Doctrine of the Mean*.

WANG SHIH-CHEN   王世貞   (1526–1590)

Ming official and man of letters; collaborated with Li P'an-lung in
advocating the "revival of the ancient"; ranked as the most prominent
representative of the classicist school in the history of Ming literature;
stimulated Sorai to extend this literary classicism into a method of
interpreting Confucian doctrines.

YAMAZAKI ANSAI 山崎闇齋 (1618–1682)

Early Edo Confucianist and Shintoist; born in Kyoto; first a Buddhist monk then a Confucian who tried to apply the metaphysics of Chu Hsi Neo-Confucianism to Shintoism; despite his particular synthesis, his school split into the Suika Shinto and Kimon school of Neo-Confucianism; a forceful educator; said to have had 6,000 disciples.

YANG CHU 楊朱

Hedonist philosopher; probably lived in the fourth century BC; one of the Hundred Schools; largely known through the criticism of Mencius; quoted to the effect that he would not sacrifice a hair from his body to benefit the whole world; believed that man should satisfy all desires possible.

YELLOW EMPEROR 黃帝

Third of the Three Sovereigns of the legendary period *c.* 2300 BC; credited with inventing bricks for construction, with correcting the calendar and with introducing the sixty-year cycle.

Guide to further reading

*

Traditional Chinese thought remains a difficult field of study today as it was in Sorai's time. A sophisticated treatment of the various ancient schools is Benjamin I. Schwartz, *The World of Thought in Ancient China* (Cambridge MA: Harvard University Press, 1985). The most complete coverage is provided in Fung Yu-lan, *A History of Chinese Philosophy*, 2 vols. (Princeton: Princeton University Press, 1952). A controversial work that emphasizes the religious dimension of ancient Confucian thought is Herbert Fingarette, *Confucius – The Secular as Sacred* (New York: Harper and Row Publishers, Inc., 1972). Discussions of Sorai's primary target of criticism, Chu Hsi within the context of a diverse intellectual history are: Hoyt Cleveland Tilman, *Confucian Discourse and Chu Hsi's Ascendancy* (Honolulu: University of Hawaii Press, 1992); Benjamin A. Elman, *From Philosophy to Philology – Intellectual and Social Aspects of Change in Late Imperial China* (Cambridge MA: Harvard University Press, 1990); and Thomas Metzgar, *Escape from Predicament: Neo-Confucianism and China's Political Culture* (New York: Columbia University Press, 1977). Also of interest are Wing Tsit Chan ed., *Chu Hsi's Neo-Confucianism* (Honolulu: University of Hawaii Press, 1986) and Wm. Theodore de Bary and Irene Bloom eds., *Principle and Practicality* (New York: Columbia University Press, 1979).

English language references to the establishment and subsequent development of the Tokugawa Bakufu as a political system, include the following. The best coverage is found in works by Conrad Totman, *Politics in the Tokugawa Bakufu, 1600–1843* (Berkeley: University of California Press, 1988, first published 1967); and *The Collapse of the Tokugawa Bakufu: 1862–1868* (Honolulu: University of Hawaii Press, 1980). Informative essays are in John W. Hall, ed., *The Cambridge History of Japan*, vol. 4 (New York: Cambridge University Press, 1991); John W. Hall, Nagahara Keiji and Kozo Yamamura, eds., *Japan before Tokugawa – Political Consolidation and Economic Growth* (Princeton: Princeton University Press, 1981); and John W. Hall and Marius Jansen eds., *Studies in the Institutional History of Early Modern Japan* (Princeton: Princeton University Press, 1968). I have written overview essays: *Japan, The Intellectual Foundations of Modern Japanese Politics* (1974; Chicago: University of Chicago Press, 1980); and "History and Nature in Eighteenth-Century Thought," in Hall, ed., *Cambridge History of Japan*, vol. 4 (chapter 12). For essays on developments in the countryside, see: Thomas C. Smith, *The Agrarian Origins of Modern Japan* (1959; New York: Atheneum, 1996); Anne Walthall, *Social Protest and Popular Culture* (Tucson: University of Arizona Press, 1986); and Stephen Vlastos, *Peasant Protests and Uprisings in Tokugawa Japan* (Berkeley: University of California Press, 1986).

The reader might consider the following brief list of works related to Tokugawa political thought in addition to those mentioned in notes 3 and 4 of the introduction: Robert N. Bellah, *Tokugawa Religion* (1957; Glencoe, Illinois; The Free Press, 1985); H. D. Harootunian, *Things Seen and Unseen – Discourse and Ideology in Tokugawa Nativism* (Chicago: University of Chicago Press, 1988); J. Victor Koschmann, *The Mito Ideology – Discourse, Reform, and Insurrection in Late Tokugawa Japan* (Berkeley: University of California Press, 1987); E. H. Norman, *Andō Shōeki and the Anatomy of Japanese Feudalism* (Tokyo: Transactions of the Asiatic Society of Japan, 1950, reprinted Washington, D.C.: University Publications of America, Inc., 1979); Peter Nosco, ed., *Confucianism and Tokugawa Culture* (Princeton: Princeton University Press, 1984); Herman Ooms, *Tokugawa Ideology* (Princeton: Princeton University Press, 1985); Mary Evelyn Tucker, *Moral and Spiritual Cultivation in Japanese Neo-Confucianism* (Albany: State University of New York Press, 1989); Toshinobu Yasunaga, *Andō Shōeki* (New York: Weatherhill, 1992).

Glossary

*

ANALECTS (LUN YÜ) 『論語』

A collection of the dialogues and sayings of Confucius and his disciples; consists of 20 chapters, divided into 497 sections; the most widely read of all Confucian works.

ANCIENT KINGS 先王

Sages; the founders of the Way; Yao, Shun and the rulers of the Three Dynasties (Yu, T'ang, Wen, Wu, and the Duke of Chou).

BAKUFU 幕府

Military government of Japan; the administration headed by a shogun, the emperor's military deputy, from 1192 onwards; there were three shogunal governments in Japanese history: the Kamakura Bakufu (1192–1333), the Muromachi Bakufu (1338–1573) and the Tokugawa Bakufu (1603–1867).

BAKU-HAN SYSTEM 幕藩体制

The semi-centralized political system founded by Tokugawa Ieyasu in 1603; placed the shogunate (*bakufu*) at the head of the government and lords or daimyo who governed regional domains (*han*) on an autonomous basis conditional to their observing the terms of their charter with the *bakufu*.

BENDŌ 『弁道』

A Discourse on the Way; completed in 1717; philosophical treatise by Sorai on the Way of the Sages to dismantle Sung Neo-Confucian metaphysics.

BENMEI 『弁名』

The Clarification of Names; completed shortly after the *Bendō*; in two vols.; Sorai's rectification of basic Confucian terms; grounded in his thesis that words, embedded in the Way, change historically; calls for a return to the ancient Six Classics.

CH'IN DYNASTY 秦 (221–206 BC)

Established by the Emperor Ch'in Shih Huang-ti; China was unified under its first imperial system; notorious for the "burning of the books"; from which the word "China" is derived.

CHOU DYNASTY 周 (1122–255 BC)

Feudal period of China, divided into three periods: Western Chou (1122–771 BC); Spring and Autumn period (771–484 BC); Warring States period (484–255 BC).

DAIMYŌ 大名

Title given to all lords who controlled regional domains (*han*) of Japan during the medieval and early modern eras; required during the Tokugawa period to spend every other year or half-year in Edo (alternate attendance, *sankin kōtai*) to confirm pledge of loyalty to the shogunate.

DOCTRINE OF THE MEAN (CHUNG YUNG) 『中庸』

One of the Four Books of Confucianism; believed to be the work of Confucius's grandson Tzu Ssu; an essay emphasizing moderation and sincerity and dealing with the character and duties of a true gentleman.

EDO 江戸

Former name (until 1868) of modern Tokyo; chosen as the seat of the Tokugawa shogunate in 1603; site of a population of over 1 million in the eighteenth century.

FOUR BOOKS (SSU SHU) 四書

Great Learning, Doctrine of the Mean, Analects, Mencius; a set of Confucian classics established as the central Confucian canon; grouped together and reinterpreted by Chu Hsi; selected as the basis of a classical education and as preparation for government service; de-emphasized by Sorai in favor of the Six Classics.

GAKUSOKU 『学則』

A Treatise on Instruction; composed by Sorai and published in 1727; a short work that tells where to find the Way, how to read the classics, and how to study them; emphasizes the individual virtue of each student.

GENROKU PERIOD　元祿時代　(1688–1704)

Period marked by a dynamic and literate popular culture that
accompanied the rise of a wealthy urban merchant class.

GI /RIGHTEOUSNESS　義

Since rites were fixed in concrete forms, righteousness was necessary to
deal with a wide range of actual circumstances; put together with rites
for a more precise approach to the Way of the Ancient Kings.

GREAT LEARNING (TA HSÜEH)　『大学』

First of the Four Books; originally the 43rd chapter of the *Book of Rites*;
attributed to Tzu Ssu; consists of seven steps to learning; the investigation of things, dedication to study, sincerity in thought, rectifying the
heart, cultivation of the self, the regulation of the family, and the
governing of the country.

HAN DYNASTY　漢　(206 BC–AD 220)

Divided into the former of western-Han (206 BC–AD 8) and the Later or
Eastern Han (25–220); noted for its many contributions to Chinese
culture.

HUNDRED SCHOOLS　百家

Proliferation of philosophical schools in the Warring States period;
included Confucian and Taoist ideas, Naturalists, Legalists,
Dialecticians, and followers of Mo Tzu and Mencius.

JIN/BENEVOLENCE　仁

A virtue that to Sorai did not reside in each individual but in the Ancient
Kings who pursued the political goal of maintaining peace among the
people; a virtue that is a fundamental value on which much of
Confucianism is based.

KANBUN　漢文

Classical Chinese language used in Japan for literature and official
documents; often with diacritical marks to be read in accordance with
Japanese grammar.

KEI/REVERENCE　敬

Attitude of great respect for those above the self; most notably,
reverence for Heaven, the ultimate basis of the Way.

LAO TZU (TAO TE CHING) 『老子』

Major work of Lao Tzu and the most important work in the Taoist canon; probably compiled in the fourth or third century BC; a collection of maxims and aphorisms about the Tao.

LEGALISTS 法家

Pragmatic authoritarian school of philosophy; derived from Hsun Tzu; argued that since man's nature was essentially selfish harsh laws and strict rule were necessary to avoid conflict; adopted by the Chi'n dynasty.

MEIJI ERA 明治時代 (1868–1912)

The period of the modernization of Japan; identified with the Emperor Meiji.

MENCIUS 『孟子』

Philosophical work of Mencius; expounded the theory that social betterment could only be achieved through moral cultivation to fulfill the original goodness of human nature; for him, all humans possess the "four beginnings," the feelings of commiseration, aversion, modesty, and righteousness.

NATIONAL STUDIES (*KOKUGAKU*) 国学

Literary movement created in the eighteenth century in opposition to Confucian and Buddhist doctrines, called for a return to ancient Japanese morality through the medium of the native classics; represented by such figures as Motoori Norinaga and Hirata Atsutane.

NEO-CONFUCIANISM 朱子学

A system of Confucian thought elaborated by Chu Hsi; argued that principle is a natural, metaphysical law; the official ideology of the Tokugawa Bakufu for ordering of society.

REIRAKU KEISEI 礼樂刑政

Rites, music, law-enforcement, and political administration; created by the Sages; specific products of history which consists of the Way; objective and concrete, not abstract.

RITES OF CHOU (CHOU LI) 『周礼』

An idealized description of the bureaucratic system which was supposed to have been in effect during the Chou dynasty; attributed to the Duke of Chou, composed probably in the Spring and Autumn period; consists of six parts; utilized by statesmen to justify reforms they wished to make in later times.

SAGES　聖人

Creators of rites and music and other regulative institutions; Yao, Shun, and the rulers of the Three Dynasties (Yu, T'ang, Wen, Wu, and the Duke of Chou); identifiably human, rather than divine figures, though Yao and Shun are more problematical than the others.

SEIDAN　『政談』

Discussion of Politics; Sorai's treatise on political economy for the use of Tokugawa Yoshimune; probably written around 1725–1727; a long and detailed four-volume, issue-by-issue response; spelled out concrete policy proposals; Sorai wished to end the samarais' habits of urban luxury and recommended their transfer from castle towns to the land.

SENGOKU ERA　戰國時代　(1467–1568)

Period of the Country in War; ended with the unification of the country by Toyotomi Hideyoshi and Tokugawa Ieyasu.

SIX CLASSICS (LIU YI)　六经

Confucian canons that existed prior to Confucius; believed by Sorai to be the only true guide to the Way of the Ancient Kings; came to the fore with the rise of the exegetical schools of the Han and T'ang periods.

BOOK OF SONGS (ODES) (SHI CHING)　『詩经』

One of the Six Classics; anthology of poems dating from the 11th to the 6th century BC; includes folk songs, love songs, political poems and longer ritual hymns, many of which were sung or chanted in Chou dynasty ceremonies.

BOOK OF HISTORY (DOCUMENTS) (SHU CHING)　『書经』

One of the Six Classics; first Chinese work of history; edited by Confucius; only 58 chapters from the 100 original ones are extant.

BOOK OF RITES (LI CHI)　『礼記』

One of the Six Classics; work based on codes and customs in the Chou dynasty; in 49 sections; put together in the early part of the first century BC from various texts of late Chou, Ch'in, and Han times;

contains minute descriptions of the etiquette to be followed at
ceremonial occasions in ancient times.

BOOK OF MUSIC (YÜEH CHI) 『樂記』
One of the Six Classics; no longer preserved as a separate work and is
now lost; considered to be pre-eminent in harmonizing power; its
merit was to secure internal harmony.

BOOK OF CHANGES (I CHING) 『易经』
One of the Six Classics; handbook of divination based on a system of
hexagrams; probably composed in the Chou dynasty; influential in
both Taoist and Confucian traditions.

SPRING AND AUTUMN ANNALS (CH'UN CH'IU) 『春秋』
One of the Six Classics; official records of the state of Lu between
722 and 481 BC; supposedly edited by Confucius; deals mainly with
politics; written in a difficult style requiring editorial commentaries;
of these the best known is the *Tso Chuan*.

SUNG DYNASTY 宋 (960-1279)
One of the most highly regarded dynasties in Chinese history; famed
for its poetry, painting and ceramics and for unprecedented economic
growth; movable type appeared in about 1030 stimulating the
development of scholarship and literature, notably the works of
Neo-Confucianism.

TAIHEISAKU 『太平策』
A Proposal for Great Peace; written by Sorai; a general response to a series
of consultations; composed probably in 1721; identified the Tokugawa
system with early Chinese feudalism; assigned economics a central
role in public affairs; discussed the utilization of men of talent and
merit.

TAITOKU/GREAT VIRTUE 大德
Supreme virtue of Benevolence attributed to the Sages; the virtue with
which the superior ruler supports life and brings peace to the people;
also used to mean the great virtue of the natural order.

T'ANG DYNASTY 唐 (618-907)
Dynasty of the Li family; reestablished a Chinese military presence in
Central Asia; marked the end of the classical and the beginning of the

early modern phases of Chinese history; Buddhism reached its zenith during this period.

THREE DYNASTIES (HSIA, SHANG OR YIN, CHOU)　三代（夏・商/殷・周）
Period of the Hsia (2205–1766 BC), Shang-Yin (1766–1122 BC), and Chou (1122–255 BC) dynasties; known for their feudal states, whereas the Ch'in and later dynasties, down to the T'ang, Sung, and Ming, were all centralized bureaucratic regimes.

TSO CHUAN　左傳
Commentary on the *Spring and Autumn Annals*; written probably in the 4th century BC; a mixture of legend and fiction, reputedly written by Tso Ch'iu-ming; work of primary importance for the study of Chou history and society.

WARRING STATES PERIOD　戦国時代　(484–221 BC)
Last period of the Chou dynasty; marked by continual rivalry between the states; the state of Ch'in gradually defeated all the other states and unified China.

WAY OF THE ANCIENT KINGS (WAY OF THE SAGES)　先王の道（聖人の道）
The Way created by the Ancient Kings; consists of concrete political systems and methods of rule; distinguished from a universal Way of nature; the way by which all under Heaven are provided peace and nourishment; used as the original historical reference for the rest of the Confucian tradition.

Bendō
A discourse on the Way

*

OGYŪ SORAI

1. The Way is difficult to comprehend and explain to others because it is truly vast. Confucian scholars of recent eras claim their own individual perceptions to be the entire Way, but these perceptions are all only aspects of it.

The Way is in fact the Way of the Ancient Kings. From the days of Tzu Ssu and Mencius, however, the Confucian School has contended for supremacy among the Hundred Schools, inevitably diminishing the full meaning of the Way.

When we consider Tzu Ssu's *Doctrine of the Mean*, we find that it is a critique directed against Lao Tzu, who had said that the Way of the Sages was a fabrication. Tzu Ssu countered with the view that the Way conformed with human nature and that it was not a fiction. In the end his argument came to rest on the concept of human "truthfulness." The Mean, however, refers to only one among several forms of moral behavior, and therefore is said to be "chosen." Tzu Ssu relied on the idea of the Mean to explain the meaning of the Way and to show that Lao Tzu's views were not in accordance with his [own] ideas. However, the conclusion drawn by later scholars that the Mean is identical with the Way is erroneous. Those who were first to create things in the ancient world are called "Sages." Confucius was not one of these creators. Thus, to defend Confucius against the

The translation is from Yoshikawa Kojiro and Maruyama Masao eds., *Nihon shisōshi taikei* 36: *Ogyū Sorai* (Tokyo: Iwanami Shoten, 1973), pp. 10–36. An earlier version of this translation prepared for student use appeared in Select Papers (9: 93) of the Center for East Asian Studies at the University of Chicago.

criticism that he was not a sage, Tzu Ssu advanced the view in *The Mean* that "realizing truthfulness" is a sagely virtue and that this also meant respect for goodness, for responsible behavior, and for status. Still, the concept of "truthfulness" is only one of the virtues of the Sages and certainly cannot be seen as exhausting the meaning of the Way.

When we examine Mencius's theory about the goodness of human nature, we find he follows the same trend of thinking as Tzu Ssu. Mencius erred in distorting the view of human nature explained fully by Kao Tzu through the metaphor of the pliant willow. Even Tzu Ssu, whose main intent was to show that the Sages relied on human nature in building the Way, did not ask each individual to conform to his own nature so as to realize the natural Way within himself. Unlike other trees, the willow can be shaped into cups and bowls. But surely these utensils are no longer the same things as the willow in its natural state. Mencius uses the ideas of compassion and shame to substantiate the point that benevolence and propriety are essential to the human self. In truth, compassion does not suffice as an explanation of benevolence, and shame is not always in accord with propriety. Once these distorted ideas were set forth, small discrepancies became enormous fissures. The idealist schools of later times find their beginnings here. Actually, Hsün Tzu's critique of Tzu Ssu and Mencius was well taken. Thus, while Tzu Ssu and Mencius may be seen as defenders of Confucianism against its critics, Hsün Tzu is in our eyes a loyal sentinel for having spoken the truth.

The era we are dealing with, however, is not far removed from Confucius's own time, so that the customs of his age are still around and names and the things to which they refer are still very much in accordance with each other. With Han Yü in the T'ang Dynasty, an enormous change in the language takes place. When we come to Chu Hsi and the Ch'eng brothers, who were great men in their age, we find that they can no longer understand the ancient language. Finding that they cannot read and grasp the Six Classics, they rely on the easily understandable *Doctrine of the Mean* and on *Mencius* and persuade themselves that the polemical views found there explain the basic meaning of the Way of the Sages. They also filter the ancient tongue through the expressions of their own day and are unable to comprehend actual meanings: they separate name from reality and follow only abstract arguments that are disconnected from the original language. Thus it is that the teachings of the Ancient Kings and of Confucius fade from view.

In recent years the eminent scholar Itō Jinsai presented some ideas that were close indeed to the central meaning of the Way. However, he examined the *Analects* through *Mencius* and interpreted ancient texts in the light of modern language, so that, in the end, his position remained similar to the Ch'eng brothers and Chu Hsi of the Sung period. Also, he made a distinct division between the Way of the Ancient Kings and the Way of Confucius, and he favored the *Analects* over the Six Classics, which reveals that he had still read these Classics in a Japanese manner. When I peruse his treatise on the ancient meaning of the *Analects* (*Rongo Kogi*), I doubt very much that it uncovers the meaning of things in ancient times.

Alas, with the passage of time the Way of the Ancient Kings splintered into the narrow interpretations of the schools of Confucian scholars. Chu Hsi and Lu Hsiang-shan followed Hsün Tzu and Mencius and contention among factions became increasingly intense, each splinter group becoming more narrow in its focus. How lamentable.

Blessed by the wondrous spirit of Heaven, I managed to obtain the writings of Wang Shih-chen and Li P'an-lung and through them discovered, for the first time, the existence of ancient literature. Since then I have read the Six Classics in small amounts over a long period of time and gradually acquired the ability to comprehend the relationship between terms and reality. Only after succeeding in this could I understand the meaning of the vocabulary I encountered and to speak with some confidence about the Six Classics. These Six Classics contain descriptions of essential things that comprise the Way. The Han *Book of Rites* and the *Analects* interpret their spiritual meaning. These explanations together with concrete examples constitute the Way. If concrete things are disregarded and only general explanations are stressed, the result, aside from exceptional cases, will be arbitrary thinking. Han Yü, Liu Tsung-yüan, the Ch'eng brothers, and their disciples all exhibit this failing.

I am now already past fifty. Should I die suddenly without having made the effort to achieve my aim in life, I will fail to realize Heaven's calling. In my spare moments, therefore, I write down my thoughts ever mindful of Heaven's grace. I have noted some of my basic ideas in several sections for students who may wish to study with me.

2. The Way that Confucius taught is the Way of the Ancient Kings, and the Way of the Ancient Kings is to bring peace into the world. Confucius always wished to restore the order of Eastern Chou in his home kingdom of Lu. In his teachings, therefore, he urged each of his students to fully develop his individual talent in order to best serve the administration.

But because he could not become a political leader, Confucius devoted his energies toward compiling the Six Classics and transmitting them to later generations. The Six Classics embody the Way of the Ancient Kings. It is erroneous to separate them from Confucius's teachings as has been argued in recent years. To bring peace throughout the land personal self-cultivation is essential, but the self must be nourished to want peace. This is what is meant by Benevolence.

With Tzu Ssu and Mencius a certain kind of Confucian school was established. A fanciful idea came to be promoted about the mission of the teacher: by studying and becoming a sage, it was said that a teacher could then dedicate himself to the kingdom and naturally bring about peace. This reminds us of Lao Tzu and Chuang Tzu who saw the virtue of the sage as being eternal, and treated external things, as compared to things of the self, lightly. This of course differs greatly from the actual teachings of the Ancient Kings and of Confucius. It is for this reason that Confucian teachers have not been able to fully develop the internal talents of the disciples in their schools, and have also failed to shape a tradition of effective rule. They stand to be criticized for arguing only in the abstract with a disregard for practical applications. Surely this situation is a result of the discrepancy between what they perceived to be the Way, and the Way as it actually is.

3. The term "Way" encompasses all things created by the Ancient Kings, such as rituals, music, the law, and statecraft. The Way does not exist apart from these concrete things. One gains a sense of this relationship in the saying "the wise understand the large frame of reference and those of

lesser mind comprehend the details; yet in each of these details resides the Way of Wen and Wu." To cite another example, Confucius once chided Tzu Yu, one of his disciples, for governing the little town of Wu Ch'eng with majestic music, saying that it reminded him of a heavy-handed cook shredding a chicken with a cleaver. Tzu Yu responded correctly, however, by saying that both princes and ordinary human beings had access to the Way. The Han scholar K'ung An-kuo used this anecdote to explain that the Way was ritual and music. This suggests that Confucian thinkers in Han times continued to understand the meaning of ancient concepts.

In later periods, however, with such figures as Chou Lien Ch'i, scholars came to prize fine minutiae and to despise the coarse and unrefined. Lien Ch'i based his view of the Way and of concrete forms on the *Book of Changes*. The Way as specifically discussed in this book, however, referred to the idea that forms correspond to arrangements of yin-yang symbols, and various instruments are fashioned out of specific standards of measurements. Lien Ch'i seemed quite oblivious to the fact that the *Book of Changes* is really a book of divination and cannot be seen in the same light as the other Classics. Sung scholars, moreover, understood the Way to be the universal principle operative in all things. Each of them equated his subjective intention as being that principle, however, and from that perspective sought to design rites, music, the law, and government. The Ancient Kings, however, were sages. It is wholly presumptuous, a failure to comprehend human limitation, to assume that anyone can grasp the extraordinary power of the Ancient Kings to create rites and music.

In recent years some scholars have based their teachings exclusively on the *Doctrine of the Mean* and the *Mencius*. They see the Way as being a combination of filial piety, brotherly respect, and the other five forms of virtuous behavior: benevolence, righteousness, propriety, wisdom, and trustworthiness. They simply do not understand that in the *Doctrine of the Mean* the five ways of behavior originally referred to a premise in the Way of the Ancient Kings – that there are five essential items that are applicable to everyone from the king on down to commoners. These items did not, however, explain the entirety of the Way. In addition to the reference in the *Mencius* – that the Way of Yao and Shun can be reduced to two points: piety to parents and respect for elderly brothers – it is actually saying, as did the *Doctrine of the Mean*, that one must always begin at the bottom to reach a high place. Surely it does not mean that piety and brotherly respect exhaust the various meanings in the Way of Yao and Shun. Consider also that in equating the Mean with the Way one tends to choose the Mean according to one's subjective wishes. Without identifying with the Way of the Ancient Kings what would one use as the normative basis to substantiate the Mean? There is the further view of the Way as ceaseless flow, which Itō Jinsai describes as the natural interaction of life and death, but here too is the same sort of thinking that prizes fine minutiae and despises the coarse and the unrefined. None of these views recognizes that the term "Way" is a broad, inclusive term.

4. The Way was constructed by the Ancient Kings. It is not natural. Possessing extraordinary intelligence and wisdom, these Kings received Heaven's mandate to be rulers. With total dedication, they set forth to establish peace under Heaven, and, committing their enormous spiritual and mental powers to the task, they created the Way to guide the actions of later generations. How could the Way of the Ancient Kings be located in nature?

Fu Hsi, Shen Nung, and the Yellow Emperor may be said to be Sages. What is important, however, is that they did not go beyond providing practical advice about survival, whereas the ancient regimes of Chuan Hsü and Ti K'u and those of Yao and Shun brought ritual and music into existence for the first time. With the following dynasties of Hsia, Yin, and Chou, the Way was shaped into its finest splendor. The Way was created over hundreds of years by a number of brilliant Sages and was not the achievement of a single individual over one lifetime. Confucius himself understood the Way only after much study. Regardless [of this] how could one say that the Way of the Ancient Kings is located in nature?

The Doctrine of the Mean says that by conforming to one's essential human nature one discovers the Way. When this view was stated, Lao Tzu had already denounced the Way of the Sages as artificial. Tzu Ssu thus wrote the *Doctrine of the Mean*, defending Confucian tradition, explaining that the Ancient Kings conceived of the Way by conforming to the realities of human nature. He did not say that this Way is to be found in nature, nor did he maintain that the Ancient Kings, by relying on human nature, did not engage in the creation of concrete things. This is best illustrated when a tree is cut to build a house. The natural essence of the tree must be relied upon, but the structure itself is no longer the same thing as the natural tree. In nature, things continue as they are in their natural form. Human beings build and order things that they take from nature. Later Confucian scholars did not understand this notion, and confused Nature and the Way to be the same thing, thus reducing their thinking to those of the Taoists Lao Tzu and Chuang Tzu.

5. Great wisdom and intellectual power was given at birth to the Ancient Kings by Heaven. Human beings do not ordinarily achieve this kind of virtue with their own strength. Therefore, the theory that through study an individual might transform himself into a sage was never advanced in ancient times. Although the Virtue of the Ancient Kings embodied many different meritorious elements that are difficult to express with a single term, the use of the word "Sage" pertains primarily to one virtue: to their having created things; it is without question the only reason why the Ancient Kings are called Sages. Had they acted only in terms of their internal (private) virtue, they would not be worthy sons of Heaven. And if the name "Sage" was applied to all the wise kings of later ages who ruled on the basis of benevolence, then there would be no difference between them and the Ancient Kings. Because the creation of rites and music was such a magnificent thing, the honorific Sage was used. However, it designates only one aspect of their Virtue. For example, in the *Book of History*, both "sageness" and cultural ability are prized as virtues. In the *Book of Songs* sageness and reverence are paired. And in the *Rites of Chou*, sageness is listed third among six virtues. How then can sageness be synonymous with the Virtue of the Ancient Kings? Once the Virtue of the Ancient Kings was termed "Sagely," the term "Sage" was considered the most dignified way of referring to them.

Tzu Ssu upheld Confucius as a Sage. There is no known evidence, however, that Confucius created anything. Tzu Ssu also made the outlandish assertion that the Way conforms with human nature so that he found himself arguing that through scholarship one could develop one's nature and become a sage. He concluded by thus identifying a sage as one who is in accord with internal human truthfulness. Later he postured as a sage for the political purpose of persuading King Liang and Ch'i to realize the glory of the kingdom of Chou. Even as he did this, however, he clearly doubted himself as being a true sage of the same order as Yao, Shun, Wen, and the Duke of Chou. Hence he even referred to mediocrities such as Po I and Liu Hsia-hui as sages.

Tzu Ssu lived at a time when the customs of Confucius's era were still within memory. Tzu Ssu's language, therefore, conveys a tone of reverence. In referring to the Sages, he spoke of godliness and mystery. Mencius saw the sage as one who primarily avoids unrighteous action and does not kill a single innocent human being to seize an empire. But this designates a benevolent person merely, and not a sage. If we look at Mencius closely, however, we find that he too made allowances of the sort just mentioned about Tzu Ssu, because his time was relatively close to Confucius's time. But since these two figures were hasty in their reformatory polemics they relied on volatile language, so that the ancient meaning of the sage became obscured. It is a pity.

To repeat my point, kings and princes in later dynasties maintained and practiced the rites and music of Ancient Kings without criticism. These rites, music, laws, and government embody the Way through which the Ancient Kings promoted peace in their kingdoms. This is Benevolence. Kings and princes in later times are called "benevolent men" precisely because they relied on the rites and music of the Ancient Kings. One does not become a sage by studying, although through study one might become a benevolent person. Thus, while Confucius taught his students the idea of Benevolence, he did not once urge them to become sages. The foregoing is indicative of the greater faith that later generations, in general, have placed on Tzu Ssu and Mencius, the Cheng brothers and Chu Hsi than on the Ancient Kings and Confucius. This is, of course, an unfortunate mistake.

6. Confucian scholars direct their students to strive toward distant and ideal goals, which an ordinary human being cannot possibly attain. They

say that these goals are the ultimate norms discovered by the ancient Sages. What a reckless idea. The saying that the Ancient Kings built norms refers to rites. Han Confucian scholars interpreted norm to denote the Mean. They knew moreover that Tzu Ssu used the Mean to convey the essential meaning of rites. Now, while this view is not entirely correct, its central theme does not divert too far from the original idea so that the ancient meaning could still be communicated from teacher to student.

The Ancient Kings created rites in such a way that the wise from above as well as the ignorant from below could identify with them. This is the meaning of norm – to be easily within the grasp of ordinary human beings. If this were not so, then ordinary people would find themselves seeking goals they could not attain and if they were urged to seek such goals mankind would be frustrated in its yearning for goodness. Certainly, this was not how the Ancient Kings intended to bring peace to the world. Therefore theories that say that the natural principle of all things represents an absolute ethical norm, or that human beings can transform their specific character to become sages through scholarship are all foreign to the teachings of Confucius and of the Ancient Kings.

In recent years, Itō Jinsai demonstrated his awareness of these erroneous ideas. However, he continued to identify the concepts of filiality, brotherly respect, benevolence, and righteousness as true norms found in human conduct. Is this a reasonable view to take? Do human beings in fact determine internally the meaning of norms such as filiality? What, indeed, is the normative basis of any ethical concept? Much of what we are told is merely arbitrary, as in calculating a meter without centimeters or using a ruler without gradations.

7. For Confucius, Benevolence was the most important idea, because Benevolence embodied the essence of the entire Way of the Ancient Kings. The Way of the Ancient Kings is to bring peace and well-being to the world. There are, to be sure, many facets to the Way, but what is crucial is the promotion of peace among men. What underlies the idea of Benevolence is reverence and devotion toward Heaven's imperative. When Heaven calls on individuals to become princes, lords, or retainers, they must have subjects below them to direct. When Heaven calls on

persons to become gentlemen, they must support wives and kinsmen. These men must all dedicate themselves to the goal of achieving peace. Retainers and gentlemen, moreover, support the prince as they respond to their calling from Heaven. Benevolence is the greatest single virtue in the Way of kingly rule.

It might be added that it is a normal human feeling to love and be affectionate as it is to nourish, support, and protect others. Mencius himself taught that "an individual should behave as a human being ought to, and that the collectivity of such human behavior is called the Way." And Hsün Tzu observed that "the prince always means society." The Way of human existence, in short, never refers to a single individual but invariably to a myriad of individuals living together in some coherent manner.

If we looked far and wide in our world today, would we find a person living totally in isolation? Retainers, farmers, artisans, and merchants mutually support each other; they would not survive otherwise. Even thieves organize themselves in groups, or they too would languish. The figure who unifies a multitude of individuals is called the King. In unifying the people, the encouragement of generous feelings toward each other and nourishment in developing their natural abilities correspond to the Way of the Ancient Kings. Each individual who seizes this idea of the Way of the Ancient Kings and develops fully the virtue in himself may be called a benevolent person.

It should be added that the gentleman who develops his own virtue by studying the Way of the Ancient Kings must also be aware that this Way has numerous facets. Human nature is also highly plural. If each individual, grasping the peaceful intention of the Way of the Ancient Kings, strives to develop himself in light of Benevolence, then he will be able to discover in his own special character an identification with an aspect of the Way. Examples of individuals who fully realized their own special talents are Confucius's disciples: Yu in his courage, Tzu his pure intelligence, Ch'in his artistry. For realizing their own virtues, they may be seen as benevolent men who were capable of promoting peace and well-being. An additional point should be stressed regarding individuals seeking to realize their own virtue. When I and Chi realized their virtue of high-mindedness, Hui his gentleness, and Yin his loyalty, they did not sacrifice the specific character that they possessed, and this in no way undermined their ethical stature as benevolent individuals. Had they not consciously identified themselves with Benevolence, they would not have been able to realize their special talents and virtues. The Hundred Schools disputed with each other because they failed to understand this. Yet it is for these reasons that Confucius and his disciples taught the value of Benevolence.

In Mencius's concept of compassion, benevolence is explained as tender human feeling. Since in his theory human goodness was assumed to be essential to the human self, his reliance on the idea of affectionate feeling was unavoidable. Individual human beings do possess the spirit of loving others, but since political nurturing does not extend to all people, affectionate feeling cannot really be described as Benevolence. Mencius himself was aware of this and therefore spoke of benevolence as the basis of governance. Later Confucian thinkers, however, failed to take into account the fact that Mencius sought to incite the people of his day. Entirely convinced by the appropriateness of Mencius, these thinkers endeavored to achieve benevolence. They believed that by cultivating the feeling of compassion in themselves, they would realize the Benevolence of the Sages. This is of course mindless illusion.

The proponents of this view have said that "there is benevolence in Buddhism too, although not righteousness." How can this be so when there is no principle in Buddhism that concerns itself with establishing ordered peace on this earth? In the case of Mo Tzu, benevolence was deemed to be the highest ideal of the Way of the Ancient Kings. But then he proceeded to believe that benevolence permeated all things. While it is true that the Great Virtue of Nature is called Life, and Benevolence is the Great Virtue of the Sages, Mo Tzu misunderstood the plurality of virtues. If the virtue of nature were "life" alone, how can the different seasons be explained? If the Sages' Virtue were only Benevolence, how would we account for courage, wisdom, trust, and righteousness? Mencius was thus correct when he cited the virtue of righteousness to refute Mo Tzu's exclusive emphasis on benevolence. However, when Mencius placed benevolence and righteousness side by side, this move lessened the previous important position of Benevolence. Thus we see what happened to the idea of Benevolence as the Great Virtue. Seeking to somehow make consistent the idea of Benevolence as the Great Virtue and benevolence as that which compares with righteousness, Confucian scholars of Sung times proposed two categories of explanation, the one general, and the other particular. The general represented a comprehensive rendering of all of the virtues, while the particular referred to virtues that might be listed as separate items. They felt that this approach would reconcile the general view of Confucius with the particular one of Mencius, a reflection of the tendency of Sung scholars to seek knowledge through abstract ideas and to rely on linguistic terms. How could the Way of the Ancient Kings be comprehended through such an approach?

The Way of the Ancient Kings is made up of many elements. To name specific examples, governments everywhere forbid insurrections and use force and punitive means to execute people. Is this Benevolence? The main aim, however, is to maintain peace in the kingdom. The teachings of the Ancient Kings are truly manifold. They teach of wisdom, courage, righteousness, benevolence, which should not be confused one with the other. The essential point, however, is that these separate references do not undermine the central intent of the Sages to provide peace and wellbeing for the people. It is for this reason that "wisdom," "courage," and "righteousness" are called virtues. Confucius's saying "conform to your own personal virtue and rely on Benevolence" is an instructive one. What he meant was that no individual would lose his own special virtue if he conformed to his true nature. He meant too that while human nature may be infinite in variety, no human virtue can be harmful to Benevolence. It is only when human virtues cannot be nourished and consummated that there is deviation from the Way. The Way of Human Nourishment is captured in Confucius's words: "Rely on Benevolence and gain mastery of an art." The meaning of "rely" is expressed in the phrase, "to sing one must rely on the voice." Music is the blend of poetry, of clear and deep tones, and of rhythm and melody, each relying on the other. This is the meaning of "rely," and it has the same sense as when used in "rely on Benevolence." Although human beings possess a virtue that is distinctive to each one, by relying on the Way of Peace and Well-being of the Ancient Kings, all humans can realize fully their own personal virtues. This was the teaching of Confucius and his disciples.

The Way of the Ancient Kings and Confucius was constantly dynamic and active. The vital aim is to enhance the human nourishment and growth. However, superficially, with abandon, scholars in later times explained all phenomena in terms of Benevolence, even with complete leaps of reasoning, calling it the universal principle underlying all things. A close examination of this concept reveals it to be the Buddhist idea that Buddhahood permeates all beings and natural things. This is poor thinking indeed.

8. Many believe that benevolence and righteousness are as night and day are to the universe. They go on to say that these virtues express the Way in its entirety. But this is a view of later times. In examining the Ancient Kings and Confucius, how could we seek to explain the Way in a word or two? Those who wish to do this impose inappropriate distinctions on the Way of the Sages, which would have been unacceptable by the Ancient Kings and Confucius. In ancient times, for example, the concepts of ritual and righteousness were classed together. Benevolence, on the other hand, was the Great Virtue of the Sages and was not treated as belonging to the same order of things. Thus in Confucius's school, Benevolence was considered to be of the highest importance. Later, however, Mencius classed benevolence and righteousness as comparable ideas. Although such a strategy was useful in arguing against the mistaken views of Yang Chu and Mo Tzu, it is not at all permissible in the instruction of scholarly thinkers. The grouping of benevolence, righteousness, ritual, and wisdom also began with Mencius and is not to be found in Confucius. The technique here was to arrange together ideas not present in the thinking of Yang and Mo and thereby argue the superiority of the Confucian Way. In actual fact, ritual and righteousness are important elements in human existence, but Benevolence transcends these ideas.

Now for a few words about wisdom. Human beings enjoy their own intellectual abilities and like to see themselves in the best possible light. Such a tendency is due to their passionate nature. The Sages, therefore, avoided the concept of wisdom for purposes of instruction. References to wise or benevolent persons are descriptions of individuals who have realized their own special virtues, which differ according to the natural endowments granted by Heaven to each individual. I have not heard of a person who simultaneously possessed all the virtues: benevolence, righteousness, intelligence, propriety, and wisdom. In Han times, Confucian scholars tried to connect these virtues with the five natural elements of wood, fire, earth, metal, and water; for example, wisdom has been equated with earth, faith with water, sometimes wisdom with fire or water, and the like. As yet, there are no established theories to support these claims. It should simply be observed that such ideas did not exist earlier. In the *Analects* there are frequent references to a fondness for benevolence, righteousness, ritual, virtue, goodness, learning, and the ancient past. But in Confucian instructions there is not a single reference to a fondness for wisdom or faith. Wisdom and faith, in other words, are not central to the teachings of Confucius. Hsün Tzu was not being outlandish at all in criticizing Tzu Ssu and Mencius for their ethical interpretation of the five elements.

9. Benevolence is the Way of Nourishment. In governing the kingdom, therefore, it is proper to elevate the upright over the perverse so that the crooked will come to be straightened. Likewise, in regard to cultivating the self, what is virtuous in the self should be nourished so that evil will disappear of itself. This is the method of the Way of the Ancient Kings. Later Confucian scholars did not comprehend the Way of the Ancient Kings, thinking erroneously that by developing one's personal wisdom one would part from evil and, through realizing the natural principle of goodness in the self, eradicate passionate desires. Once these ideas were firmly implanted a spirit of reckless criticism spread throughout the land. After all the world of Yao and Shun no longer prevailed, human beings were no longer Sages, and evil tendencies always outnumbered the good ones. People could not tolerate the oppressive ideas imposed by Chu Hsi in his criticism of governance in the treatise called *T'ung Chien*

and by other Sung scholars in their prescriptions of self-cultivation. They finally became convinced that Confucian scholars enjoyed being abusive. How sad. Actually since the days of the legalist Shang Yang, not only the imperial government but various scholarly schools have relied on legalistic methods. Surely these later ages cannot compare with the ancient dynasties of Hsia, Shang, and Chou.

10. The Way of the Ancient Kings is to establish peace and well-being under Heaven. In ancient times scholars of political economy unfailingly subscribed to this view. After the ancient period, however, the non-centralized form of governance was transformed into a centralized bureaucratic rule, and the Way of the Ancient Kings became mainly decorative. Those who referred to the Ancient Kings merely used classical scholarship to embellish bureaucratic rule. In general, non-centralized rule fostered the feeling of family relationships such as that between parents and children. Centralized bureaucracy relied on the law alone. Unduly formalistic and strict, it extinguished human feelings of kindness and affection. In addition, after the Sui and T'ang dynasties, an examination system was instituted which greatly altered the tradition of learning among scholars. Primary attention came to be given to such skills as writing conventional lines with a clear hand. The scholars of that age were influenced to the marrow by legalistic thinking. Although these scholars discoursed on the Way and analyzed the Classics, their ideas were drawn from their own particular age. How could they, therefore, come to grasp the actual workings of the Way? Sung scholars excelled in constructing grand outlines and compiling minute details. While it cannot be denied that these scholars were careful in their deliberations, their accomplishments can hardly be compared with the Way of the Ancient Kings.

11. It is in accordance with the Way of the Ancient Kings that, when the essential principles are in order, other lesser considerations will proceed of their own accord. Thus, Tzu Hsia remarked in the *Analects*, "Since the Great Virtue never exceeds normative bounds, the little virtues may come and go as they wish." If this were not the case one could not move about within the guidelines of the Way. Tzu Kung said, again in the

Analects, "Wise men perceive the breadth of the Way, while the unwise see only narrow limits." Thus to know the vast scheme leads one to be wise; to seek only small portions of it leads one to be a fool. Later scholars failed by seeing only the fragments. If one weighs everything by the smallest gauge how can one accurately weigh a large mass? And if one relies on the shortest standard of measurement one is bound to err when it comes to calculating great distances. In developing their arguments by seeking ever more refined examples, they busied themselves with splitting silk threads and ox hair and were totally unaware of having missed the essentials. How then could they nourish human talent and promote peace in the realm?

A similar type of thinking can be seen in their view of the Sages. While identifying the Sages with the all-embracing principle of nature, later scholars denied them even the smallest amount of private human passion. This is simply an arbitrary viewpoint. The *Book of Rites* says, "To be serious and to be relaxed are both in the Way of Wen and Wu." In Confucius's words, "Should I finally get to study the *Book of Changes* in my fifties, I might then begin to rid myself of some of my grave faults"; while Tzu Ssu observed, "Even Sages do not know everything and cannot do certain things." We know this is so from such examples as the following: Shun executing Kun, who Yao had previously entrusted with hydraulic projects; Yu withdrawing his troops even though Shun had ordered him to attack the three Miao tribes; the Duke of Chou ordering Kuan Shu and Ts'ai Shu killed; and Confucius failing to lead a punitive campaign against three recalcitrant towns.

The Sages cannot be defended against derision for committing these errors. To cite an example of such a foolish defense, Confucius is said not to have set aside the ginger roots in his food, eating them instead because he liked the taste of ginger. King Wen too, according to the chronicles, liked marinated iris roots. Now even if the Sages had their likes and dislikes about food, what difference could this make; yet, we find Chu Hsi explaining in his gloss on the *Analects* that Confucius was fond of ginger root because of the divine nature of ginger. How far-fetched can one be?

The Virtue of the Sages may be likened to the movement of nature. The

Way of the Sages embraces vast and great elements, and its essence is the nourishment of all beings and things. If the grand principles are in order, the small items will naturally fall into place. Later generations saw only the immediately visible details and understood only the trivial.

12. There is a method with which to cultivate one's virtue. Establish what is essential; lesser concerns, of their own accord, will find their proper places. This is why the disciples of Confucius focused their thinking on the essential concept of Benevolence. There is also a method to eliminate one's evil traits. Let us compare it with covering the horns of a young bull or castrating a boar to blunt its tusks. People today seek, in a day, to embody all sorts of goodness, taking in one trait after another and being proud of themselves. This reminds us of the fable in which young seedlings are pulled from the ground to extend them and make them grow faster. Are they not aware of the natural tendency among human beings to do good? Thus, people today also strive to cleanse themselves of evil all at once and sometimes even bring physical damage to themselves. We are reminded of the false doctor who pretends to cure an illness while paying no heed to its deeper cause. The general point is even of greater importance when it comes to teaching others.

13. The discussion about innate human nature began with Lao Tzu and Chuang Tzu, and is not to be found in the Way of the Sages. Let us assume someone aspires to discover the Way. Hearing that human nature is good, he will dedicate himself with increasing diligence to refine his nature. And if he hears that human nature is evil, he will strive to transform it into something good. On the other hand, supposing a person does not aspire to the Way, hearing that human nature is evil, he will simply resign himself and do nothing. Should he hear that human nature is good, he will simply rely on this and likewise do nothing. It was for these reasons that Confucius placed great emphasis on custom and not on human nature.

Aroused by the words of Lao Tzu and Chuang Tzu, Tzu Ssu and Mencius, therefore, formulated a theory of human nature as one that was innately good in order to challenge the formers' views. Meanwhile, fearing that the concept of innate human goodness would surely result in the destruction of rites and music, Hsün Tzu therefore countered Tzu Ssu and Mencius with the idea that human nature was inherently evil. These are all polemical views aimed at influencing the debates of their age and ought not be taken as absolute and unchanging principles. Ou-yang Tzu's advice was farsighted when he said, "The problem of innate human nature should not be a central concern of scholars. The Sages rarely spoke of it."

14. The concept of "transforming one's essential and specific character" was fabricated by Sung scholars. Its origins may be traced to the *Doctrine of the Mean* but it is not to be found in the Way of the Ancient Sages and Confucius. The so-called "change" in commentaries on the Ancient Kings is the way of bringing peace to the kingdom. This is not a goal that can be achieved by a single individual. It can be realized only with the combined strength of many. We are reminded that only after the seasons have run their course can the whole year be completed; only after the hammer, chisel, knife, and saw have been assembled can the carpenter do his work; and only when there are drugs to cool fever or warm the body, and to nourish and cleanse the stomach, can the physician practise the art of healing. The awl must be sharp, and the hammer blunt. Gypsum is a mineral substance that produces great coldness and can be used to reduce fever; aconite is a plant that can generate warmth. The Ancient Kings would not have been able to govern society without relying on the specific character of each thing. Moreover, gypsum is prepared in fire and aconite is baked in ashes, reminiscent of the reliance by human beings on specific rules as in rites and music. Yet, while gypsum is fired, its essential character of producing coldness is not lost; and although aconite is buried in hot ashes, its inherent capacity to generate heat is not lessened.

Thus we learn the error of the idea that human beings can change their essential and specific character. Indeed, one's fundamental nature is endowed to that person by the grace of Heaven. However desirous, human effort cannot oppose and overcome the will of Heaven. Should a person be forced into striving to do something as humanly impossible as this, the result will only be bitterness toward Heaven and hatred toward one's parents. Certainly this is not the Way of the Sages. We need only observe that each of the disciples of Confucius fulfilled himself according to his own specific talents. The saying from the *Analects*, "A true gentleman is not a mere instrument," means that a gentleman is a benevolent man who has realized his personal virtue. Princes and ministers use instruments, roughly comparable to the use of tools and drugs by carpenters and doctors. There is no truth in the saying that "an instrument can be both a boat on water and a cart on land." By identifying with their personal virtues and by relying on Benevolence, human beings realize their specific talents. By grasping this essential principle all can certainly become benevolent human beings. And this is surely the meaning of the phrase in the *Analects*, "A true gentleman is not a mere instrument."

15. Since Tzu Ssu and Mencius there has been a deceitful tendency to explain difficult ideas with many little details, thereby simplifying matters for the audience. This was the rhetoricians' technique in argumentation: to persuade others to accept their views as quickly as possible. The capacity to accept or reject their views, however, resided outside of them, in the audience. This is not the way to teach others. The capacity for conviction should reside in the teacher who should rely on his own strength and not on the listener's capacity to decide one way or another. The Way, after all, rests with those who are princes and teachers. Accomplished teachers always take their audiences into consideration and, applying gentle care over a long period of time, foster the intellectual growth of the listeners and alter their way of thinking and of understanding things. Thus the audience comprehends spontaneously, without any explanation. For those requiring additional assistance all that is necessary is a suggestive word or two and remaining doubts will dissolve like melting ice. Teachers should thus not exert themselves vigorously, since students learn on their own with deep understanding. This is because even before teachers make assertions, students already understand much of what is about to be said.

The Ancient Kings and Confucius relied on this approach. Thus the Ancient Kings relied on concrete facts in presenting their ideas and did not rely on such terms as "rites" and "music," which had no explanatory significance. And Confucius was quite correct when he said, "I will not try to enlighten anyone who is not angry with confusion. Nor shall I teach a student who does not feel deep frustration within himself."

Mencius, however, sought to overcome his listeners by arguing in an authoritarian fashion when queries were raised and by carping over minor details. Those who rely on words to overpower audiences invariably fail to teach them how to understand reality. In the final analysis, a teacher can instruct only those who trust him. The populace trusted the Ancient Kings; the disciples of Confucius trusted him; consequently, their teachings were accepted. Mencius's ambition was to convince people who did not trust him on the basis of sheer rhetorical skill. Itinerant lecturers of the Warring States period used this technique. It is unsuitable for teaching the people. Mencius and Tzu Ssu debated with scholars of other schools. Later Confucian scholars used their polemical ideas to instruct students. They failed to distinguish debating from teaching.

16. Confucian scholars of later ages have clarified and classified such ideas as "pure goodness and human passion," "the identification of self with natural principle," and the "fostering of goodness in the self." But my readings have not uncovered discussions of these subjects by the disciples of Confucius or for that matter by Confucius himself. How then are we to explain the shortcomings of these scholars? The Ancient Kings and Confucius taught as they did in contrast to the Sung scholars, because the former knew that the fundamental way of teaching ought to be otherwise. How could later generations, however, have placed greater faith in Tzu Ssu, Mencius, Ch'eng Tzu, and Chu Hsi than in the Ancient Kings and Confucius?

The Ancient Kings relied on concrete artifacts and not on abstract theories in their teachings. When instruction is based on specific things, the teaching must conform to the facts themselves while a reliance on abstractions makes the language of explanation convoluted in its detail. A concrete artifact is a convergence of ideas. It can be comprehended only after a thorough examination. A reliance on rhetorical expressions is not adequate, since rhetoric can express only one portion of what is true. Even if one happens to throw light on a subject without close study of facts free of abstract arguments, deep understanding cannot be gained. Even Sakyamuni said, "One can tell whether the water is cool or warm by drinking it." How could the Sung Confucianists believe that the Ancient Kings fell short of Sakyamuni! It is rare indeed for a person to be effective in life without first engaging with concrete facts. This is true not only of the Way of the Ancient Kings, but also of all the 100 other human arts.

17. In ancient times the Way was referred to as Culture. "Culture," in point of fact, was another expression for rites and music. Culture consists of a myriad of concrete artifacts that are inextricably woven together. It simply cannot be exhausted with a single abstract term. Ancient scholars believed that, "the Way of Confucianism is broad and its essential element elusive." This is true of the fundamental character of the Way. Later Confucian scholars, however, prized simplification and reduction. To think in such manner, on the basis of emotional impulse, is the way of uncultivated minds. It is not the Way of the Ancient Kings. Confucius said, "although King Wen of the Chou Dynasty is dead, King Wen still remains with me." Later Confucian scholars interpreted this as an expression of humility. Actually the reference to Wen was not to the King himself but to his Culture. Supposing Confucius humbled himself: does this mean that he referred condescendingly to King Wen himself? Confusion arose when Sung scholars divided the Way ("high principle") and Culture ("somehow demeaning ordinary detail") into antagonistic dualistic categories.

There is also the confused view regarding the concept of culture and quality. Culture actually means the Way and refers specifically to rites and music. Quality, on the other hand, means the basic character of human intelligence.

Special value is placed on truthfulness and trust only because they are basic to human learning. However, even if a person should be "truthful" and "trustworthy," he would remain an unsophisticated country bumpkin without Culture. Thus, even in little villages and hamlets, Confucius did not admire "truthfulness" and "trustworthiness" and prized instead the pursuit of knowledge. Later Confucian scholars sought to explain the differences between the high and the ordinary (and the basic and the peripheral) with a single unifying principle; but upon closer observation it becomes evident that they merely favored the subjective over objective and high principle over ordinary details, emphasizing always the simple, the clear, and the symmetrical. After this unfortunate misinterpretation, the Way of the Ancient Kings faded like autumnal leaves and intolerance spread throughout the world. The road led inevitably to the paths of the uncultivated. Surely the people have been led astray because of a failure to understand that in the ancient world the Way was called Culture, and that this meant the encouragement and nourishment of human virtues.

18. Both good and evil characterize the human spirit. Mencius was certainly correct in observing that, "When evil grows in the human spirit, there will be failure in governance." However, there is no specific structure to the human spirit. It cannot order itself. In the Way of the Ancient Kings, therefore, rites are relied on to regulate the human spirit. To speak of a method of managing the spirit totally divorced from rites is an arbitrary and subjective idea. This is because the regulator and the regulated become identical. In short, the idea of regulating one's self with one's own spirit simply reminds us of a madman trying to cure his own madness. How is this possible? The various theories of later scholars, then, regarding the management of human spirit all lack an understanding of the Way.

19. The idea of "universal principle" has no form and thus is not a fixed norm. Sung scholars referred to the *Doctrine of the Mean*, justly regarding it as the highest example of refinement which pays close attention to detail. Their position would be more acceptable, however, if they had first understood the Way of the Ancient Kings and then pointed to the *Mean* with praise. To choose the *Mean* on a purely subjective basis and then to equate it to the Way of the Ancient Kings is a totally erroneous procedure. It would have been acceptable, too, had they interpreted the Way as the principle of acting as one ought to and equated it favorably with the Way of the Ancient Kings. But since they sought to discover this ethical imperative on the basis of their subjective views and then identified it as the Way of the Ancient Kings, they were again in error.

It is obvious, after all, that "principle" is formless and lacks a normative reference. To take this concept and equate it with the *Mean* or to see it as the basis of ethical imperatives is nothing more than the imposition of one's subjective wishes. Perceptions differ from one individual to the next, and it is simply subjective to state dogmatically that this is the Mean or the Principle upon which one ought to act. In our world, when one views things from the north all else is to the south. Where should the normative reference be placed?

The explanation of a universal principle and of human desire by Sung scholars is overly refined. Again, there is no normative reference here. To clarify by analogy, when two villagers are involved in a boundary dispute, there is no explicit norm to refer to without calling on an official to adjudicate the dispute. As a consequence, there are no theories about a universal principle in the thoughts of the Ancient Kings and Confucius. The Sung Confucian scholars fabricated these useless arguments, relying invariably on the useless methods of the Logicians of the Warring States epoch to make distinctions between things on the basis of a play on words such as "hardness" and "whiteness."

20. The Way of the Ancient Kings was originally called the "Way of Artistic Technique." This referred to rites and music. Later Confucian scholars came to dislike the term "technique" and avoided its use. It would seem that they were completely unaware that under the Ancient Kings the people were nourished toward goodness without feeling spiritually coerced. Similarly, they were ignorant that those teachings enhanced the knowledge of scholars who, over the days and months, slowly and naturally came to realize their personal virtues. This is the meaning of "technique." It is similar to the example of the master of court music establishing the four arts of song, history, rites and music, and prescribing that rites and music be taught in spring and autumn, and songs and history in summer and winter. The concerns advanced by later Confucian scholars about the intensive observation of the principle of things, and about overcoming oneself to achieve spiritual unity with the Way, are brilliant concepts to be sure. But the scholarship of these men was shallow as they did not understand the Classics and failed to study

the ancient age. They simply absorbed every idea they encountered and made it their own. Their thinking was often quite strained.

Generally, when human beings and natural things are nourished properly they grow and flourish. If they are not they perish. Not only is this true in regard to the physical body but to human talent and virtuous behavior as well. The Way of the Sages, therefore, is indeed to nourish and foster all things. The Way of Nature is to move ceaselessly as in a state of flux, yet within it, as if guided by a divine spirit, each specific event brings about an inevitable effect; what is set in motion in the present reaches fruition in the future. Similarly, all activities within the Way of the Sages are carried out in terms of a design, not as if the results can be realized immediately but always with an eye toward consummation in the future. And if the results cannot be achieved within days, a year or more is an acceptable period, and if this still does not suffice, then the lifetime of an entire generation may be necessary. This is the attitude that encourages princes to nourish their minds and realize their virtues, and leads ordinary people to shape the customs within which they spontaneously seek goodness and avoid wickedness. The Way of the Sages, therefore, is intertwined with Nature, actively, continuously and endlessly developing both human and natural things into the vast and infinite future.

In recent years, the scholar Itō Jinsai has pointed out some of the errors of the Sung Confucian scholars. When we examine his view on morality all that we can say is that, having discarded the extreme views of the Sung scholars, he demonstrates a somewhat healthy purpose. He has not, however, departed from the tradition of relying on rhetorical arguments and it is thus a pity that in the end he was not able to escape the charge of confusing fifty strides with a hundred.

21. The Way of the Ancient Kings was based exclusively on a reverence for Heaven and the mystery of spirit. Quite simply, they valued the primacy of Benevolence; but because Confucian scholars of later generations prized knowledge and strove to investigate the principle in things, the Way of the Ancient Kings and Confucius fell into ruin. The evil of investigating "principle" was that heaven and spiritual mystery were no longer viewed with awe and the individual now came to assume an arro-

gant position between Heaven and Earth. This flaw is common to all later Confucian thinkers and it is not at all unlike the idea expressed in the Buddhist phrase, "Above and below Heaven I alone exist." Furthermore, where, I wonder, is the absolute ultimate norm in the vast universe to be located? Does "principle" completely solve this problem? When individuals claim to have total comprehension, this must be sheer illusion. And while they all ostensibly pay obeisance to the Ancient Kings and Confucius, they inwardly disregard them. They are convinced that they have focused on elements that had not been made clear by the Ancient Kings, and in so doing, seem not be aware of their selfish intent to surpass and rise above the Ancient Kings and Confucius. The teachings of the Sages are complete in themselves. They cannot be surpassed. The Ancient Sages refrained from discussing subjects that could not possibly be explained. If something required commentary, they would have already done so and not have left it for posterity to clarify. Later scholars simply have not given much thought to these matters.

22. The four arts of the Ancient Kings were songs, history, rites, and music. These were used to foster gentlemen scholars during the Shang, Hsia, and Chou dynasties. What Confucius transmitted were these four arts only. Each of these classical arts teaches something different. In a simplistic fashion, Confucian scholars of later times treated all of them as being alike. Why then should they be called the Four Classics?

In general, the *Book of History* contains the great precepts and norms set forth by the Ancient Kings. Confucius addressed it as such, with deepest reverence, as true utterances of the Sages themselves. In ancient times there were no books, so that references to the "book" always meant the *Book of History*. Kings and princes believed in and revered this book, as did the scholars who read and gained knowledge from it. The Way of the Ancient Kings to establish peace in the kingdom is to be found in this Classic. Later Confucian scholars, however, found it simplistic and looked elsewhere for more brilliant and elegant writings. This erroneous attitude simply reflects their superficial minds. Even the briefest expression of the Ancient Sages was related to enormous problems in the real world, such as the rise and fall of empires and such as order and disorder in human society. Without comprehending things in terms of its profound implications and without viewing distances with a broad vision, this Classic cannot be properly understood. Mencius had no faith in the *Book of History*. Yet where did he acquire the information to make comments on Yao and Shun? He was curiously uninformed of the Way of the Ancient Kings as the Way of promoting peace among humankind.

The *Book of Songs*, however, is different. It contains lyrical language arranged to be sung and bears much resemblance to what later generations would call poetry. Some have said that Confucius deleted some of the songs but in fact he merely revised a few expressions. When scholars study the *Songs* it is solely to cultivate their [linguistic] expression. We are reminded of Confucius's comment: "Without having learned the Songs, one will not be able to express himself in a proper manner." Later generations, however, read the *Songs* in the manner that they read the *Book of History* and came to the conclusion that the *Songs* had been compiled for the moralistic purpose of "promoting good and punishing evil." Their explanations inevitably faltered when they stumbled upon passionate love poems such as those by Cheng and Wei. The didactic precepts they actually advanced were barely enough to fill a page. If their interpretations were correct one would have thought that the Sages would surely have created a separate book of ethical admonitions instead of using such a roundabout method.

The explanations offered by these scholars tell us that they knew precious little about the *Songs*. For instance, the "prefaces" of the various songs, they say, demonstrate how the ancients spontaneously understood the songs, describe the situation in which the songs were written, and explain the contents of the songs so as to make them easily understandable. In such cases, then, what need is there to rely on an understanding of the content itself? However, since the songs originally did not have explicitly detailed meanings, there is no reason at all for later scholars to accept the views suggested in the prefaces as if they contained unchanging truths. A case in point is the Great Preface. It explains the poem *Kuan Sui*. The ancients merely expanded on the original preface, commenting on the specific song itself as well as on some of the other songs in the

Book, thus making it an extensive preface. Being unaware of this fact, later Confucian scholars called it the Great Preface as compared with the lesser prefaces of the other songs. This is truly absurd.

In general, the *Songs* embody subjects that deal with the court above and continue on down to the byways of towns and also to the domains of princes, the noble and the humble, men and women, the wise and the ignorant, the good and the wicked. The *Songs* make us perceive, as if we were eyewitnesses, the changing conditions of society, the local customs, the human passions, and the natural landscape. The language is elegant and graceful and meshes with true human feelings; sung melodiously, it easily moves the human spirit. The Songs, moreover, deal with a wide variety of small and large things; and they do not provoke feelings of narrow-mindedness. It is from within this frame that rulers gain an understanding of plain folk, of husbands, of their wives, and of the courts of lower society; and, in a time of tranquility, people gain [through the frame of these songs] an insight into the customs of a world in decline. Another good reason for appreciating the *Songs* is that, while not important in and of itself, the praise and criticism of politics and of customs that are found in them are to the point. Should the reader view them with an open mind, interpret them in terms of their broadest implications, and pry out the analogies embedded in them, he will find an endless source of inspiration in them. The ancients, therefore, relied on the *Book of Songs* to develop their hearts and minds, to promote the cause of governance, to give elegance to their expressions, and to be decorous in words and convivial in exchanging toasts as envoys to foreign lands. The *Book of History* describes actual things and events. The *Book of Songs* uncovers delicate and hidden meanings. The *History* announces grand principles while the *Songs* is full of delicate nuances. They are like the sun and the moon shining alternately, or like the positive and negative forces of the universe. Together, these two Classics therefore are justifiably called the repository of human virtues.

Rites and music are the regulatory underpinnings of human virtues. The concept of Central Harmony may be taken to mean the maximal point of virtue. It is the highest example of refinement and nothing can be added to it. But it does not have actual form and its substantive content can never be fully explained. Thus, rites are relied on to teach what is Central; and music is used to explain Harmony. The Ancient Kings gave concrete shape to the idea of Central Harmony. Without relying on words, rites and music nourish human virtues and alter the way humans think. When one's thinking is altered, one's perceptions naturally change. There is no better method to nourish human intelligence than through rites and music.

Moreover, the Ancient Kings relied on rites to establish criteria for governance and guidelines for human activity. Wise men reflect on and comprehend this meaning about rites; the unwise may not be able to do so but they will nonetheless rely on them. Wise men identify with rites from above and the unwise reach for them from below. Whenever one commits an act or expresses a thought, one weighs its propriety in accordance with rites; and one also knows thereby whether they are in accordance with the Way of the Ancient Kings. Rites are never unspecified. They are explicit prescriptions of the Way of the Ancient Kings.

Now despite the foregoing discussion, if rites are upheld with mindless rigidity without the ameliorating mixture of music then the nourishment of virtue will be devoid of human enjoyment. Music gives life to the realization of virtue. Nothing is superior to music for stimulating the human mind and nourishing the growth and expansion of individual virtue. Thus rites and music may be likened to the Way of Nature in its creation and nourishment of the ten-thousand things in the universe. Rulers use rites and music to nourish their virtues. Ordinary people use them to give shape to their custom. The kingdom thereby lives peaceably and its spiritual life continues into the future. How divinely marvelous are the four arts: they give complete expression to the teachings in the Way of the Ancient Kings.

23. When Confucius said "Our Way is unified by a single concept," he did not intend these words only for his disciples Tseng Tzu and Tzu Kung. All of his other disciples heard them. In praising Tzu Ssu and Mencius, the Sung Confucian scholars drew on Tseng Tzu as their basis for doing so, and thereby established their version of the lineage of the Way. I

wonder, though: can this serve as a ground for their thinking? They interpret the phrase "single concept" to mean "universal principle" or a single
"spirit" or "truthfulness." The theory of a single principle joins Heaven
and earth and men and things all into an undifferentiated whole. It is
identical with the Buddhist notion of an unchanging soul embracing all
beings and things. The ideas of a unifying spirit and truthfulness place
due importance on two of the virtues of the Sages, but they do *not* ascribe
importance to the entire Way of the Ancient Kings. Confucius explicitly
said "Our Way," by which he surely meant the Way of the Ancient Kings.
We gather this from Confucius's comment: "Although King Wen is dead,
Wen's culture is still with me now."

The Way of the Ancient Kings brings peace to human beings in the
world. The Way of Peace rests on Benevolence. This is what Confucius was
referring to when he said that "a single concept integrates all." What
might be the basis for his saying this? Benevolence is one of the virtues. It
is also, however, the Great Virtue: it integrates all of the other virtues.
Although the Way of the Ancient Kings is truly many sided, Benevolence
alone permeates all their teachings. We might liken it to stringing coins
together, which makes it possible to speak of a unifying idea. On the other
hand, the ideas of "principle" or "spirit" or "truthfulness" are single and
exclusive concepts; they do not integrate other ideas. Thus when Tseng
Tzu said there is only sincerity and generosity in Confucius's Way, he
actually implied that these were means by which to carry out
Benevolence. The term "only," used by Tseng Tzu, is similar to Mencius's
use of the term in his comment that "the Way of Yao and Shun is only filial
piety." How can filial piety be the entire Way of Yao and Shun? Similarly,
sincerity and generosity cannot be said to express the entirety of the Way.
It is true, of course, that one may, if one seeks it, somehow perceive the
broad Way by depending upon sincerity and generosity. The language of
the ancients is full of such allowances. The advocates of a universal
principle in later times, however, manipulated things and facts without
deliberation, so as to penetrate the "principle" in things. They spoke all
too easily of sincerity and generosity as a manifestation of a "principle,"
and referred to the sincerity and generosity of Heaven, of the Sages, and

of scholars and the like. The language at the time of Tseng Tzu, of course, had a very different meaning.

24. Being unable to decipher ancient vocabulary, scholars of later times relied on the language of their own day to interpret ancient terms. The Way of the Sages has been obscured for this reason. An example will illustrate this important point. The idea of the "absolute ultimate," which is taken from the *Book of Changes*, simply means that the Sages referred to this idea in organizing that Book. It is said in this Book, therefore, that there must be an "ultimate" explanation of change, but there is not the slightest hint that this "ultimate" must exist in nature. Phrases such as "investigating principle" and "clarifying subtle movements" only celebrate the concept of change formulated by the Sages. It is unfortunate that later Confucian scholars would see these as prescriptions of scholarly duty.

There are other such examples relating to the *Book of Changes*. The term for "Heaven" refers simply to the vast natural sky above. The word "human nature" means the specific quality of a person. The term "pure" means *constant*, and to read it to mean *truthful*, affiliating it with the virtue of wisdom, is a farfetched interpretation. The compound "festive gathering" refers to such events as marriages and entertaining guests, and uniting it with the concept of rites means nothing more than creating harmony, as when voices unite in concert. There is no hidden meaning beyond the fact that affairs such as marriages and receiving guests frequently require rites. As for the "utility of things," it means simply using an object, or making a tool useful, as in sharpening it. The phrase "harmony with righteousness" means just that, harmonizing oneself with righteousness. It is erroneous to interpret those to mean that righteousness is always located at a harmonious or convenient point. Not altering one's point of reference is the method by which one "maintains a basic position." But this is not necessarily identical with "wisdom." Thus, later in the *Book of Changes*, there is the phrase that one should practice being original, effective, useful, and firm; but to equate these activities with the normative virtues of benevolence, righteousness, ritual propriety, and wisdom is excessive and beyond reasonable bounds.

The phrase in the *Book of Changes* that says "Those who inherit this are said to be good" means inheriting and giving continuance to Heaven's will. "Good" simply refers to a "good person." Sung scholars interpreted "inherit" to mean the "continuous forward flow" of nature, and lost thereby the meaning of the term "inherit." The phrase "it is human nature that fulfills" what is inherited means that each person responds to his divinely endowed specific character and thereby dedicates himself to purposeful accomplishments.

In conventional terms, when people speak of virtue they contrast it to malice and sometimes to material wealth. Quite certainly, however, when "virtue" is used by itself, it means exclusively the "virtue" of one's Heaven-endowed human nature. Otherwise, the prescription in the *Analects* that one should "rely on one's virtue" would make no sense.

As for "human spirit," its original meaning in the *Book of History* is "the spirit of the people." Having no sturdy reins to guide it, the "human spirit" is said to be unsteady. The spirit of the Way guides the spirit of the people; but because the spirit of the Way moves in an extremely subtle fashion it was said that the spirit of the Way, like the human spirit, could only be faintly perceived.

The principal meaning of the title *Great Learning* comes from a sentence in the *Historical Records* which said that in the great learning of ancient times, rites were created to nourish the elderly and to regulate relations of respect towards age in society; the phrase did not refer to the scholarly activities of princes as interpreted by Chu Hsi. The term "Brilliant Virtue" mentioned in the *Great Learning* is the Virtue of the Monarch. This is verified in such works as the *Tso Chuan*. To clarify the Brilliant Virtue was to display it for all to see. It did not mean, as Sung scholars suggested, polishing it so as to make it shine. It meant quite specifically caring for the aged and showing respect in relation to age. In Mencius's words, "if human relations are clear above, the people below will interact with mutual affection." Thus we also find in the *Great Learning* the phrase "making the people affectionate." Chu Hsi understood this phrase to mean "renovating the people," which is surely an error. The term reno-vating the people comes from the K'ang Kao chapter of the *Book of History* and it refers to the revolutionary overthrow of dynasties. There is no discussion of this subject in the *Great Learning*.

The term "thing" means concrete items that are appropriate for use in rites. The character *kaku*, used often in combination with "thing" to mean the investigation of things, indicates drawing things together. The character to realize, *chi*, means taking an act to its logical conclusion and does not mean an ultimate culmination. In the Way of the Ancient Kings, when the appropriate things which are to be used in rites are in proper order, human intelligence naturally realizes enlightenment. This was how the Ancient Kings taught their people. In citing the phrase "thoroughly comprehending principle" in the *Book of Changes*, Chu Hsi interpreted the verb "to draw things together" to mean the "intense investigation" of principle. Misunderstanding the meaning of key phrases in the vocabulary, he formulated a deceptive theory. Wang Yang-ming used the same term "to draw things together" to mean "correcting what is wrong," as in his reference to Mencius's comment about "correcting the wrong thoughts of a monarch." This term, however, implies the sympathetic attraction of things, so that Wang Yang-ming, too, was in error.

As for "reverence" which Chu Hsi used in the formula "disciplined investigation of principle," the foundation of it is reverence for Heaven. Reverence for the order, the people, and oneself all stem from this basic idea. How can one vaguely maintain reverence without an object of reverence? As for the compound "self-control," the correct interpretation of it is to discipline oneself and gain humility. The first character of the compound, *koku*, indicates providing order as one does in one's own home. It would seem, therefore, that Chu Hsi's interpretation of the compound as "overcoming the self" is utterly opposed to the concept he advanced about relying on the self to become benevolent.

In sum, all the previous are egregious examples of how the meanings of ancient phrases have been misunderstood.

25. The Six Classics have not survived intact. Even if they are accessible in their entirety the language is ancient and the meaning of each word cannot be recounted precisely without error. It is thus easy to understand why later interpretations of the Six Classics are all seriously distorted.

Later Confucian scholars tended to think it shameful not to know every little detail. They failed to realize that in ancient times, "to know" meant valuing the knowledge of Benevolence. Not once did Confucius teach the idea of cherishing knowledge for its own sake. With this in mind, scholars today should dedicate themselves to the study of ancient languages. To understand those languages they must examine the meaning of ancient terms in a systematic manner. Since the former Han Dynasty was not too far removed from the time of Confucius, many of the ideas handed down from the ancient period are still to be found in the interpretations of this era. From the Later Han onward, ancient ideas steadily lost their original meaning. It is true, of course, that the scholar Han Yü had not yet appeared to so drastically alter the language of the ancients. Old terms were still being used. If one reads a wide variety of books from the Ch'in and Han up to the Six Dynasties period and diligently examines and appreciates these writings, one might gain insights into the meaning of ancient language.

I do not wish scholars to disregard the theories of Sung Confucianism and other later schools by uncritically accepting what I have to say. There is a vast expanse of time between the ancients and us. Portions of the Six Classics have been lost over time, so that it is perhaps unavoidable that one should come to use the abstract concept of "principle" to speculate on the meaning of these Classics. The Sung scholars were the first to employ this concept; a concept which unfortunately lacked precision. Even less fortunate is the fact that they became captives of the abstract idea itself and could not go beyond it. If the scholars of Sung Confucianism and other schools had been more exact and meticulous in their method of study, they would not have committed so many errors.

In the end, of course, thoughtful reflection is crucial to scholarship. And this means appreciating all forms of thinking because they may be helpful and these include even Taoism, Buddhism, and certainly Sung Confucianism and the related schools.

Kyōhō 2 (1717)
fifteenth day of the seventh Lunar Month

Benmei I
The clarification of Names

*

OGYŪ SORAI

Names have been given to things ever since human beings came into existence. Names were originally established by ordinary people for objects with concrete shapes. When it came to things without form, which ordinary people could not assess, the Sages gave expression to these and assigned them names so that even ordinary people could see and understand them. This is called teaching with names. Names contain teachings, and the Sages were respectful of this. Confucius observed: when names are not true then the order of words cannot be set. Thus when things are improperly named, the people will not be able to grasp their meaings to make use of them. This deserves careful thought.

When Confucius passed away, the Hundred Schools flourished, and according to each of their differing viewpoints, established various names. Thus for the first time names and things came to be confused. Only his seventy disciples protected with great care the views of their master and passed them down to the future.

During the Han Dynasty, each scholar chose different classics and each scholarly house similarly focused on different classics. However, while the teachings of each differed, in general they were all drawn from the teachings of Confucius' disciples, so that what was lost in one school still existed in another. By combining views, it was indeed still possible to bring names and things into close accord. This is because the views of the

The translation is from Yoshikawa Kojiro and Maruyama Masao eds., Nihon shisōshi taikei 36: Ogyū Sorai (Tokyo: Iwanami Shoten, 1973), pp. 38–158.

ancients were still being conveyed. With Ma Jung and Cheng Hsüan, scholars respected among all the schools, a synthesis was shaped which appeared acceptable to the various points of view. In so doing, the distinction between names and things could no longer be determined, because many important elements were excluded. This was truly regrettable.

From that time onward the world underwent change carrying language along with it. In the T'ang era, Han Yü separated ancient language from the prose of his own day. In the Sung period, Ch'eng Tzu and Chu Hsi altered ancient meanings with their scholarship. Possessing outstanding ability, these various gentlemen were all viewed as heroes by their age, and, moved by a concern for the world, they saw upholding the Way of the Sages to be their personal mission. However, they relied on their subjective feelings and theorized about their age without any hesitation. That is, they assumed their subjective views to be one with universal principle, and claimed this to be the Way of the Sages. How erroneous they were. They especially did not understand that the language of the present is not the same as that of the ancients. As we live within our times and seek to understand the ancients from this context, how rarely then might we grasp the names in those times. Principle, moreover, is pervasive. Should we reach conclusions from our subjective point of view, how then can we say these things to be the concrete things of the Sages. The relationship between names and things were lost. Those who seek to fully understand the Way of the Sages have never done so in this manner. Thus even though their names be Ch'eng Tzu and Chu Hsi, their views are simply their own personal ones. They are not in accord with the Way of Confucius as taught by his seventy disciples. And therefore they are also not in accord with the Way of the Ancient Kings. Those who wish to discover the Way of the Ancient Sages must seek it in the Six Classics and to know the references to things in them, and then by examining texts prior to the Ch'in and Han dynasties come to understand the names. Only when names and things are not in discord, then can the Way of the Sages be spoken with certainty. It is for this reason that I have written this *Benmei*.

THE WAY [DŌ] — TWELVE DEFINITIONS

1. The Way is a comprehensive name. This statement is based on reliable sources. In sum, it refers to the construction of the Ancient Kings which later generations of governments relied on to carry out their tasks, and thus individual people relied upon this as well. This is like the roadway that people walk on; hence it is called the Way. It is a name that is inclusive of the values that range from filiality, brotherhood, compassion, and justice to rites, music, laws, and governance. Thus it is called comprehensive. The Ancient Kings are the Sages. For this reason, it is referred to alternatively as "the Way of the Ancient Kings" or "the Way of the Sages." All princes seek to identify with it. Hence it is sometimes called "the way of princes." Those who protect the teachings of Confucius are called jusha, and so it is also referred to as "the way of the jusha." The substance of these is single. However, each of the epochs of the Ancient Kings differed. Hence, those who speak of the Way of the Ancient Kings refer to Hsia of the Hsia Dynasty, Shang of the Shang Dynasty, and Chou of the Chou Dynasty. These terms all refer to the Way in each of the dynasties. The reference to Confucius was to distinguish him from other people, and the term "jusha" was applied to distinguish themselves from the Hundred Schools. As disagreements arose, the terms used were reduced. Thus it seems that princes came to use these terms only occasionally. Such phrases were not ordinarily used.

The Way came into existence with the most ancient of sages. With Emperor Yao and Emperor Shun the Way was built, and through Yin (Shang) and Chou Dynasties it steadily gained perfection. It was achieved as a result of the dedicated efforts of several dozens of sages over 100 years. It was not produced by a single sage in a lifetime. It was for this reason that Confucius worshiped Yao and Shun and held in esteem King Wen and King Wu and prized the ancients through scholarly study. Sung scholars misread the *Doctrine of the Mean* and *Mencius* and then speculated that because human nature was good, the Way was naturally in accord with one's inner nature. They failed to understand that the followers of Lao Tzu were active at that time in criticizing the ideas of benevolence and justice as artificial. Tzu Ssu [author of the *Doctrine of the Mean*] simply replied by saying that the sages built the way by responding to the natural condition of the nature of humans. But he certainly did not say that by conforming to one's nature the Way would be naturally found.

Mencius said only that benevolence and justice were rooted in human nature. With regard to goodness, he generally said the same. But where did he say that people in general were not any different from the sages? Suddenly the Way was said to reside in all humans and was no longer identified with the sages. As an inevitable conclusion, rites, music, law, and governance were trivialized. How misleading is this view for these are not trivial but essential to the Way itself. In the annotations of the Sung scholars, the Way is said to be the principle of actual practice. If we are to support the Way based on these words, then this is entirely laudable. But these words are surely inadequate for they encourage people to practice the Way only in a brief manner.

When one relies on the Way, the journey through life is easy. When one does not, one steps in thorns and encounters dangerous obstacles. Are these not reasons to follow the Way? Should one take one's subjective preferences as "true principle" of carrying out everyday practices and call this the Way of the Sages, then this is only being simply superficial. How can this be the true meaning of those words? How can this be what Confucius sought to study? Based on his understanding of the wisdom of the Sages, Confucius knew their thoughts. How truly incredulous.

In general, the Way of the Sages is as though vast and distant. It cannot be known by ordinary people. Thus Confucius said, "The people should rely on it. It cannot be taught to them." He also said, "The person who composed this poem must have known the Way," for the Way is difficult to know. And again, "our Way is single and runs through all." But he did not say exactly how this happens. That is because this is too difficult to be said. Precisely because it cannot be spoken, the Ancient Kings established words and facts and taught that the relationship between them be maintained. These teachings are in the Classics of *Songs*,

History, *Rites*, and *Music*. Thus although Yen Tzu sought to understand these with his mind, he still read widely into the texts themselves, and sought the essentials through *Rites*, and only then saw the extraordinary construction that was there. If the Way can be simplified to a single term, then the Ancient Kings and Confucius surely would already have said it. There is absolutely no single term like "principle" for this. This is delusion in the extreme.

The teacher, Itō Jinsai, drew from the *Book of Changes* the idea of a single process of darkness and light, yin and yang that pervades everything. This is misleading. The so-called yin and yang originally speaks of the way things undergo change. The *Book of Changes* thus says: "When there is any opening and closing there is change. When things move to and fro without cessation, there is engagement between them." In the process of change and engagement is the way of *Changes*. Yet how can this exhaust the meaning of the Way of the Ancient Sages. His language moreover is oriented to rhetorical completeness. Anyone who argues with rhetorical intent does so from a subjective position. While he critiques Sung scholars for this fallacy, Jinsai repeats the same error. He tried in a phrase to express what the sages would not say. This is identical with the legacy handed down by the Sung scholars themselves.

K'ung An-kuo wrote on the *Analects* that "The Way is about rites and music." Scholars in later times have not attained this insight. On the Classics on Filiality, he said the following: "The Way sustains the natural order with its ten-thousand things, and sees each life through its end. When left to humans, only the way of doing changes departs from the true path. Thus when one is with the Way, then words are also in order, and practices are also accurate, services to a lord are of their own accord loyal, doing things for the father is filial, there is trust in relating to other people, and results are realized in the ordering of things. When one carries things out in this manner, it will not be said to be excessive. If the entire kingdom does this, it will not be said to be inadequate. If this is pursued in small amounts, small degrees of well being will be realized. When done so on a large scale, much well being is to be gained. The kingdom that practices this will be at peace." This may seem like a shallow point of view. But the ancient meanings have not been lost.

Thus when the Ancient Kings constructed this Way, it was their intent to provide peace and well being for future generations. The Classic of *History* puts it this way: "Relying on honesty and truthful understanding of texts, peace is brought to the people as it ought to be." This was their intent. Thus, of the virtues of the Ancient Kings, none is greater than Benevolence. The teachings of the Confucian School are based on and do their work through Benevolence. Thus the Ancient Kings relied on the spirit of mutual affection, nourishment, assistance, and the efforts of people for each other and on their ability to manage their personal activities. Thereby they built the Way and carried it out for future generations to rely on. Each and every life would be seen through to its end. Given this purpose, how can it be said that all human beings should seek to be sages? Moreover, is it sensible to try to teach this to everyone? And why force upon people a concept [principle in nature] that is difficult to know and hence to practice. To summarize, the Way is bringing peace and well being to the people. Scholars must think about this.

2. Now there are those who speak of "The Way of Hsia," of "Shang," or of "Chou." The Way was built first by Yao and Shun and all ages have since relied on this. However, changes were made in accordance with the times. Thus, a sage in a certain era established new rules and rendered these to be of the Way. Lords and retainers in this era relied on this. This does not mean a revision was made due to inadequacies of the previous epoch. Nor did it mean that because the Way of the previous era had realized its fullest achievement that a sage personally sought to alter things so as to gain anew the attention of the people. Nor again did it mean that each age should view the previous achievement and then alter the Way depending on circumstances. The Sages in any one of these dynasties possessed a vision of several hundred years to come and sought to order their worlds so as to not head in a direction of decline. Without the wisdom of the Sages, it is not possible to grasp fully the reasons for the establishment of new reforms. When perusing the commentaries about the Six Classics, one encounters phrases such as "a certain person is good" or

"that is still good"; or "Hsia Dynasty stands for loyalty, Yin Dynasty for quality, and Chou Dynasty for culture." These are all fragmentary comments by Confucius with which to discuss rites and music in different eras. Each era represented different personal creations. Confucius did not say one was superior or inferior to another. Even in the case of Yen Yüan – transmitting *Rites* and *Music* in the period of the Four Dynasties, should not be seen as the moment in which a permanent system was built for all generations to come.

3. There are things referred to as "the Way of Heaven" or "the Way of Earth." The reference here is to the sun, moon, stars, and comets, and to the wind, thunder, clouds, and rain that are generated and cold, heat, day, and night that rotate without end. Their deep origins cannot be fathomed, nor can their breadth. The ten-thousand things originate here. We do not know why good and bad luck, fortune and misfortune happen. When we view all this quietly it appears that these things are reliable, and so we call this "the Way of Heaven." Carrying mountains it feels no weight. It holds rivers and seas and yet does not leak. Its vastness, depth, and breadth cannot be exhausted. Creatures arise from it, yet are not diminished. Every creature dies and returns to it, yet the earth does not expand. We should know about these things through our familiarity with them. Yet there are things that we cannot know. When these are examined piecemeal, there seems to be regularity in them. So we call this the Way of the Earth. It is because of the existence of the Way of the Sages that the name of the Way is simply borrowed and applied to all of these.

4. There are the phrases "the way of the small person is less extensive" and "the way of the barbarians." These phrases depend on the fact that in carrying out ordinary life there simply seems to be a way; thus the phrases are used.

5. There are also the phrases "the way of good people"; "no change in the way of fathers." These, too, are merely references that people use. They are not necessarily the Way of the Ancient Kings. Basically, the meaning here is that these phrases were used to refer to the Way. Thus people came to rely on them as the Way.

6. A saying goes, "Are these not the totality of the Way?" The *Songs*,

History, *Rites*, and *Music* are all the Way of the Ancient Kings. Thus even fragments of terms and phrases from them are referred to, in brief, as the Way.

7. Another saying says, "With a total transformation, the Way is realized." This refers to carrying out the Way of the Ancient Kings in the world. It is said, "We should travel together on the Way." This means identifying personally with "The Way of the Ancient Kings."

8. When we say, "the ultimate Way" and "the great Way," these are terms with which we revere the Way of the Ancient Kings.

9. There are phrases such as the following: "Seeking the way"; "Listening to the way in the morning"; "The way is in the world"; "The country has the way"; "The country does not have the way"; "The prince who does not know the way"; or "Correcting things according to the way." Generally, the way, as used in such phrases, is conceived of with the Way of the Ancient Kings in mind. To say "not of the Way" means being completely devoid of the Way of the Ancient Kings. "Possessing the Way," however, does not mean completely possessing it. Someone such as a "gentleman of the Way" is one who has internalized arts of the Way. Yet the Way of the Ancient Kings is external to the self. Thus the six arts are the Way of the Ancient Kings. That is why in ancient times the Way and the arts were equally esteemed. There is but a small difference. Though a person may possess virtue, without knowing the Way of the Ancient Kings this person may not be called a gentleman of the Way. Later generations confused the names of "way" and "virtue." Scholars shall keep the distinction clear.

10. The following phrases all refer to different aspects of the Way of the Ancient Kings. "The way of great learning"; "the way of fathers"; "the way of mothers"; "the way of ministers"; "the way of children"; and "the way of the divine."

11. Phrases such as "There is a way to being promoted from above"; "there is a way to relate to friends"; and "there is a greater way to generate wealth" all refer to the practice of certain arts or methods. The arts are something to be relied on, as they lead you to a goal without stress or strain. This is the meaning of statements like "the people should rely on

through the human character with which one is endowed or through study. Every human being has an inner nature and is different. Thus virtue, too, is different from one person to the next. Such is the vastness of the Way. Had it not been for the Sages, how then would individuals be able to identify their individual selves with the Great Way? Thus the Ancient Kings established the name "virtue" so that scholars could each rely on what was close to their inner nature and protect, nourish, and promote this. Nine virtues in the *Book of Yü*, six virtues in the Book *Chou Kuan*, and virtues cited in the *History*, such as benevolence, cleverness, filiality, brotherly affection, loyalty, trust, reverence, thrift, generosity, restraint, bravery, courage, integrity, and honesty are all examples of such virtues. Certainly the differences in human nature may be compared to the differences in the world of plants and trees. Even the teachings of the Sages, however wise, cannot be forced upon the people. Therefore, each and every one stays close to his inner nature and nourishes it to realize its virtue. When virtue is realized, and one's talent is achieved, then one may be given public duties. We should understand that even the Sages could not achieve all the very same ends. For example, the achievements of Hou K'uei in music, King Yü in irrigation, and Chi in the art of planting, could not be attained by Yao and Shun. When we turn to Confucius we find that he taught his seventy disciples according to their specific talents. Thus we can see that in teaching Tzu Lu, he emphasized courage, and for Tseng Tzu, filiality. We see clearly among Confucius's leading disciples the specific virtues of compassion, decisiveness, and diplomacy. The sources of nourishment and encouragement for these virtues are in the *Rites* and *Music*. In *Music*, it is said: "rites and music encourage all to achieve. This is called realizing one's virtue." It is said in the *Analects*: "Tsang Wu-chung's wisdom, Kung Ch'o's restraint, and Pien Chuang-tzu's courage and Jan Ch'iu's skill will develop into fruition in adulthood if embellished with rites and music."

If these four immersed themselves in rites and music they will realize their virtues as adults. A mature individual is one who has realized his virtue. To "embellish" here means to realize virtue and thereby achieve honor and distinction as an adult. It is not superficial glitter. It means each has realized a single virtue. They do not mean the accumulation of many virtues. The Sages did not wish that people realize many different virtues. In the *History* the following is said, "By reciting the three virtues daily and seeking to reflect on these from morning to night, one will maintain one's house. By strictly practicing the six virtues with deep intent, the country will thereby be governed." These refer to the virtues of governors and lords, and these clearly should not be imposed on the people. Thus the Sages in ancient times established the name of virtue to teach the populace.

Chu Hsi commented as follows, "The term virtue means to realize. By practicing the Way one realizes it in the spiritual self." The Way, however, is the Way of the Ancient Kings. It says in the *Tso Chuan*, "If the effort is not from within that specific person, the Way as a goal will be in vain." In other words, if one's virtue has not been developed the Way cannot be practiced. The meaning here is that the Way as an inevitable principle is the principle of practice and not of nature. This is the only interpretation possible. Thus virtue basically cannot be discussed apart from the individual spiritual self. However, if this is discussed exclusively in terms of the spirit, how can it be taught as realizing virtue. It is said in the *Book of Rites*, "Virtue is realized by the physical self." Chu Hsi thought it superficial to speak of the body and not the spirit. This error is due to the lack of knowledge of ancient language. In ancient days, the body and the spirit were not opposed to each other. When the term body was used, it always meant oneself. How can the spirit be outside the self? Mencius says, "it is alive in colors, bright and clean, it appears in one's face and spreads to the back and to the four limbs. The four limbs do not speak but feel its force." These words speak of virtue as an actual condition. How can virtue be only of the spirit? Virtue certainly is not simply making language more clever and embellished. But to speak of realizing virtue only as a matter of spirit is a comparable error. Hence they rely on the idea of spirit and not on rites and and music. There is absence of knowledge and method. They do not abide by the Way as taught by the Ancient Kings and Confucius.

The teacher, Jinsai, is prideful of his view on virtue. But this is simply putting the names of inner character on the level of virtue. Moreover, he misreads Mencius by expanding his interpretation of the 'four inner resources" as realizing virtue, thus not differing at all from Chu Hsi. Beyond this, Jinsai did not attribute these to the Ancient Kings nor realize that virtue and inner character were not the same things. It is as though he is casually saying that medicine has a healing virtue and fire the virtue to heat water. The issue is whether one realizes virtue through nourishment or whether one has the virtue from the beginning. Thus for him virtue refers to something that is entirely not yet realized. It is a name without substance. Again he reverts to the views of the Sung scholars.

2. Sayings such as one who "does things with virtue," "reveres virtue," "knows virtue," "does not isolate himself from his virtue," "reflects on virtue," "desires virtue," and "knows that clever language disrupts virtue." All these phrases refer to one who has realized virtue.

3. It is also used in response to anger, as in "respond to malice with virtue"; and "it seems to have a veneer of virtue." These usually indicate the incurring of emotional benefits.

4. The "achievement of virtue" is the idea of virtue being consistent among all individuals. Tzu Ssu drew these words from Confucius's saying that "there are three bases to the way of princes." However, if you talk about the foolishness of parents that allows them to be aware of their children's follies yet still take care of them, this is a diminishing of the concept. How can this be the ancient thinking of Confucius' school? Mencius moreover relied on Tzu Ssu's language and also said, "Benevolence, righteousness, propriety and wisdom-all people have these in themselves." These are all polemics against Lao Tzu, who said that benevolence and righteousness were artificial. Thus the names of the Way and virtue became confused. Tzu Ssu and Mencius both centered their ideas on warding off theories directed against Confucius. This explains their errors. Scholars should reflect on this.

5. "Reaching the ultimate virtue" refers to those who are able to realize their own specific virtue to the fullest. Confucius discussed this by referring to T'ai Po in terms of his generosity, and to the Duke of Chou in terms of his respectfulness. In the *History*, the King Shun is referred to as one

who was "truly and respectfully generous." These are about the virtues they were able to realize. However, if respectfulness and generosity are not practiced by the Sages, they cannot be said to be "reaching the highest virtue." T'ai Po's "generosity" was done in terms of governance as was the Duke of Chou's respectfulness. Thus they were said to have realized their own ultimate virtue. The reason "filiality" is seen as reaching virtue is because compassion is at its basis of practice. The virtue realized by the officials of the Chou dynasty means the virtue of Sages as the standard of the ages. "Active virtue" refers to virtues that vary with the inner character of each person.

6. "Clearly apparent virtue" means virtue that is made manifest. It describes virtue that is conspicuous for all to see. In many references, therefore, it refers to gentlemen. In the *Tso Chuan*, Ch'eng Chuan quotes from *Songs*, "his virtue is brilliant," and interprets this as the glorious provenance of the Lord over the entire domain. The prince of Ch'i announced that peace had been achieved among the Three Kingdoms. The Lord of Lu responded through the nobles saying, "How can I not accept the illustrious virtue of the prince of Ch'i." Kung Chih-ch'i said, "If the kingdom of Chin joins the kingdom of Yü and through clear virtue makes its rule like a fragrant offering, not even the gods will object." Tsang Wen-chung said, "Even the clear virtue of the Ancient Kings was not without complexity, but this should not be viewed with concern. Even more so regarding a small country such as ours." Ta Shi K'o said, "Emperor Chuan Hsü had an untalented son and it was impossible to teach him. His speech was poor. When talked to he was unresponsive. When left to his own he would not speak the language of loyalty. Defiant of clear virtue, he thus caused disturbances in the kingdom." Tsang Wu-chung said, "When the large conquers the small, prizes are taken and sacrificial vessels are inscribed with great achievements for the future to see. This makes clear virtue visible as against impudence." Yen P'ing-chung said that "the ruler of Chin Dynasty proclaimed this clear virtue before other lords. Concerned about their inabilities and losses, he mediated between them and ended their conflict. Thus he is known as a brilliant leader." These examples refer broadly only to the virtue of rulers,

and they do not necessarily relate to the ideographic term "clear" as in "clear virtue."

Wang Sun-man said, "Since King Chieh of Hsia Dynasty possessed debased virtue, the throne was usurped. When virtue is clear, it is too weighty to be moved. When virtue is scheming and disorderly, while enormous it is light. When Heaven is blessed with clear virtue, there will be balance and order in the Land." Liu Tzu said, "How marvelous is the achievement of King Yü. His clear virtue will last forever. If not for King Yü, I would have become a mere fish in a flood." Meng Hsi Tzu wrote, "Although the Sage of clear virtue may not govern the land, among his progeny there will surely be one who is truly outstanding." These are all broad references to the virtue of Sages. They do not necessarily relate to the word "clear." However, here again these things are said because the virtue is outstanding and easily visible for everyone to see.

Chu Hsi's idea of virtue as "mystical yet visible in its movement" is based on spiritual studies and is not present in ancient times. Jinsai viewed the virtue of the Sages as bright eminence. It is merely drawing on the poem from the *Doctrine of the Mean* about "reflecting deeply about one's clear virtue." Both Chu Hsi and Jinsai misinterpreted virtue because they sought too deeply into its meaning. The *Tso Chuan* is not a work of much complexity. It is difficult to understand why these two thinkers did not consult it.

BENEVOLENCE [*JIN*]: FOUR DEFINITIONS

1. Benevolence refers to the virtue of the head chief who brings peace to the people. This is the Great Virtue of the Sages. The great virtue of the natural order is Life. The Sages modeled themselves on this. Thus this is also sometimes called "the virtue that is supportive of life." The Sages are the head chiefs who ruled the world in ancient times. Hence there is nothing else that can augment this virtue. It is said in the *Great Learning*, "The virtue of the ruler is fulfilled with Benevolence." Sages did not realize this virtue through study. Gentlemen of later times who study the Way of the Sages and practice virtue are said to realize benevolence. Thus

Confucius said, "should a ruler abandon Benevolence, how can he enforce the naming of names." This means that it is benevolence that gives meaning to the name of princely ruler. Thus the teachings of the Confucian school rely necessarily on Benevolence. This spirit cannot be separated from the Benevolence of the Sages. Benevolence is the Great Virtue of the Sages and princes and rulers practice it as a virtue. However, the virtues of the Sages are complete and inclusive. How then can it be said to be only benevolence when benevolence is actually but one among the virtues of the Sages? The reason the Sages are Sages is that they bequeathed the virtue of Benevolence to all generations thereafter. Thus Benevolence is the Great Virtue of the Sages. The Way of the Sages resides with the many virtues of the people in their interaction with one another. Is this not why there is only Benevolence? Also since everyone who studies the Way of the Sages possesses a different virtue, why only Benevolence? This is because the Way of the Sages is only bringing peace and well being to the people. The Way includes the many fine qualities among the people, and they all support Benevolence and its actualization. Though the nature of human beings is different, still regardless of their intelligence, ignorance, wisdom or foolishness, all nonetheless are similar in seeking mutual affection, nourishment, aid, advancement, and the means to manage ordinary affairs. Governance is for rulers to sustain the ordinary people in their engagement in agriculture, craft and trade and to nourish all to aid each other in living their lives. It is inevitable for human beings to live together and avoid being isolated. The ruler is a social ruler. Only with Benevolence can the people be brought together effectively into a unity. Those who seek to realize their virtue through study all possess different natures from one person to the next. But what they all seek to study is the Way of the Sages. And the Way of the Sages is in bringing peace and well being to the people. How can the ruler identify himself with the Way of the Sages and nourish his own virtue without relying on Benevolence? This is like seeking to support life without relying on the five grains. Only emaciation and death will result. And then what is the reason for the people to study and realize these virtues? It is because the ruler relies on the different talents found among the which is called the principle of love is received from Heaven and is a given of the spirit. This is then taken to be Benevolence, and as the virtue of the inner spirit, and as confirmation that when humans are born they are no different from the Sages. But then the material character of passion gains the upper hand and prevents Benevolence from being fulfilled. Once study is completed then whatever one does, it will be in accordance with Benevolence. There is further the view that the way of the natural order is only an active process of unending life, and that humans are given this life and become benevolent. This view expresses the meaning of continuous life in the flow of things. And within this is the further view that Benevolence represents the entire virtue of the inner spirit. Thus it contains justice, propriety, wisdom, and trust. This is an overly expansive use of language. And when justice, propriety, wisdom, and trust are distinguished from each other then Benevolence is used as a limited concept. But how wrong this is.

Benevolence is a virtue, and not the inner spirit of human beings. Nor is it principle. "To love is the basis of benevolence," is only one particular statement. How can this explain the whole meaning of Benevolence? Furthermore Confucius's so called "loving of people" refers to becoming parents of the people. Without bringing peace and well being to the people, how can one become "parents" of the people. Sung Confucianists centered their ideas on the human spirit. When speaking of love by emphasizing spirit, then Shakamuni Buddha is also a benevolent person. When there is no virtue of peace or well being for people, then it is not Benevolence as we use the concept. Does the basic material nature in the human self undergo change? Can human passion be eliminated? Is there a virtue not related to the human spirit? If Benevolence is made to be inclusive of all virtues, why are there diverse virtues among people. Is not the reliance on the comprehensive and particular meanings of Benevolence inadequate? All reflect the erroneous reliance on the arbitrary concept of principle without seeing the precise meaning of the Way.

Jinsai discusses this in the following way: "The virtue of compassion and love extends everywhere fully complete and extensive, far and near, within and without." This again is from reading Mencius and wanting to expand the idea of compassionate inner spiritual resources to include achieving benevolence. He did not connect benevolence with the Ancient Kings, but to all human beings. Not realizing that benevolence means only bringing peace and well being to the people, he recklessly interpreted it as compassion and love. Thus his defect extends to rendering Shakamuni as a benevolent person. What an error this is. Especially since Mencius's "expansion of the four inner resources" were mere polemics and did not discuss how to realize benevolence. This is analogous to a spark turning into a prairie fire, or a tiny sapling growing to the heavens. When one shakes the sapling at its roots, or forces it to grow, it dies. Blowing makes a spark flare to burn the field, and watering the sapling makes it grow, to reach the skies. So too for human beings. Slowly cultivating oneself with rites and music a human being realizes benevolent deeds. Those who do not know this will think that rites and music are only external objects and not within the self as well. These are the ones who do not believe in the teachings of the Sages and seek to realize benevolence based on their own personal intelligence. Truly they do not know that wind and rain, while external, exercise great influence on things. In the Way of rites and music, it is as though one comes to conform to the rules of nature gradually and effortlessly. Is this not like the wind and rain coming from Heaven to nourish us? Jinsai and the Sung Confucianists are equally without learning or method.

2. Sometimes the designation of "benevolent person" is said to be the same as "benevolence" itself. For example the reference to the three benevolent men of virtue or Kuan Chung's ingenuity, are in both cases about specific ways of bringing peace and well being to the people. The Sung Confucianists sought benevolence in the human spirit. Thus they went totally awry in explaining Kuan Chung. Jinsai too sought it in the human spirit. His difference with the Sung Confucianists was simply that he did not speak of natural principle or human passion. In explaining Kuan Chung his explanation was also totally wrong. One need only glance at these errors.

3. Benevolent government is sometimes said to be the same as benevo-

lence. Thus: "One became a prince with wisdom and sustained one's position with benevolence." "People's yearning for benevolence is infinitely greater than that for water and fire." "In attending to benevolence do not concede even to your master." These and other related queries, by Confucian students refer to this same issue. Generally, matters of governance and benevolence are mutually related. Those concerned with governance manage villages. They become administrators and address what needs to be done today. Those concerned with benevolence govern domains. They ask beforehand about the purpose in another future day in order to govern the entire domain. Confucius's conveyances to Yen Tzu and Tzu Chang, as though in preparation to govern the country, are a case in point.

Basic to carrying out benevolent governance is the cultivation of oneself. Without this cultivation, although one may attempt to carry out benevolent government, the people will not abide by it. This idea is expressed in the *Mean*. The cultivation of the self begins with acceding to the nine principles. Thus Confucius's responses all point to self-cultivation. Later Sung scholars did not realize this and mistakenly emphasized doing benevolence. This is an egregious error. The teaching of the Ancient Kings is based simply on *Songs*, *History*, *Rites* and *Music*. Without words one learns from *Rites* and *Music* to carry out virtue. This cannot be replaced by another way to realize virtue. The Way of the Ancient Kings was built originally to bring peace and well being to the people. Hence the cultivation of the self is also basic to carrying out this virtue. It is not simply for self fulfillment. Later Confucian scholars became accustomed to learning Chuang Tzu's idea that if one realizes sagely virtue in one's inner self one can become a king, and applied this idea to governing the kingdom. Benevolence was interpreted through the idea of heavenly principle, or of love, placing weight exclusively on the human interiority and the completion of self realization. This is pitiful.

4. The "way of the arts" is also discussed in terms of benevolence. This does not apply to the virtue of the Ancient Kings. Nor is it referenced to benevolent people or benevolent governance. It merely embellishes the virtue of the Way. Later Confucian scholars did not grasp this, and

confused it by combining it with Benevolence. Further details are in the discussion below on benevolence and justice.

WISDOM (*CHI*): TWO DEFINITIONS

1. Wisdom is also a great virtue of the Sages. The wisdom of the Sages cannot be gauged. Nor can it be realized through study. Hence it might be divided into two parts, namely, "sageliness" and "wisdom ". Generally, the references to wisdom in the Classics are to the virtue of princely rulers. These include the understanding of "rites," "language," "the way," "mandate," and "other people." "Understanding the Way" means knowing the Way of the Ancient Kings. It is inclusive of all the other forms of knowledge. A person with true comprehensive knowledge is rare. Confucius's saying, "Does the composer of this poem know the Way?" exemplifies how rarely such knowledge can be acquired. "To understand rites" means knowing the rites of the Ancient Kings. "Understanding language" means knowing the standard of language set by the Ancient Kings. Rites and language are viewed as two parts of the Way. To divide it in this way is for the convenience of later scholars. The teachings of the Ancient Kings are made up of *Songs, History, Rites,* and *Music. Songs* and *History* are the texts for understanding "language" as the repository of righteousness. To know language is to know righteousness. When one understands rites and righteousness, this comes close to knowing the Way. The reason why music is not spoken of resides in the fact that few people can attain it. Confucius commented that Tsang Wen-chung is ignorant of three things. All three pertain to not understanding rites. In ancient times ignorance was seen as a failure to understand rites. The phrase in Mencius "to know language" also refers to the standard of language of the Ancient Kings. When one has this knowledge of language, then one comes to possess a standard of measurement within the self from which to assess the utterances of other people. Through this one can gauge the meanings of terms such as "licentiousness," "wickedness," "deviance," and "evasiveness." Later Confucian scholars did not understand the Way. Thus they said Mencius understood the words of other

people. When Confucius said, "In listening to an appeal I am like any other person," he meant that even he could not say with complete assurance that he knew the words of others. How then could Mencius realize this? Here his discussion of terms such as the "licentiousness," "wickedness," "deviance" and "evasiveness" of others are cases of rhetorical exaggerations. Still, since he used a consistent standard, he did understand that the phrase "to understand language" meant the rules of language of the Ancient Kings.

"To understand the mandate" refers to the "Mandate of Heaven." It means knowing what might be Heaven's imperative. The Way of the Ancient Kings is based on Heaven, and is carried out in revering Heaven's Mandate. Rulers who study the Way also seek to carry out their responsibility to duties mandated originally by Heaven. Even an individual who studies the Way and carries out virtuous deeds, but is unable to achieve official status, may still teach the Way to the people as Heaven's calling to him. The gentleman takes learning and teaching as his task, and does not feel disturbed even though the ruler fails to recognize his talent and appoint him to office. This is what is meant by knowing one's calling. In general the power of an individual is capable of realizing certain things and not others. One who forces himself to realize things he is incapable of is foolish in the extreme. Thus it is said, "Without knowing one's mandate or calling, a princely ruler will not be able to perform his duties." Later Confucian scholars said this meant, "knowing the inevitable principle," and "knowing a good or bad future," and others to mean being imperturbable to the rise and fall in human fortune. These are words of those who do not understand the Way.

"To understand people" refers to knowing the people with benevolence and sagacity. This is the substantial portion of wisdom. The *Book of History* says: "Wisdom is in knowing other people, and in bringing peace and well being to the people." Kao T'ao established these two virtues of Wisdom and Benevolence and rendered them as norms for all ages. However, it was the wisdom of the Sages that led them to create rites and music, and these were not possessions to begin with among commoners. The basis of providing orderly rule in the kingdom did not go beyond these two terms of Wisdom and Benevolence. Even rulers in later times who were engaged with military hegemons would not have been able to provide orderly governance without relying on these two ideas, Wisdom and Benevolence. What more might be said about these terms? Confucius said: "To cultivate the self and thereby bring peace to the common people, even Yao and Shun struggled over realizing this." King Yü said, "Difficult for everyone, it was certainly trying for emperors as well." Therefore, even Yao and Shun were not able to realize these two ideas very well for are they not terms of perfection. Further, since the Way of the Ancient Kings is to bring peace and well being to the people, there is no greater thing than realizing this goal, which must be preceded by first knowing other people. Confucius in discussing Wisdom and Benevolence, again saw wisdom as being prior to virtue. There is no other way, for without knowing people through benevolence and sagacity, the Way of peace and well-being cannot be carried out. For this reason, Confucius noted that from ancient times rulers with sagely wisdom invariably took men of wisdom as their ministers, and saw the other forms of good governance as not equivalent to this. Hence, there is no greater virtue of wisdom than knowing the virtues of other people. Most Confucian scholars truly take "understanding people" to mean exclusively assessing their intelligence and ignorance, strength and weakness, beauty and homeliness.

They speak of despising small achievements. This is an enormous error. In the ancient world, "understanding people" meant grasping the strong points of others, without claiming to know their weaknesses. In its ultimate meaning, "understanding people" necessarily meant being able to recognize Wisdom and Benevolence in others. Thus when Fan Ch'ih did not fully understand the phrase, "understanding other people," Tzu Hsia intervened and said to Fan, "Emperor Shun promoted Kao T'ao and King T'ang promoted I Yin." This indicated that the Way of ancient times was exactly as I have explained it here.

People's understanding of others is first realized among people of the same kind as themselves. Thus only the noble recognize nobility in others, and thus also the wise recognize the wise. When comparing human talents, they all vary from one another, even when you consider hundreds or thousands of people. Thus, it would surely be difficult to know what exactly is the sagacious person. And it would be difficult for us to understand a more intelligent person than ourselves, as King Kao Tsung's recognition of Fu Yüeh's intelligence and King Huan Kung's of Kuan Chung. Then should we view it as evidence of Yao's inability to understand others that he appointed Kun by looking only at his talent but not his deficiencies? Thus Yao's understanding of other people is in his knowing Shun, not in his knowing Kun. This was the way in ancient times. Later scholars obfuscated this, wanting to emphasize their knowing all the strongest and weakest, successes and failures without leaving anything out of the discerning eye. Ts'ao Meng-te was praised for this. But it is not the Way of the ancients. To seek out the origin of this error, it was probably in Mencius. It was Mencius who said: "Wisdom originates from within, from wanting to know right and wrong." His aim was to say that the Sages built the Way by drawing on human character. However, due to his extreme fondness for rhetorical style, he was unaware of the distortion in his language. Later Confucian scholars did not grasp this. They simply went on to interpret wisdom as "knowing the principles of the world with clarity and completeness, beyond any possible doubt." How wrong they were in not knowing that this is wisdom in the ordinary sense, and not what was prized in the Way of Ancient Kings.

Confucius said, "without choosing to rely on benevolence, how can one gain knowledge of wisdom." Then again, "One who has knowledge turns benevolence to an advantage." What he meant was that nothing surpasses Benevolence. Those who do not appreciate this say that first one must exhaust the meaning of "principle" in the natural order. After this, one comes to realize that nothing surpasses Benevolence. Here is the theory among Sung Confucianists to "observe things and penetrate principle." They did not know that this idea of penetrating principle was used to praise the Sages for compiling the *Book of Changes* and not a matter of comment by scholars. The idea of "observing things" is from the *Great Learning* and means that if one studies things for a long time, one can come to master them. Only after this can one have a clear idea of what one has learned. By first encountering things in nature, what one knows is made evident. Thus the wording: "Observing things directly, one then gains knowledge." There is nothing here about exhausting the understanding of the principle of all things under Heaven. Indeed, without relying on the teachings of the Ancient Kings and studying them over a long period, knowing things is merely vulgar knowledge. On what basis then can we come to know that Benevolence ought to be respected? The basis is the Confucian ideal of knowing "rites," "language," "way," "mandate," and "other people," all of which refer to the Way of the Ancient Kings. Sung Confucianists' approach to knowledge, the direct and diligent observation of things, saying clearly that "right is right and wrong is wrong," relies on ordinary wisdom. Because it is said that the ordinary person relies on physical strength and the gentleman uses his mind, the gentlemen of this world enjoyed the reliance on their own knowledge and did not feel it necessary to rely on the Way of the Ancient Kings. They are all alike in this regard. It was for this reason that Confucius often spoke of "being fond of benevolence and of virtue and rites and righteousness, but never did he speak of being fond of 'wisdom.'" Moreover, he noted, "To be fond of study is to be close to knowledge. Unless one follows the Way of the Ancient Kings, one will not realize knowledge. Scholars must reflect on this.

2. In Mencius there is a phrase on "virtue, wisdom, method, and knowledge." These are ancient terms. They were not created by Mencius. Wisdom began with reliance on virtue, knowledge on the way of a method. In ancient times knowledge always depended on a method to realize a virtue in attaining constructive knowledge. This is what is meant by "observing things and realizing knowledge." Without a reliance on virtue and method, knowledge will not be attained. Such was the Way of the Ancients.

SAGELINESS (*SEI*): FOUR DEFINITIONS

1. Sageliness refers to those who first created concrete systems. In the *Book of Rites* it says: "The creators of systems embody sageliness. The documenters of systems embody clarity." Also in this same text, "While there

may be creative persons in later times, they will never approximate the achievements of Shun." The emperors of ancient times possessed the virtue of extraordinary brilliance and wisdom. Understanding the ways of the workings of nature and fully aware of the inner qualities of human beings, they created systems of things. Their creative achievements are like those of gods. Thus they built the Way of promoting the well being of human life so that all generations thereafter would benefit from their virtue. Fu Hsi, Shen Nung, and the Yellow Emperor were all sages. But in their times the way of true virtue had not yet been constructed. Rites and music had not yet been created. Thus, later generations had nothing to narrate. Then Yao and Shun appeared to create rites and music. Thus the way of true virtue first came into existence. Gentlemen relied on it to attain virtue and commoners to shape their customs. Without reliance upon punishment, order was realized throughout the land. This was the origin of the Kingly Way. Being supremely gifted, they participated in and helped the generative process of Heaven and earth to realize and support the Way, thereby constructing that which would serve as the ultimate norm for every generation. Thus in his introduction to the *Book of History*, Confucius calls for a clear break to be made at the time of Yao and Shun. Sages of the three subsequent dynasties also oriented themselves to the Way of Yao and Shun and created rites and music and built the rules for their respective dynasties. Time, however, cannot be reversed. People pass away and the world changes. Customs grow thin with each day. And thus they are corrupted and undergo decline. This may be compared to a river as it flows ever forward without pause. The sages of the three dynasties were fully aware of this process. Thus they relied on the rites and music of the previous dynasty, gauged the benefits and losses of doing so, and maintained custom over several hundred years so that there would not undergo swift deterioration and decline. The virtues of Yao, Shun, Yü, T'ang, Wen, Wu, and the Duke of Chou were all truly broad and profound. They were complete and beyond full description. Because their creative achievements were so vast, as though the workings of the gods, and beyond which nothing more could be added, they were named Sages.

Confucius was not born in the right era and was unable to take part in

2. Among the six virtues in the *Rites of Chou* there is reference to wisdom and to sageliness. The virtue of sages is here separated into these two, and upon them princes seek to realize their virtues. The inner nature of humans, however, is not the same. Thus wisdom refers to a familiarity with the way of politics. It was named wisdom for this reason. There is also that element that connects well with rites, music, and spiritual matters. This is named sageliness. This so-called sageliness is not as though it is the virtue of the sages. The nine ministries of Yao and Shun expressed nine different virtues. The six ministries of Chou also contain six virtues. Virtue differs in accordance with inner human nature. After one's virtue has been manifested, then he is entrusted with office. Thus the differences between the administrative systems of Yao and Shun and Chou are due to the fact that the virtues that constituted the systems were not the same. In the Chou Dynasty wisdom was the special talent required for the official position of Chung Tsai. In managing the kingdom's offices, understanding other people was essential. Benevolence was the talent of Ssu T'u. He directed education and knowing people was his duty. Sageliness was the talent of Tsung Po. He oversaw the religious rites, and familiarized people with rites, music, spirits, and gods. Righteousness was the talent of Ssu Ma. He administered law and matters of rewards and punishments, promotions and demotions, military planning and hunting. He needed to be righteous to do his job well. Loyalty was the talent of Ssu K'ou. He carried out punishments. Without being considerate and mindful, how could he carry out this duty? Harmony was the virtue of Ssu K'ung. He directed the construction works of the country by harmonizing the hundred occupations, in accordance with the actual conditions of the land. Viewed in this manner, the division between sageliness and wisdom can be readily seen. It is said in *Songs*: "Everyone sees sagelinesss in the self. But how does one know one from the other, such as between the male and female crow." And in the *Tso Chuan*, Tsang Wu-chung walked in the rain and people criticized him for not acting like a sage. From ancient times on people picked on small traits in wisdom to define sageliness.

3. Later Confucian scholars say that King T'ang and King Wu were not sages. This is a totally unfounded view. They mistook Confucius's words,

"Wu had not yet realized goodness," and Mencius's, "Yao and Shun had goodness as their inner natures," but, "T'ang and Wu came to internalize it as part of their physical selves." Confucius discussed music, but did not comment on the virtue of Shun and Wu. And Mencius simply said that Yao and Shun were born with wisdom and that T'ang and Wu developed their virtues by studying the way of Yao and Shun. Neither spoke of their superiority or inferiority. In sum, Yao, Shun, Yü, T'ang, Wen, Wu, and the Duke of Chou are the seven creative individuals, and the rites, music, politics, and teachings that they created are what gentlemen study. Thus these are enshrined in our studies. In the *Tso Chuan*, it is written, "Homage is extended to the sages and former teachers." And further: "The emperor leaves for battle and performs a sacrifice to Shang Ti and to the gods of each of his ancestors; and at his destination he receives his command from his ancestors to whom he owes his life and from his school to whom he owes his knowledge of strategy. When he carries out the campaign he will capture the guilty and punish them, and present to his academy for review the evidences of the fallen enemy." Should there not be gods to perform rites where then does he receive his command and present his results. From the *Book of Songs*: "After the great learning had been created, distant and undeveloped lands conceded to the way of virtue. Brave leaders went forth to dispense of enemies. Fair judgements were dispensed with while criminals were dealt with and military order put in place." These lines are about such affairs. In the *Book of Rites*, "The Mi Lin was the school of Shun. Hsü was the school of Hsia; Ku Tsung the school of Yin; P'an Kung the school of Chou." Again from *Rites*, "The Emperor established four schools. Clearly these great schools of the emperor combined the systems from the four dynasties, and enshrined in them were all the sages."

In ancient times when sacrifices were offered to ancestors this was a worshipping of Heaven, so that ancestors and Heaven were one. When the emperor set out to conduct great events, he received his mandate from Heaven and the previous sages. Thus it is said, "The gentleman has three fears. He is in awe of Heaven's mandate, the person with great virtue, and the words of the sages." The gentleman is thus in awe of only Heaven and

Tzu Ssu was the grandson of Confucius and viewed Confucius with intimate understanding and affection. What Confucius had conveyed still remained intact. Thus when Tzu Ssu discussed the Way he always maintained the 300 courtesies and the myriad forms of expressing dignity, and when he discussed Confucius he noted that though Confucius was truly good, he did not possess political rank and thus could not be a creator of things. This is because the Way of the Ancients still existed intact.

When it came to Mencius's time, the schools of Mo Tzu, Tsou Yen, and Legalists each constructed positions and considered their own to be the Way. Confucius said of them that they were "people who fabricated without understanding." Mencius also spoke of sagehood in terms of a single virtue and did not once refer to creating. Nonetheless, he seemed to think that the Ancient Sages were creators and that Confucius was not. He thus found it difficult to compare Confucius with the Ancient Sages. He drew on the great virtues and deeds of the wise men of old and compared these to Confucius, thus using this approach to praise Confucius for his greatness. Mencius viewed Po I and Liu Hsia-hui as sages, which was not the view of the ancients. He drew them into his writing as a temporary convenience, not realizing the problems that would come later. While this does not make him guilty of a crime, he committed the error of exaggeration.

The virtues of brilliance and wisdom of the Sages were received from Heaven. They cannot be gained through study. Their virtues were mysterious and beyond calculation, and surely unattainable through ingenuity. Thus, those who studied the ancients and became sages were only T'ang, Wu, and Confucius. Those who truly study the Ancient Sages must rely on their teachings, and through rites and music realize their own virtues. This was all that Tzu Ssu had to say. Though Mencius did not speak of *Rites* and *Music* when he said, "humans can become like Yao and Shun," he simply meant, "people could appear as Yao did and speak as Yao spoke, do as Yao did." He did not mean that one would become a sage thereby. Later Confucian scholars did not grasp the intent of these two scholars. Thus they blindly sought to become sages. And they argued the details of sagely virtues and wanted to make these the standard of scholars. Soon they were saying, "The spirit of the Sages was clearly identical with the principle of the heavens," that " Yin and yang are one with virtue" and that the Sages were "without personal preferences or entanglements." In these audacious thoughts Sung Confucianists claimed to possess sagely wisdom and attempted to measure what could not be measured, and imposed on people in general what in fact could not be studied. In its extreme, standards as to what virtue should be were mandated, and eventually the virtues of the Ancient Sages were distinguished according to superior and inferior. This too is the inevitable result of their thinking. These theories are rooted in Mencius, but the further distortions made by Sung Confucianists are not minimal. They are, in sum, the excesses of poor scholarship. It is truly regrettable.

4. As for the names of Sages and wise men, these were not ranked in ancient times. The sole difference was that Sage was the name given to creators. A wise man referred to a person's talent and virtue, and was a name given to distinguish him from the rest of the people. The Sages too stood out from all the others. Thus when we begin to establish ranks the number of the wise men becomes the larger of the two. Tsai Wo said, "When I look at Fu Tzu, there is a distance from the wisdom of Yao and Shun." In the *Book of Divination*: "The virtues of wise men are eternal, and their accomplishments are grand." If people of later ages had written the above in their own words, they would have said, "sage." Hence wise man is a term widely applied. Yang Tzu-yün was the first to say; "The words of the sage are like those of Heaven. Those of the wise man are of the earth." From then on sageliness and wisdom became ranked names. With the naming of Confucius as the great sage, Yen Tzu as the wise sage and Mencius just behind him also as a wise sage, they unwittingly came to resemble the ranking of the bodhisattvas by the names of Futo, Nyorai, Bosatsu, and Hosho. All this must be seen as falsification.

RITES [*REI*]: THREE DEFINITIONS

1. Rites is a name for the Way. It is a single term for the Four Teachings of songs, history, rites and music, and the Six Arts of rites, music, archery, writing, horsemanship and calculation that were created by the Ancient

Kings. The so-called 300 basic rites and the several thousand variations are the specific objects. Of the six arts writing and calculation are especially for commoners with official positions, archivists, historians, foremen, and lower officials; horsemanship is for knights, and archery for lords, but archery is executed with rites and music. Thus, it may not be compared with the archery of the people in which striking the target dead center is the main objective. Above all, rites and music are the greatest of the arts and it is these to which rulers devote themselves. However music is managed by the music master, and the princely ruler relies on it to nourish virtue. Rites are the special activity of the ruler. Hence it is said that when Confucius was young he became familiarized with rites. He called on Lao Tzu in the kingdom of Chou and asked him about rites, and visited T'an, Ch'i, and Sung, all to seek the meaning of rites. This view of rites can be seen in the documentations of Tzu Hsia, the queries of Tseng Tzu, the earnest discussions of the seventy disciples, and the various chapters of *Rites*. It is clear that the gentlemen of the Three Dynasties also concentrated on rites.

Indeed, the Ancient Kings realized that they could not rely on words alone to teach the people, and hence created and taught rites and music. Realizing too that laws and punishments would not suffice to provide order among the people, they created rites and music and taught people to follow these. The fundamental form of rites prevails everywhere between Heaven and earth, setting details in place, providing norms for all things and order to every twist and turn, and the Way does not reside apart from it. Princely rulers study it and commoners rely on it. To study rites is to learn about them through diligent effort, and gradually realize their meaning. To realize their meaning after long effort means to leave no part unknown. This cannot be realized through words only. When one relies on rites one undergoes change. In changing, it is without realizing or knowing it that one comes to rely on the emperor's rules. There is nothing wrong with this. Most assuredly, the same cannot be realized through legal punishments.

People generally understand when things are explained to them with words. Without these words there is no understanding. Yet, while rites and music are wordless they are superior to teaching with words, because they alter people. When one is learning something and concentrates on it, the spirit and body quietly undergo change without one's awareness. One then suddenly understands this. But when one gains awareness through words, one simply stops at the accuracy of what has been said, and does not think beyond that. The problem is that the listener simply is not made to reflect. In rites and music, there are no words; so that if one does not reflect, nothing is gained. And even if one reflects but does not gain understanding, or if one does not inquire into why one lacks understanding, nothing can be done about it except by studying another form of rites. By broadening what one studies and by steady exploration from different angles, one gradually gains understanding in the course of things. Such study is already spread broadly, thus the understanding gained does not exclude anything. Further, the understanding gained through words can be explained, but it is only one fragment of the whole. Rites are concrete things. They both contain and overflow with myriad meanings. There may be clever words, but they can never exhaust meaning. This gain is realized from silence. In the teachings of the Ancient Kings this is the best route. While the teachings of rites and music are understood silently, some people gain knowledge, and others do not. Thus on occasion Confucius discussed elements of the meaning of propriety. In fact, the propriety of rites was created by the Ancient Kings and hence the *Book of Rites* refers to these only. People's knowledge always extends to some areas and not to others. Thus those who believed in the Ancient Kings of the seventy disciples did not believe in the Ancient Kings as Confucius saw them. And those who believed in the seventy disciples did not believe in Confucius as the seventy disciples saw him. Thus, out of the urgent desire to have people understand, much effort was given to explaining the righteousness of rites, and as this discussion spread down into the period of the Warring States, righteousness came to be separated from rites and gained an independent life. Rites, too, came to be spoken of without discussions of righteousness. These tendencies are clearly evident in Mencius's writings. Following this, the distancing from the ancients took place rapidly. Discussion of righteousness and principle idea that sees physical phenomena and unchanging underlying reality as ultimately identical. These views reflect a poor reading of Mencius. When we look at Mencius, he says, "The heart of reverence is rites," and moreover, "the spirit of generosity is the source of rites." The crux of his knowledge is whether rites are said to be internal or objective, and again his words are chosen and spoken with casual abandon. Thus he uses words such as reverence and high-mindedness without clarification of their basic premises. Even Mencius did not realize that reverence and high-mindedness could not adequately explain rites. He simply explained it in terms of the spirit with which to carry out rites. If he did not grasp the objective truth underlying them, he did not grasp the obvious truth that the Ancient Kings drew on the nature of human beings to build the Way, and they did not view rites as being the same thing as human nature.

Jinsai's view of benevolence, righteousness, rites, and wisdom as being contained in virtue also simply places inner human nature on the same level as virtue. It actually has not gone beyond the views of the Sung Confucianists. Hence, in explaining rites, he spoke of them as "clarifying high and low and differences in statuses and not overstepping these bounds in the least." To depart from the rites of the Ancient Kings and say this makes Jinsai no better than the Sung Confucianists. And further he spoke of rites as being simply external, which did not correspond with Mencius's ideas of reverence and generosity. It also clearly contradicts his own idea of realizing virtue from within one's self. How, then, can one expect this to encompass the rites of the Ancient Kings.

Truly the thoughts of the Ancient Kings were profound. Living thousands of years ago, they already knew that words alone would not suffice to explain the Way. Thus they created rites and music with which to teach the people. Scholars in later times, however, discarded this legacy and relied on rhetoric only. Abandoning the rites without studying them, they sought to rely on their own words to explain the meaning of the rites of the Ancient Kings. Clearly they were not aware of their own limitations. This resembles discarding tools of measurement and then saying, "If you rely on what I say, even if you discard your measuring tools you can still make accurate angles, circles, curves and straight lines." This is truly chaos.

2. It is said in *History* that "Heaven made order in the universe and rites came into being." This means Yao and Shun created rites, and by dedicating themselves to the Heavenly Way carried out these rites. Thus they rendered the teaching of rites sacred. In the same way, when the emperors of the Three Dynasties commenced a new policy or activity, they also revered their ancestors and submitted it to Heaven. Then with the mandate of Heaven and their ancestors, they initiated the new activity. This was done through divination. The ancient way was done in this manner. The later Confucianists did not understand the meaning of this. They said that Heaven was the same thing as nature, and that rites were natural. This was the theory upon which they based their idea of the principle of Heaven. But they did not know that those who said Heaven was nature were Lao Tzu and Chuang Tzu. This idea was not present in ancient times. If rites really were one with nature, what then does one make of the differentiation of rites among the Three Dynasties? The inevitable result was that the principle of Heaven' had to be rendered as detailed and fine and rites as coarse. Hence when the fine and detailed came to be adopted these rites, as coarse things, were divided and said to be now to the left and then to the right. If this was so, what might the meaning have been of sayings such as, "The Ancient Kings created rites and were careful not to go beyond these bounds;" and "The Ancient Kings created rites and they always realized their goals". The Sung Confucianists, nonetheless, strictly defended their view of the coarseness of rites. And in the end they put aside the rites of the Three Dynasties and felt compelled to erect a theory of a single and timeless "rite." Thus, Ch'eng Tzu said: "The claim that King Ch'eng passed on rites and music and that Po Ch'in received them is incorrect." The *Rites of Chou* were built by the Duke of Chou, and King Ch'eng and Po Ch'in received them directly from the Duke. If, however, these were not the rites, then how can Ch'eng Tzu's so-called rites be anything other than the rites of Chou themselves. Indeed, he put aside the rites of the Ancient Kings and replaced them with another set of rites determined by subjective judgment alone. Plainly such confused reasoning brought the way to extremes of disorder.

special entity. Hence it is said, "Rites and righteousness are the great reference points of the people." Rites regulate inner spirit, righteousness orders events. Rites maintain the normal flow. Righteousness responds to changes. These two come close to fulfilling the Way of the Ancient Kings. For this reason, the ancients often put the concepts of rites and righteousness together. People often recognize rites as the rites of the Ancient Kings, but often do not recognize righteousness as the righteousness of the Ancient Kings. Hence, as explanations, these are incomplete.

Righteousness was presumably derived as a portion of the Way. It can have 1,000 different applications each one good. Thus it is said, "Righteousness is appropriateness." The Ancient Kings brought together many of the thousand different applications and ordered them into rites. Scholars seek the meaning as to why this ordering took place. This is due to the righteousness of rites. Hence in contrast to rites, that are concrete, what is called righteousness are the things that are spoken of in abstract terms. Hence rites and righteousness have been passed on together from ancient times. Righteousness is truly of the Ancient Kings. Han Yü said, "To act and render a good is righteousness." And Chu Hsi said, "Righteousness is regulation of the spirit, the appropriateness of events." These do not show understanding of the righteousness of the Ancient Kings. They simply took their subjective thinking and called it righteousness. In doing this, they gave rise to an understanding of righteousness that was not righteous. Chu Hsi based his ideas on Mencius's "righteousness within." But Mencius's point was simply to say that the Ancient Kings relied on the nature of human beings to build the Way and thus that righteousness was in accord with the spirit of human beings. He did not say that righteousness was identical with inner human nature. It is true that the Ancient Kings defined the meaning of righteousness with their reasonings. But the aim of the Way of the Ancient Kings was to bring peace and well being to the people. Moreover, this brilliant and wise virtue interacted smoothly with the way of the natural order and thus with knowing thoroughly the natures of both humans and things. Thus, because righteousness is so diverse that it varies in thousands of different ways, it is appropriate to the needs of any circumstance. This cannot be firm judgment. It is called so simply because the meaning of the poem and ideograph has been understood in the same way since ancient times. For instance, in poems there are six elements of righteousness. How can this view of firm and clear judgment be the same thing as righteousness. This simply means that there have been different ways of composing poems from ancient times. However, after Lao Tzu's "After the way was lost, scholarly interest in virtue emerged. After virtue, interest in benevolence emerged. After benevolence, righteousness, and after righteousness, rites." This was said to criticize the Way of the Sages, but one should be aware that this was said in the language of the ancients. The meaning here is that benevolence, righteousness, and rites were created by the Ancient Kings and that it was not the way of nature. That is why Lao Tzu uttered the above words. Kao Tzu's "righteousness that is outside the self" is also the same. Had Kao Tzu not understood the meaning of righteousness, Mencius would have argued righteousness. When one looks at the fact that Mencius only discussed whether righteousness existed within or outside of inner human nature, one will know that what Kao Tzu said is not wrong. Lao Tzu, Kao Tzu, and Mencius all understood righteousness as the righteousness of the Ancient Kings. Mencius said, "The sense of shame is the origin of righteousness." And further: "People do not do that which they should not do. Righteousness, then, is realized in this way. Thus, the idea of righteousness need not be relied on." It is this argument that supports the unreliable view about clear and firm judgment coming from within. Since all people possess the spirit of shame, people in the lowest dregs of society will fall by the wayside and take their own lives. This certainly cannot be righteousness. What people should not do is always not in accord with righteousness. If Mencius meant it to be so, his own theories would be viewed as being erroneous. Thus we know Mencius did not mean this. The gentlemen of ancient times did not make subjective choices in carrying out a deed or making an assessment. They invariably reflected on the prior ancients and drew upon the rites and righteousness of the Ancient Kings in reaching conclusions. And when they decided to develop an argument, they always relied upon the ancient songs and history. This was their way of doing things.

Furthermore, Jinsai in rendering righteousness as a virtue had this to say: "Doing what one must do and avoiding what one must not do is called righteousness." This view is based on Mencius. However, in doing or not doing what one must do, the question remains as to whether Jinsai meant inner self or the righteousness of the Ancient Kings. Should he choose from within, this is simply changing the wording of Chu Hsi's thoughts. And should he rest on the righteousness of the Ancient Kings, how then can he call righteousness an inner virtue of human beings? The error involved here is obvious. Indeed, when the Ancient Kings erected righteousness on their own, they did not have precedents before them to which to turn, and had to make choices from within themselves alone. This is why they are Sages. Gentlemen in later times who studied what the Sages created to carry out virtuous practices made one or two choices by relying on their own thinking. This, however, is not what people can do well, because there is no standard of true agreement to rely on. Late Confucian scholars, in teaching the people, discarded the righteousness of the Ancient Kings and taught them to make subjective choices from within. How mistaken this is. There is no other cause than that Mencius used language for polemical purposes. Without knowing this, Sung Confucianists drew on Mencius's words to understand righteousness. This is akin to a physician who needs a particular medicine to cure an illness, and continues to prescribe the same medicine even though the illness has been cured. The confusion is extreme.

2. The ancients did not refer to righteousness as a virtue. It was first included among the six virtues in the *Rites of Chou*. They referred to the ability of Ta Ssu Ma for this. Ta Ssu Ma oversaw the execution of rewards and punishments, promotions and demotions, and military and hunting matters. Hence rewards and promotions were said to be appropriate to righteousness. Military and hunting matters involve making quick judgments. If he was not thoroughly acquainted with the righteousness of the Ancient Kings, he might not be able to respond to actual changes taking place and avoid making errors to carry out his duties. This is the primary duty of knights and princes and appropriate to all those who serve. Hence in other texts it is not referred to as a virtue. There is reference to

"righteous knight" or "righteous person," but in these cases what is actually done is said to accord with righteousness, and the person praised accordingly. These are used only in particular cases. The specific act itself is not given the name of a virtue.

3. In references such as, "Princes and stewards are righteous," the emphasis is on the steward. The prince is responsible for the entirety. The Way of the Ancient Kings is in peace and well-being of the people. Unless the ruler is a benevolent person, he will not be able to carry out his task. Thus it is said, "To become a princely ruler benevolence is everything." The steward also serves according to the Way of the Ancient Kings. The princely ruler, however, oversees the entirety, while the steward is responsible for a segment of it. There are many particular offices, each with different duties. Without righteousness, duties will not be done well as they divide in 1,000 different ways. Hence righteousness is said to be the duty of stewards. The saying, "The teaching of young servitors is done with particular righteousness," refers to teaching the way to stewards. Each duty has its own way to be followed. It is said that all the duties are not of the same nature. Only righteousness serves to draw clear boundaries between them. The *Analects* says: "In carrying out his duties, the gentleman seeks to practice righteousness." And further, "By carrying out righteousness he realizes the Way." In serving, the princely ruler studies the righteousness of the Ancient Kings and carries out his duties.

4. It is said in the *Book of Changes*: "With what should the ruler govern the people. With wealth. Through managing wealth and ruling the populace with correct language, the prince prevents people from doing what they ought not do. This is righteousness." The *Analects* says: "When one sees advantage, one thinks of righteousness." Further: "The princely ruler immerses himself in righteousness; the ordinary people in profit." This is because people must regulate their daily lives as their duties. Hence to seek wealth and profit is the occupation of the people. The princely ruler studies the Way of the Ancient Kings and fulfills his mission endowed by Heaven. Here righteousness is viewed as the Way. "To manage wealth, use correct language, prevent ill deeds among the people." These are also the duties of those who serve in the various offices.

To manage wealth means the policies of reclamation, public education, and construction. To use correct language means to engage in divination and military matters. To prevent ill deeds means to administer justice, to police, and to punish.

5. In ancient times *Songs* and *History* housed these ideas of righteousness. *History* contains the great instructions of the emperors, and it serves all ages to seek through it an understanding of the Way. One need but draw from it and make decisions on events. Thus to claim righteousness as being contained in *History* is entirely appropriate. With regard to righteousness being contained in *Songs*, many find it difficult to decipher this. The songs of the ancients were truly much like the songs of today. The language was centered on the feelings of the people. There is no call to speak of them as righteousness or principle. Later Confucian scholars understood these as the rewarding of the good and punishing of the wicked. These are only words of those who do not understand. In sum, the Way of the Ancient Kings was erected with direct ties to human feelings. Hence, without knowing human feelings, how can one attempt duties or policy and not fail? Scholars must know human feelings well and then gradually change accordingly the spiritual force in the *Book of History* itself. Hence, also those who see righteousness as being in the *Book of Songs* must also confirm their readings with the *Book of History*. This is the mystery of the teachings of the Ancient Kings. It cannot be understood with superficial knowledge.

6. Sometimes righteousness is used in the phrase "the determining of virtue and righteousness." Virtue is with regard to people in general, and righteousness refers to events. It was used this way in ancient times. It is said, "*Songs* and *History* are the house of righteousness, and *Rites* and *Music* provide the norms of virtue." They are also examples of virtue and righteousness used as a pair.

7. There is also the reference "longitudinal connective of Heaven; righteous details of the earth." These are words used to embellish rites. The longitudinal connective means the greatness of rites, holding large segments of the people together, like the warp that is woven with the woof. Righteousness refers to the small details of rites. It refers to the ordering

of the various different aspects of rites. Referring to these terms as Heaven and earth means honor and praise.

8. The compound, benevolence and righteousness, is not to be found in the Classics and the *Analects*. This is because the emphasis is on doing things. After the seventy disciples, the idea of the various arts being in the Way itself became a central concern. As the argument persisted, people's attentions were drawn closer to this to the extent that the view increasingly came to be celeb rated, and moreover, the Way of the Ancient Kings itself came to be tampered with. The flow in this direction was inevitable, and the Way came to be degraded. Benevolence and righteousness were put together into a compound, and named as the product of the Way of the Ancient Kings. However, when this process began, the Sages had not been gone very long and that language was not yet distorted. The following are examples. In the *Book of Rites* it is said: "Righteousness is part of the arts. It regulates benevolence. It coordinates the arts, and harmonizes benevolence. Those who realize this are firm and stable. Benevolence is the foundation of righteousness and the substance of harmony. Those who realize this are to be revered." In the addendum to the *Book of Changes* it is said: "In building the way of humankind, there is benevolence and righteousness." Thus the Way of the Ancient Kings is broad, but in sum it boils down to bringing peace and well being to the people. However, Benevolence is not realized with words. Thus was created rites and music to teach the people. This is properly the meaning of the arts. Righteousness was also created by the Ancient Kings and it is documented in the *Songs* and *History*. The teachings of the Ancient Kings combine rites and righteousness as the great pillars of the people. Thus *History*, *Analects*, and *Mean* all combine rites and righteousness, but not benevolence and righteousness, because Benevolence is the great virtue of the Ancient Kings. It is not comparable to righteousness. Rites and righteousness belong to the Way. They are not the virtues of the Kings. When benevolence and righteousness are used together it is forgotten that they do not belong to the same category, and instead rites go with righteousness. Thus this was not done in ancient teachings.

However, within the themes of the Way and the arts, benevolence and righteousness were sometimes discussed together. It can be found in the *Books of Rites* and *Divination*. Those who emphasized rites spoke of benevolence and righteousness as virtues; they praised the virtue of rites by referring to benevolence and righteousness. Though the rites of the Ancient Kings have 1,000 ways, its ultimate purpose is to bring peace and well being to the people. Thus it is Benevolence that maintains unity in rites. The 300 basic rites and 3,000 detailed variations exist because of righteousness. Benevolence unifies them all while righteousness constitutes different parts. Hence the phrase, "Righteousness is the various arts and Benevolence forms one unit." When various elements of righteousness are gathered, rites are put into place and Benevolence is realized. Thus it is said "Arts combine them and Benevolence harmonizes them." The meaning of harmonize is like that in the phrase, "harmonizing is synonymous with standardizing." Those who emphasized divination located its teachings in the *Book of Changes*. Hence they praise divination by referring only to righteousness and benevolence. The yang is great and leaves nothing beyond its unifying frame. And as an analogy to this the idea of benevolence is advanced. Yin is small and divides into many parts. Hence righteousness is posited as analog. Yin and yang interact constantly and are inseparable. Without complete unity it is not benevolence. When it separates without clear division it is not righteousness. *The Books of Changes* and *Rites* discuss benevolence and righteousness together. And yet, benevolence and righteousness have not been divided into two separate entities. Hence they do not deviate from the Way.

Again in Music, it is said, "Benevolence is the basis of loving others. With righteousness this is made true. In the spring things are cultivated and they grow in the summer. This is benevolence. In the fall things are harvested and in the winter they are stored. This is righteousness." In *Rites*, "embracing benevolence one takes parents as being of prime importance and traces back through them to ancestors. This is named lightness since benevolence gets weaker as one goes from parents to ancestors. Putting emphasis on righteousness, one takes ancestors as being of prime importance and works back to parents. This is called weightiness since ancestors receive higher respect than parents. In *Rites*, "The energy of the stern freezing winds of nature begins in the southwest and flourishes in the northwest. This is the majestic energy of nature. It is the righteous energy of nature. The gentle and warm energy of nature begins in the north-east and flourishes in the south-east. This is the flourishing energy of nature. It is called the benevolent energy of nature." Language such as this is part of the debate over the Way of Ancient Kings, but they already divide benevolence and righteousness, and reveal the deterioration from the older rites of the Confucian school. Towards the end of this process, the benevolent gift of the Sages became separated from the Way. The teachings of Confucian scholars declined with each day during the period of the Warring States and struggled amongst the 100 schools who simply involved themselves in verbose debate. They did not express the true words of the Ancient Kings, and sought advantage by assuming a subjective viewpoint. Mo Tzu prized benevolence and Yang and the other Legalists denied the validity of benevolence and righteousness. Thus the Confucianists soon named benevolence and righteousness together as the Way of the Sages to distance themselves from the others. And thus they too were unaware of their having abandoned the way of rites. For instance, in the *Book of Rites* it is said, "One who is close to benevolence is distant from righteousness. One may be humane but not honor it. Alternatively one may be close to righteousness and cool toward benevolence. One may honor it and not be humane." Or there is Mencius's discussion of commiseration from within in terms of benevolence and the spirit of dishonor in terms of righteousness. The idea in all of this is that benevolence is the basis of saving the people and suppressing rebellion is righteousness. Just as the sun and the moon interchange in providing light so is the meting out of punishments and rewards. And it is said after that that the Way does not favor one or the other. These words were said as though there was a timeless principle and everything was crystal clear. But these scholars are not aware of the grave departures that were being made from the Way of Ancient Kings and Confucius.

In nature there is the sustaining and killing of life, and among human beings there is good and evil. Sages from the outset favored goodness and despised evil. Punishments and rewards began from this. However, in supporting goodness and despising evil, only benevolence served as the underlying reason for rewarding one thing and punishing another. Thus the Sages relied on Benevolence to erect rites and righteousness to this end, and gentlemen, too, relied on it to carry their duties out. Thus those who speak of benevolence and righteousness as one are mistaken. Mencius and the various schools followed the idea that there were differences in righteousness, and, interpreting "not to do" as "ought not to be done," further impressed this view of righteousness in people's minds and made it stand for the spirit of despising wickedness. They eventually combined righteousness with the idea of benevolence and came to call them together the Way. However, once rites were embellished by benevolence and righteousness, they were always concrete things. But when the Way became identical solely with benevolence and righteousness, the concreteness of rites was lost. This is because scholars sought the Way based only on the names of benevolence and righteousness. Arguments flourished over the details of speech, and righteousness ceased to be close to rites and gained an independent place. In short order, ancient language was simply disregarded and the Way of benevolence and righteousness became a conventional phraseology among Confucianists over the countless generations. Here again is the failure to reflect on the ancients.

The gentlemen of later generations, especially when viewing the various venerable teachers of the Sung era, presented their scholarly views about earnestly internalizing goodness and desisting from wickedness, and they extended heavenly principle to suppress human desires. They did not realize that in the teachings of the Ancient Kings when the Way is paved for goodness, wickedness disappears of its own accord. Similarly in discussing politics, they earnestly spoke of rewarding gentlemen and punishing the wicked. In the Way of the Ancient Kings, the benevolent person will simply be put forth for recognition and the wicked, of their own accord, will keep their distance. In discussing human beings, while these gentlemen spoke of strong and weak points, pluses and minuses, in the Way of the Ancient Kings only strong points are relied on to prevent wasted talent in the world. In seeking the origins of this misunderstanding, it probably originated

soon benevolence was rendered as being identical with filiality. This is erroneous. Filiality is filiality. Benevolence is benevolence. The gentleman disliked the method of taking one idea and destroying 100 other concepts. If filiality alone suffices as an equivalent of all the others, Chiang Ko of the Han dynasty and Wang Hsiang of Chin Dynasty, famed for his filiality, must have been a sage. Confucius thus said, "Beyond one's daily activities, one should study letters." The idea here is that even though there is filiality and brotherly affection, if one does not study, one remains a rustic country fellow. Scholars should know this well. Even so, the Chou dynasty built the way of supreme virtue and sensitive personal virtues to realize all the things that needed to be done, and beyond that erected the filial virtues with which to teach the people. Even though one might have committed wrongdoings if one possessed the virtue of filiality, the Ancient Kings accepted him. It can be said that the Ancient Kings placed great emphasis on filiality.

LOYALTY AND TRUST [*CHŪ, SHIN*]: THREE DEFINITIONS

1. In loyalty, one organizes one's thought for someone else, or acts in place of someone else, thoroughly fulfilling the essential spirit of the task, and viewing this task as if it were one's own. With wholehearted dedication to the prince every detail is accounted for. It can also mean serving the ruler. Or it can mean dedicating oneself to hearing out cases. Hearing cases too means serving the ruler as an official. However, the headings under the five kinds of punishments number in the thousands, and are truly manifold in their application. In this, officials have to listen to and rely on the deceptions of people, so it is difficult to gain true knowledge of a trial and they face the resentments of this party and that. If the true picture of a case cannot be fully grasped, a fair conclusion is difficult to reach. Hence, among the virtues of the *Rites of Chou*, loyalty is included as a talent for official duty. In the *Tso Chuan*, "The severity of a prison sentence may be difficult to assess, but should always begin with the actual details. It is linked to loyalty." This is worth looking at. Confucius lists four principles, letters, virtuous action, loyalty, and trust and thought

loyalty was in the realm of politics. Politics is carrying out the prince's affairs. Hence the name of loyalty is given to such service.

2. Trust refers to the fact that words are always accompanied by evidence. Many in society interpreted this to mean that there is no deception in words. Yet while one may rely on words being accompanied inevitably with evidences, this does not suffice to mean the absence of deception. Phrases such as the following: "When trust is close to righteousness, words may be acted out" means that while words may have evidence to go with them, they should always be in accord with the righteousness of the Ancient Kings. If words are not in accord with righteousness, although one may try to carry them out in deeds, the attempts will fail. In the end, the evidences will be for naught. Chu Hsi drew on the line, "an agreement is called a pledge," and removed from agreement the ideograph for trust, and rendered it as promise. This makes no reference to evidences. This interpretation is simply mistaken.

Again, the phrase, "without faith the people cannot stand firm" refers to the people having trust in their rulers. When the orders are issued sparingly, and the people are not despised, then the people will have trust. However, when there is trust based on fear, then the trust will not be embraced. Hence, only when one is able to become like parents of the people, will people come to have trust. Sayings such as: "If one does not have trust, that person will never know what is possible," and "when words are based on loyalty and trust and actions are earnest and reverential, then even those barbaric tribes beyond the boundaries will act accordingly," all center on action based on trust. In general, the Way of the Ancient Kings was created to bring peace and well being to the people. Hence, the way of princely rule focuses on providing for the people. However, if individuals and the people as a whole do not have trust, how then can the Way be followed. The basis of distrust is in the self. Thus the princely ruler honors trust. The idea of trust in the phrase, "Words among friends are trusted"; is not to be confused with "in serving parents, the greatest efforts are made, and in serving the prince one gives his all." Although the former tends to be taken very lightly, it is friends who might help enhance one's reputation and make one advance to higher levels. Hence the *Doctrine of the Mean* says, "To advance upward one must have trust among friends or he will not rise upward." Hence the Ancient Kings honored close friendship and gave it the name of trust. Later gentlemen detested this as simply seeking advancement, and hence despised trust, but they did not realize the significance of trust. The unfortunate result of this was that they exalted their severance of ties with others and sought advancement on their own. Thus they fell into the trap of overcompensating in seeking to correct an error, and soon they were no longer in accordance with the Way of the Ancient Kings where "in carrying out the Way, one is not far from the people." Scholars should reflect on this.

Moreover, in the list of terms, "language, action, loyalty, trust," trust here is in the realm of language. The way of language respects concrete evidences. Hence the name of trust is used. The phrase "words contain concrete things" refers to the words of the ruler, which are based on specific evidence. Later Confucian scholars are elegant in their arguments, but their words are empty, lacking evidence. Why do they not seek the language of Tsai Wo and Tzu Kung. Using the words loyalty and trust as a compound also refers to planning things for others as well as to a specific person . The phrase, "Viewing loyalty and trust as central," also centers on this idea. "A person of loyalty and trust," likewise, points to a person who is capable of acting accordingly. It is said: "Centering on loyalty and trust, one moves toward righteousness," and "a person of loyalty and trust should study rites." Rites and righteousness are the Way of the Ancient Kings. Loyalty and trust are the virtues of the mean. To climb high always one begins from below, and to travel far, one always starts close by. Thus in studying the Way of the Ancient Kings, one always begins with loyalty and trust as the base. In the *Book of Changes* it is said, "Loyalty and trust are the reason virtue advances. To master written language and to establish its truthfulness is because one is dedicated to learning." To master language refers to the study of *Songs* and *History*. To establish its truthfulness means studying *Rites* and *Music*. *Songs* and *History* are vessels of righteousness. Hence the words, "to move toward righteousness" and "by studying rites, illustrate each other." Confucius said ,"To be loyal and trustworthy is being like me, one who studies. Should you not, therefore, pursue studies as I do?" That is, even if one possesses loyalty and trust, without study he remains a country bumpkin. And if one does not rely on the virtue of the mean in studying the Way of the Ancient Kings one fails to establish a basic point of departure. Then despite any desire to travel far and to climb high, one will not achieve this. This is why loyalty and trust were prized in the Confucian school. Filiality, brotherly affection, loyalty and trust are all virtues of the mean. Thus to put loyalty and trust aside and advocate filiality and brotherly affection alone means that a person has failed to study adequately and locates filiality and brotherly affection in the inner human spirit. Such a person who favors the interior and slights the external should not be allowed to minister to others. The Way of the Ancient Kings was dedicated to peace and wellbeing. Hence, in large measure it centers on the ministering of others. Loyalty and trust are terms that relate to those who govern. This means the affairs of others should be taken as one's responsibility. Thus those who advocate loyalty and trust in particular are close to the Way.

Ch'eng Tzu said: "To complete one's self realization is called loyalty. To act concretely on this basis of self realization is called trust." He felt that phrases such as "viewing loyalty and trust as central," meaning planning for the benefit of the people were too narrow and unattractive. Moreover Ch'eng Tzu did not realize that these virtues were established because the Way of the Ancient Kings was to bring peace and well being to the people, and therefore he tended to seek these within the self. But "to complete self realization" is hardly adequate to exhaust the meaning of the concept of loyalty. If today's scholars of Sung Confucianism have not heard of planning things for the good of others this is because this concept, for the most part, has been abandoned by them all and they do not reflect on it. Thus they said: "the self has already realized its own inner spirit". They said this because they were unaware that the term loyalty contained within it the meaning of careful and extreme attention to surroundings. "To act on the basis of self realization" is also not an accurate reading of the term of trust. Ch'eng Tzu tended to seek its meaning in the inner spirit, hence his interpretation. In ancient times this was discussed only with specific reference to the language itself. It certainly was not sought in the human spirit.

Jinsai said as follows: "In general when something exists, people say that it exists; when it does not they say it does not; when there is an excess amount they say so; and when it is not enough they say so too, and things are neither exaggerated nor underemphasized. Truly this is trust." This is none other than the view of the Sung scholars. Moreover, Jinsai did not understand that in ancient times this was said only to manage people. Thus he rendered "trust is close to righteousness" and "trust is knowing that just rewards and penalties will be acted out" as being about promises among the people. This is sloppy thinking. Jinsai further said: "Loyalty and trust are all realized in the interactions of people." This phraseology is still not adequate. Loyalty means serving the prince and assessing things for the people. This is not just human relations. He further says: "Loyalty and trust are plain and factual and not mere rhetorical extravagance." This is much like his interpreting the statement, "the loyal and trustworthy person should study rites" as lacking authority. His views should not be followed. Jinsai is correct, however, for criticizing the previous Confucian scholars who posited loyalty and trust as a part of mutually dependent concepts.

TOLERANCE [JŌ]: ONE DEFINITION

The term for tolerance can be seen in the Analects where its basic foundation is stated: "That which one wishes to avoid one does not impose on others." The phrase is first seen in a response to Chung Kung. This line is in the main text itself. The second occasion is in a response to Tzu Kung. This is in the commentaries to the main text. In these works the question is asked, "is there tolerance in him?" In the *Analects*, the phrase is voiced to simply interpret the term tolerance. Hence it is said in the *Mean*, loyalty and tolerance are not separate from the Way. If one does not wish to impose a thing on oneself then he refrains from imposing it on others. This is the essence of the idea. But the written form of the term combines two ideographic radicals – "to be like" and "the heart." Hence doing for others that which one wishes for oneself is also tolerance. However, this ideal cannot be easily put into practice by the student. The inner spirit of individuals is not the same. Their desires are different. Thus emphasis was placed on the part that said "that which one does not wish for oneself." Confucius said: "The ability to draw analogies with the familiar, this is the method of benevolence. That which is familiar is analogous to one's heart. This refers to tolerance. A benevolent person wishes to stand on his own and thus helps others to stand. Desiring to realize goals, he aids others in achieving them." Likewise when he is incapable of standing on his own or realizing goals, then he does not impose on others that which he is even slightly disinclined to do.Hence the phrase "the method of benevolence" is used. Those who combine the words for loyalty and tolerance practice both loyalty with tolerance, they plan things for the benefit of others, and they relate the familiar to their own hearts and selves. Having done so, they can see the affairs of others in the same light as their personal affairs. Ch'eng Tzu interpreted tolerance to mean "to infer from oneself." This is not unreasonable. However, "That which one does not wish upon oneself and hence should not do onto others" has been accepted and passed on down from ancient times, so there is no need to interpret it again. Ch'eng Tzu's renewed interpretation was made because he felt that what one does not wish was the only aspect mentioned and that which one does wish was not mentioned. He was not sympathetic to this since it seemed to limit the significance of the idea. However, when one interprets tolerance as "infering from oneself" it also means that an ordinary person can avail himself of his feelings and actually glimpse the heart of the princely ruler. There is here a single-minded dedication to clarifying and making order but no depth or breadth of thought. This is the weakness of all the Sung scholars.

Jinsai said: " There is the feeling of forgiveness. And there is also that of empathy. The meaning here is to always deal with others' feelings without a hint of cruelty." He draws here those sections from the *Books of History* and *Rites* that deal with forgiveness and tolerance. However the actual meaning of tolerance is explained entirely by the phrase, "do not impose on others what you do not wish for your self." Further as regards forgiving without being cruel, the Ancient Kings built the Way to bring peace and well being to the people and they extended it, enacted it, supported it and nourished it. To the extent that the concept does not proceed along these lines, the single ideograph of tolerance does not suffice. In other words Jinsai shaped his views under the influence of Sung Confucian scholars' idea of cruelty. Moreover he did not realize that many of the notes to the *Analects* were inserted into the main text. Hence, it is doubtful that the phrases "this is tolerance" and "Do not do unto others what you do not wish for yourself" are identical in meaning. Regarding Tzu Hsia, his statement, "I do not wish this to be imposed on others" again repeats the errors of the Sung Confucianists. In general, loyalty and trust are at the base of scholarly study. And loyalty and tolerance are means that are closely related to benevolence. Hence among the ancients, those who spoke of loyalty and tolerance saw them as greater than loyalty and trust. Scholars should reflect on this.

TRUTHFULNESS [*SEI*]: ONE DEFINITION

Truthfulness stems from the center of one's spirit and is realized without reflective effort. Should one self-consciously seek, even in the least, to be truthful, leads one to conscious effort. Truthfulness cannot be realized intentionally through effort. For this reason in the teachings of the Ancient Kings and Confucius loyalty and trust are discussed, but not truthfulness. This is because it could not be taught. Among the main classics, one finds in the *Book of Rites*, "In carrying out the ceremonies of prayer in reverence to the spirits, without rites there is neither truthfulness nor the sublime. Truthfulness is the virtue of heaven and earth, the virtue of spirits. Truthfulness is thus prized in carrying out ceremonies of prayers. However, truthfulness is not something that is realized through conscious effort . By relying on rites to carry out deeds, truthfulness will naturally be fulfilled." That is all that was said about this. Again it is said in *Rites*, "As Confucius's delegate did not arrive at his friend Po Kao's funeral on time, Jan Ch'iu borrowed one bolt of silk and four horses and offered them at the funeral to the spirit of the departed. Confucius said that it was not acceptable for himself to have been untruthful to his friend Po Kao." Po Kao had already passed away, and he could not have known what was done by Confucius. Hence Confucius detested being untruthful to the dead. To continue from *Rites*, "The funeral ceremony is performed on the third day. Basically the things that are placed with the body must be placed there in a spirit of truthfulness and belief such as one does not begrudge them. The things that are buried together with the coffin must also be given in a spirit of truthfulness and belief without begrudging them." This statement refers to the spirit of concern that stems from the depths of one's heart; when one acts accordingly, one is devoid of calculation. This is truthfulness. Trust means beyond any doubt. When there is doubt within, then one refrains from acting. This is the meaning of trust. This is the way of dealing with the deceased. It is said in *Rites*, "One relies on a calf to represent truthfulness." Lords used calves to worship Heaven and to welcome emperors visiting their lands because calves still retained purity due to their lack of desires. Hence calves were used to symbolize truthfulness. The virtue of Heaven is truthfulness. The reverence for the son of Heaven is as though for Heaven itself. Calves were thus used to worship Heaven and welcome emperors. References in the ancient texts to "truthfulness" are of this kind alone.

The followers of Lao Tzu called the Way of the Ancient Kings artificial. With this development Tzu Ssu wrote the *Doctrine of the Mean* and the term truthfulness came to be widely used for the first time. However, when we consider the meaning of truthfulness it is said to be the virtue of the acutal order, the virtue of spirit, the virtue of inner nature, the virtue of sages. Heaven and earth and the spirits do not possess the faculties of reflection and analysis. Hence truthfulness is said to be their virtue. Even with foolish and coarse men and women, all sense without deep thought something that is informed by their inner nature and realize it without training. Hence the phrase, "the virtue of inner nature." One's inner nature is received from Heaven. Hence it is said that "truthfulness is the Way of Heaven." The Sages, in carrying out the Way, all realized their goal without reflection, and realized their objectives without extensive training. Thus this process was referred to as realizing truthfulness. The saying, "this will be made truthful" means studying the Way of the Ancient Kings and changing accordingly over a long period of time. When one's knowledge is as though identical with one's own Heaven's given nature, then even those who are without knowledge and not able to do things, now realize their objectives without deep thought and effort. This develops out of the power of studying. Hence, it is said, "Making things truthful is the way of human beings." The Way is outside the self. Heaven given nature is within the self. When one behaves truthfully as though it were one's custom of Heaven-given nature, the Way and inner nature are joined as one. Hence this is said to be the "Way of joining the inner and outer." In sum, it means realizing one's virtue through learning, and when virtue is realized, that virtue is then said to be truthful. In broad terms, this is how truthfulness is used in the *Doctrine of the Mean*.

The phrase from the *Great Learning*, "making one's mind truthful" is similar as the above. What is meant here is that when one observes things carefully knowledge is acquired and the mind becomes truthful. These efforts are made only to carry out "the observation of things," and attaining knowledge is achieved merely as the effect of such labors. In the *Book of Changes* there is the phrase, "By mastering written language, one attains truthfulness." This refers to studying *Rites* and *Music* and on this basis realizing one's virtue. The Sung scholars were poor in their understanding of ancient language and additionally had a propensity for abstract and imprecise ideas. Hence their reading of the two classics of the *Great Learning* and the *Mean* loses the original intent of the language in the text. They rendered truthfulness as concrete principle and spirit, and as truth without fabrication. Their various interpretations became increasingly detailed and convoluted. All of this stems from their failure to understand language in and of itself.

Jinsai's separation of truthful mind and truthful body as though one were superior to the other is an especially egregious mistake since the body and the self are one. This contrasting of body and spirit derives from Buddhist sutras. In general in our teachings of the Sages, the body refers almost exclusively to methods. Although skills are outside the self, when one learns these skills intensively, then one realizes virtue within the self. This is referred to as "making the body truthful." When virtue is realized, knowledge is attained without straining. When knowledge is attained, benevolence is looked on with favor just as one likes the beautiful and dislikes bad odor. The efforts are required only for the purpose for learning a method and mastering it. The *Great Learning* and the *Mean* do not have a different view on this. As the saying goes, "When one is truthful from within it will reveal itself without." Scholars have had difficulties understanding this because they have been confused by Mencius's theory of the goodness of human nature. This line in the *Mean*: "As one knows one's own way, one can act it out without stress or strain" is certainly not only applicable to sages. Knowing life and acting with ease is a practice among lowly men and women too. When one is hungry, one eats, and when thirsty, drinks water. This is done without thinking and planning about it. This is knowing one's way and acting it out without effort. Hence, when one learns to do evil, and this becomes his inner nature, evil then becomes his truthfulness. The Ancient Kings, therefore, did not teach about truthfulness. Tzu Ssu in seeking to brush aside Lao Tzu was the first to advance this idea. There is no need to beautify it as a special virtue.

Jinsai contested the Sung Confucian saying, "truth without fabrication," with his statement, "truth without falsehood," to argue that his phraseology is superior to that of the Sung Confucianists. His boast reveals his unawareness that his ideas are actually no different from those of Chu Hsi. Can these phrases be said to be misleading falsehoods – "When spring should be warm it is on the contrary cool. Summer should be hot but is cold. It frosts in the summer and thunderstorms in the winter. Peach and plum bloom unexpectedly. The five stars rotate backward. The sun and moon wander off course." Sung poet Tung P'o's comment, "People do not know the limits as to what they will do. Only Heaven is without falsehood," means only that Heaven does not accept the falsehood of human beings. It does not say that Heaven does not do anything false. Why indeed should Heaven even be discussed in terms of artificiality or the lack of it. This is not understood even in the context of today's language. It is even more so with ancient language.

HUMILITY, REVERENCE, MAJESTY, HUMBLE AUTONOMY
[*KYŌ, KEI, SŌ, SHINDOKU*]: SIX DEFINITIONS

1. Humility is the name for a virtue. It means not seeing oneself in a superior light. It is the opposite of being boastful. The Sung Confucianists say, "Humility is central to one's demeanor, reverence is central to the human spirit." This view is wrong. In general, what appears on the face of things is anchored to the spirit. Absent in the spirit, humility and reverence will not show outwardly in appearance. Hence they are entirely within the spirit and reveal themselves outwardly. The difference between humility and reverence is that humility is centered on the self, while reverence inevitably has an object to revere. Hence one can say, "revering something," but cannot use "humility" in this way." Yao's saying, "true humility," and Shun's "having humility within the self" mean not being proud of oneself, not seeing oneself as a sage, and not demeaning others. Although Yao knew of Kun's disregard of a command which had thereby caused the destruction of Yao's clan, when Yao's vassal spoke of Kun's building an irrigation system Yao said, "Let him try it and see if he can accomplish it. Otherwise, remove him from the project." Therefore Yao assigned Kun the project of constructing the irrigation system. He also relied on Shun to create rites and music, and he passed on the kingship to him. This is humility. Shun liked to investigate things, and then use plain language to describe them. This is humility. Confucius, referring to Tzu Ch'an, said, "One does things with humility and serves those above with reverence." The difference between humility and reverence can be seen clearly in this passage.

Mencius said, "For one to admit his need to rely on the prince to carry out difficult tasks; this is called humility. Speaking of the good and sealing out the bad, this is called reverence." Here not treating the prince lightly is termed humility, and doing so with respect is called reverence. Mencius's comment, "What is the spirit of exchanging gifts among friends? It is humility. And why is it said that rejecting such exchanges is a lack of humility? This is because when a man of high repute offers a gift and the recipient accepts it only after first asking whether or not the gift was acquired through a righteous means, that action means a lack of humility. Hence one does not refuse exchanges." Here again the idea is that one should not treat other people with contempt. Mencius said Liu Hsia-hui was lacking in humility. Believing that there is no ruler who practices the Way, Liu Hsia-hui remarked, "Wherever one goes to serve government, one will be dismissed from office three times." Seeing a country person, he spoke to him arrogantly. Thus the country fellow said, "Why do you treat me in such a disgraceful manner?" All these are examples of treating others with extreme contempt, and so they are called the absence of humility. From them, we are able to see the meaning of humility.

2. Reverence means having an object of respect and not neglecting it. Reverence for Heaven, spirits, the ruler, superiors, parents, brothers, and guests are all examples of this. Jinsai's critique of the Sung Confucianists idea of holding to reverence within the self is entirely valid. Yet, in reviewing the Six Classics, the term reverence is used often in them. The various terms used, such as devotion, esteem, and respect, while not identical all contain the meaning of reverence. The ultimate basis for this is that the Way of the Ancient Kings is based on reverence for Heaven and their deeds were done with respect for the Way of Heaven. The people show their respect to the Way of the Ancient Kings because they wish to dedicate themselves to Heaven's calling. The people simply rely on Heaven as a base, and on parents as a base. In the Way of the Ancient Kings, ancestors are worshipped and this is offered to Heaven. Heaven and parents are joined into one. Herein the base is unified. Princely rulers are the heirs of the Ancient Kings, and thus they revered these Ancient Kings, as they stood in the place of Heaven. Heaven extends mandates to all the people and has them order their own lives. Hence they revere Heaven. Physical bodies are extensions of parents. Hence there is reverence for them. These are the reasons that in the Way of the Ancient Kings reverence for Heaven forms the base. Indeed, in the Way of the Ancient Kings, Heaven is fundamental. The spirit of the princely ruler is never devoid of this spirit of reverence. When humility and reverence are discussed in the Classics, the object of reverence for Heaven is often unspecified. For example, in such

phrases as "being humble in all situations"; and "to exist in reverence and carry out deeds with brevity," the terms "situations" and "to exist" are analogous to the "exist" in "to exist in benevolence." Here again, the physical body is present with reverence.

The scholars of Sung Confucianism centered their ideas on principle and prized intelligence. Hence although they were aware of the many references to reverence in the Six Classics, they could not explain why there are so many references, and directed their interpretations to the interior human spirit. This is the result of their idea of holding firm to reverence within the self. And thus, those who focus on principle and prize intelligence do not have faith in spirits and do not revere Heaven. Accordingly, they say that Heaven is principle, that spirits are the yin and yang, and that principle resides in the self. Thus everything is understood thoroughly in terms of principle, and Heaven is said to be in the self. The attitude here begins in arrogance and is an absence of humility. To understand reverence from this perspective explains their inability to gain a proper perspective. Uselessly holding the inner spirit firm and keeping the mind distinct from the external world, they named this "reverence." Yet, that which holds firm the inner spirit is also spirit. To use spirit to hold spirit is to set both in a state of constant struggle. This is something not even the followers of Buddha engage in. Thus those who wish to hold firm to reverence in this manner could never succeed. Chu Hsi believed he was aware of this late in life, and therefore said, "We revere because there is something to fear." However since he remained unaware of the faultiness of the idea of centering on principle and prizing intelligence, he had achieved a state that was equivalent to never having gained awareness. How truly regrettable. Jinsai was blessed with outstanding talent and possessed a very special wisdom. However he did not know ancient philosophy, and was not able to read the Six Classics. Thus he did not know that reverence for Heaven and for the spirits was the base for the Way of the Ancient Kings. Thus while he clearly saw the flaw in the idea of holding firm to reverence within, he was unaware that he himself had not fully gone beyond the framework of Sung Confucianism. Furthermore he assumed an arrogant stance of his own and considered himself to be sufficient to see the true view unassisted, and he considered the Way of the Ancient Kings and of Confucius to be separate. In theorizing about reverence he said, "The references are only with regard to reverence for the activities of the people." Thus his explication of reverence became incomprehensible. Is this not pitiful? Scholars should be aware of how pitiful this is.

3. Reflecting on comments from the classics such as the following, "setting straight one's ceremonial dress, focusing one's gaze upwards in honor, and with solemnity anticipate with respect," or again, " in ceremonial dress, with abstinency and purified body and spirit act only in accordance with rites" – these are used mainly with reference to the grand rites practiced at the ancestral mausoleum or the imperial court. There are other phrases, "In ordinary daily life, grand and elaborate rites are not put in place"; and "daily life should be lived with contentment and relaxation." There are some who do not agree with the content of these phrases. Sung Confucianists do not understand the way of tension and relaxation. They concentrate entirely on disciplining the self and distance themselves from human passion. Moreover, they do not realize that reverence is based on reverence for Heaven, and they pointlessly cling to reverence as an independent idea. The Way of the Ancient Kings is based on reverence for Heaven. This is true of the classics of *Songs*, *History*, *Rites* and *Music*. Thus, if scholars know this meaning, then in the long course of study they will gain understanding without undue effort from within. Why must one hold firmly to reverence by itself. If one understands that reverence means reverence for Heaven, it is unnecessary to rely on the idea of holding firmly to reverence alone.

4. Being humble with autonomy refers to the effort from within to realize one's virtue. In general, the Way of the Ancient Kings is on the outside and terms such as rites and righteousness refer to the governing of human beings. Many scholars, in viewing rites and righteousness as the methods of the Way, did not exert the effort to realize the virtue within themselves. Hence the wording, "being humble with one's autonomy." These words are seen only in *Great Learning*, *Doctrine of the Mean*, and *Rites*. "Autonomy" is a name used for a human state of solitude, and "humility"

means keeping the mind in a humble state. The meaning here is that while the Way is on the outside, still, indeed, one ought to retain the spirit within and work toward realizing the virtue within oneself. This is the meaning of "being humble with one's autonomy." It does not originally mean reverence. Moreover it is different from the theory of distinguishing the latent and the manifest. The Sung Confucianists did not know how to properly study the Way of the Sages, and in seeking to study the Sages, saw the phrase "the continuous realization of truthfulness." They concentrated their studies on this to establish the indicators for the latent and the manifest and to seek an uninterrupted process between these two. Thus there is the theory about awe and respectful autonomy. Here again the meaning is sought exclusively in the spirit, so that "autonomy" was rendered as "knowing oneself only and not others." By reducing their thinking to a single idea they sought to impose their authority. These are all careless and benighted ideas and are not to be found in the Way of the Ancient Kings and Confucius. The Sung Confucianists wished to define the Sages in terms of those rites pertaining to attitudes and manners. How can these be sufficient to define the Sages? Even if this could be so, the references to attitudes and manners are about studying and realizing virtue through learning, and this means doing without expectation, yet achieving. Why then include the management of methods directly in the spirit? The teachings of the Ancient Kings are like a generative system, their practices are like being one with the nature of Heaven itself. Why must effort be put into this? The teachings of the Sung Confucianists are like the making of utensils by craftsmen. Precious stones, soil and wood are first worked upon and then shaped into utensils. How can the human spirit be likened to precious stones, soil, and wood? Hence in the teachings of the Ancient Kings, the human spirit is regulated only by rites. To disregard this is truly inept. The Sung Confucianists' ideas relating to the latent and manifest, awe and humble autonomy, along with all of the categories of motion and stillness, are dealt with in minute detail. Yet by relying on these teachings they all quite obviously did not approach the realm of the Sages.

5. In the various classics the terms for humility and reverence are used

as a compound. This is because their meanings are interrelated. The Way of the Ancient Kings is based on reverence for Heaven. Hence they did not brazenly see themselves as being supreme. It is for this reason that humility and reverence are used together. Therefore, Yao and Shun refused to look down upon those below with contempt because they could not know Heaven's intent. Should the divine spirit of Heaven draw out the true inner spirit within human beings, then even the treacherous ministers Kun and Huan Tou could reform their previous ways. Even the words of the lowest servants are not necessarily inferior to ours. Confucius's refusal to dismiss lightly the world around him was also because Heaven was beyond his knowing. Thus the humility of the Sages was a complete reverence for Heaven.

6. The term majesty is centered entirely on forms of appearance. It refers to looking down to the people. Heaven shines gloriously on the earth, and sun, moon, stars and comets are sure to run their course. Those who govern others model themselves on this. This is the meaning of majesty.

MODESTY, DEFERENCE, RESTRAINT
[*KEN, JŌ, SON, FUBATSU*]: ONE DEFINITION

Modesty is similar to humility. But in humility one never assumes a superior stance. It means being lowly. Modesty means never being aggressive. It means withdrawing. Ch'en Tzu-ch'in's words, "Confucius acts humbly," relate to modesty. Deference is the opposite of contention. It means thoughtfully giving to others. Refusal and deference resemble each other. Refusal means not accepting. Meekness means being non-contentious. It means being flexible. It often refers to careful use of language. Then words are pliant and are not stated in opposition to things. "To transfer a rank or yield courteously" refers to deference. Restraint means being successful and yet not being boastful about it. These are all about virtues being fully realized. The princely ruler studies rites and music and realizes his virtue. Thus he gains harmony and his brilliance expands outwards beyond himself. Restraint is the virtue of King Yü. Deference is the virtue of Yao, Shun, and T'ai Po. Although Yü's achievements were worthy of being relied on through the ages, he did not boast. How great this is. Yao deferred to Shun. Shun in turn to Yü. The Way of realizing virtues was thus established. Thus the Way of the ancient emperors and kings was created. How truly great. T'ai Po conceded his reign and Wen and Wu brought great benefits to their age. This too was great. All these achievements were not realized through the efforts of one reign. Had they not been Sages, who could have done these things. Being fond of rhetoric Mencius emphasized the receipt of high rank by Shun and Yü and left the deference of Yao and Shun in the shadows. How deplorable.

COURAGE, PROWESS, IMMOVABILITY, STRENGTH, TOUGHNESS [YŪ, BU, GŌ, KYŌ, KI]: FIVE DEFINITIONS

1. Courage is another great virtue of the Sages. It refers to fearlessness in dealing with the affairs of the political world. Yet when identifying what is greatest among the virtues of the Sages, benevolence and wisdom are sufficient. However if courage is also added it is because the princely ruler must be militarily prepared. Thus in *History*, in celebrating the virtue of King T'ang, there is reference for the first time to bravery and wisdom as a compound term. This should certainly be noted. In the administration of Chou, there is reference to the chief of military affairs and the six ministers of Chou. They all took leadership for military events. In ordinary times, soldiers returned to their farming, rites and music embellished the performing of archery, a bow was hung at the entrance when a male child was born, and all gentlemen of the three dynasties wore swords at their sides. In *Songs* it is said, "Yin Chi Fu was skilled at both the literary and military arts." Similarly Confucius noted, "one versed in letters also is prepared in military ability." And in the Commentaries, "The grand affairs of the country are located in worship and military matters." How could it be otherwise? And so the princely ruler is also a military leader. His courage cannot be compared with those of military men and the rank and file. And such a person who nourishes courage and realizes virtue, necessarily does so with a grounding in

benevolence and in rites and righteousness. Thus Confucius said, "The benevolent person necessarily has courage." Tzu Lu queried as to why courage was prized, to which Confucius replied that this was because righteousness is prized. He further explained, "Courage without rites means there will be upheavals." In seeking a commander, Chin selected Hsi Hu because of his deep understanding of *Songs* and *History*. It is said in *Rites*, "For one who possesses great courage with great strength, when there are no disturbances in the kingdom he relies on rites and right-eousness, and when there are disturbances, he deals with them through military victories. Through military victories the enemy will disappear, and through rites and righteousness there is orderly rule. No enemies threaten from without and order prevails within – this is the fulfillment of virtue." Such was the ancient way.

Tzu Ssu in writing the *Doctrine of the Mean*, referred to wisdom, benevo-lence, and courage as the three highest virtues and said they fulfilled the way of learning. These are still thought of as a single way. In the Warring States era, the literary and the military arts were considered to be differ-ent methods; from the Ch'in and Han Dynasties they were differentiated administratively; and with the T'ang and Sung they were separated into different realms of government. Scholars today learned this and thought that it had always been this way. Since they claimed that military affairs were not part of Confucian affairs, the ancient meaning came to be obscured. To use Confucian courage for learning, as Tzu Ssu believed, is to cleave to one and discard 100 others. Scholars should reflect on this.

2. The term prowess is used with regard to crushing rebellions. How-ever, since victory is not always assured, courage is mentioned more often than prowess.

3. Strength and prowess resemble each other. Strength is the opposite of weakness and prowess is opposed to cowardice. Strength and weakness are broader in scope than courage and cowardice. Thus Tzu Lu's questions about strength are actually questions about courage. It is said in *Changes*, "The princely ruler never ceases to strive for personal strength." Strength also means study. The rising tone with which the term is pronounced is correct for it affirms the importance of study. Lu Te-ming has it as a flat

tone, but that would mean that from ancient times the Sages were virtuous without any study. But how can this be, since the Sages too were human beings. Again, the problem is one of not understanding the Sages. When "personal strength" is not enunciated properly, the term loses its true meaning.

4. Immovable contrasts with flexible, and is also different from strength and courage. It is, for example, like wood and metal: wood is supple and metal is firm and hard. Water is the supremely flexible, and it does not assert itself against anything. This is strength. It is not immovable. The difference between immovability and strength should be clearly perceived. Chu Hsi said, "Courage is the manifestation of immovability and immovability is the substance of courage." It is clear that Confucius had already included immovability and courage, along with benevolence, wisdom, trust and honesty, as being among the six virtues. Chu Hsi's view is erroneous. In his view, an immovable person is one who is decisive, implacable, and who cannot be challenged. The courage of Chang Liang is not like this. It is from this view that the distinction between courage and immovability should be understood. The virtue of mastering the practice of divination lies in the ability to interpret symbols composed of immovable and flexible elements. The way of divination in the *Book of Changes* relies on the interpretation of abstract symbols. When immovability is sought through such use of symbols, the scope of its meaning expands enormously. Thus the use of the terms immovability and flexibility are not identical with their use in the other classics. The Sung Confucianists threw them together and merged them. Hence the error. Scholars should take note of this.

5. Toughness is like immovability. It means primarily the capacity to endure difficulties.

PURITY, INTEGRITY, DENYING GREED [*SEI, KEN, FUYOKU*]: ONE DEFINITION

That which is pure is untainted by evil. Po I and Ch'en Wen-tzu are fine examples. To deny greed is to lessen greed. It means not being corrupted by money and wealth. Integrity means knowing clear limits as to what one should accept. In later generations, it came to mean not being corrupted by money and wealth, and thus has carried the same meaning as the ancient term, "denying greed." Scholars must be aware of this.

MODERATION AND FRUGALITY [*SETSU, KEN*]
TWO DEFINITIONS

1. Moderation refers to moderation, as in decorum. Decorum is always concerned with limits and what may not be overstepped, and observing decorum is called moderation. "To be moderate" means recognizing these limits and being careful not to overstep them. "Great moderation" means responding to the grand limit. These are aspects of the Way. "Sageliness is mastery of moderation. Next is the observation of moderation." Subsequent generations created such terms as "a moderate person," which denoted a gentleman. These refer to the virtue of the person.

2. Frugality means moderate use of resources. Later Sung Confucianists mistakenly used a variety of terms such as warmth, goodness, courteousness, humility, frugality, and deference all as the dignified authority of the Sages. Those who said that frugality was not confined to the careful use of resources are mistaken. Frugality, however, is the way of the benevolent person. It is part of the great virtue of the Kings. Yao and Shun did not trim miscanthus reed for their thatched roofs and lived in houses made from clay. King Yü dressed in coarse cloth, and did not eat or drink in excess. He did not decorate his kingly halls. These certainly are indications of thriftiness. Mencius's comment, "Be benevolent to other people and take good care of things," conveys something of the ancients' meaning. It means loving and caring for things. It is, however, erroneous of the Sung Confucianists to view frugality as kindly affection, as in relying on Mencius's remark about loving even the ox about to be sacrificed. The saying that "one should not fish in the ponds with small-eyed nets and trees in the forest should be cut only at certain appropriate times" is meant to caution people against damaging living things created by Heaven. If this notion is understood as merely kindly affection, how can the prohibition

of the sacrifice of oxen be explained. Mencius regarded it as a benevolent deed that the king of Ch'i requested the use of lamb instead for the sacrificial ceremony because he realized that the king had saved the ox not on the basis of love but benevolence only. Although his fondness for rhetorical language can be seen, this is what he meant. The saying, "In ceremony it is better to be moderate than luxurious," refers to frugality, as does the line, "One wears silk that is worn and inexpensive." There is moreover the saying, "While wealthy, he still follows intimately the rules of propriety." Tzu Lu said, "Poverty is lamentable, for one is unable to care for parents, and practice the proper rites for their funeral." Tseng Tzu said, "Without the Way the ruler will be uable to practice the proper rites for his kingdom." If his kingdom flourishes, he achieves it with frugality. If frugality spreads through the land, he celebrates it with proper rites. Tzu Ssu observed, "Even should propriety reign, without resources the ruler cannot fulfill his duties. Even with adequate propriety and resources, when the times are unfavorable, the ruler fails." Thus material provisions are always provided in rites. When there is poverty these materials cannot be furnished. When there is no poverty, but the uses of provisions are limited without exhausting the exercise of rites, this is called frugality. In seeking to provide material provisions with ostentation, this is called extravagance. Later Confucian scholars did not know that frugality is based on the language of ancient times, and they said that "frugality indicated insufficiency," and sought to control both luxury and frugality through propriety. Their view is unacceptable and scholars should not adhere to it.

PUBLIC, RECTITUDE, CORRECTNESS [*KŌ, SEI, CHOKU*]: THREE DEFINITIONS

1. The term public is opposite to private. The public is where people do things together. That which the individual does exclusively for himself is called private. The Way of the ruling prince is in part that which he shares with the people, and in part that which is entirely his own. In *History*, it is said: "Not favoring one party over another, the Way of Kings is broad and

encompassing. There being no favored party over another the Way of Kings is fair and just." The *Great Learning* says, "Peace was made to reign throughout the kingdom," and in the *Mean*: "The entire kingdom under Heaven was made peaceful." In the *Analects*, "It is not the lack of things that is to be lamented, but the absence of justice." And further, "When things are public, there is joy." This means that fairness and equity are public matters. And in *Rites* , "For those appointed above the rank of knights, fathers and children live in separate quarters." This indicates the fulfillment of privacy. In the *Analects*, " The father conceals on behalf of his child and the child does likewise for his father". In Mencius's words, "This I have heard: a prince will not spare expenses for his parents' funeral, even if this should cause strain on the kingdom." Among the eight basic proposals one is for parents. These are all about private matters. Both public and private realms each retain their particular relevance. Even the princely ruler has his private sphere. However, in governing the polity under Heaven the public is prized because it is the way of governing the people. Hence Confucius observed, "Revere the three selfless principles of Heaven to govern the kingdom." This refers to the Sages identifying themselves with the Way of Heaven.

Sung Confucianists formulated the theory that "the principle of Heaven is public and human desire is private." They placed exclusive emphasis on the public with such fervor that they came close to denying human feelings altogether. Jinsai criticized this correctly. Yet, by compensating for this he completely deleted references to the term public in the *Analects*. This reminds us of one who burned himself on too much hot soup and cautiously blew on cold salad. Scholars should take note.

2. Rectitude is the opposite of being inaccurate. Rectitude means abiding by the Way of the Ancient Kings. Incorrectness means not following the Way of the Ancient Kings. False strategies and false ideas can be assessed accordingly, as though using a compass and measuring stick. These are instruments for achieving correctness. With a compass one can correctly gauge a circle, with a square, one can accurately measure angles. A level sets the plane straight. The Way of the Ancient Kings is a standard of measurement. After gauging things with the Way of the

Ancient Kings, there is rectitude. Tseng Tzu said, "Should I have a fatal fall at the moment of realizing rectitude, my life will have been fulfilled." The occasion for his saying this was when an improper judgement was imposed upon him by a senior official. In *Rites*, "To rectify a nation with rites is comparable to using scales to weight things exactly, the level to keep planes straight, the compass and square to gauge circles and angles." Thus it is said in *Songs*, "As all the standards of measurement are in accord, rectify the four kingdoms." Confucius said: "If the self is correct, one acts without commands. If the self is incorrect, even with commands, the self will not respond." These are all references to rites.

In later generations the theory of universal principle arose, and the rites of the Ancient Kings were discarded and replaced by the idea of principle. To rely on principle is simply to take a subjective position. To call this subjective position rectitude was to render all human beings as innately possessing correctness. This is completely arbitrary. The *Book of Changes* uses the term "correct center." The meaning here is not the same as in the other books. The Sung Confucianists, however, confused these. Hence their error. Moreover, phrases such as "correct spirit" in the *Great Learning* suggested that the spirit was one with rites and thus means correctness. This reference explains the meaning of the rites of nourishing the elderly. In practicing rites when one is under the influence of passion, fear, affectionate feelings, sadness, and frustration, one's spirit cannot be in accord with rites. Thus it was said that "the spirit is not rectified." Nourishing the elderly involves the rites of proper eating and drinking, and hence, "One does not eat with flavor in mind." Sung scholars did not understand this in their viewpoint of rites. They erred. It is said in *History*, "The spirit is regulated with rites." This is the way of ancient times. Jinsai took the phrase "rectitude of spirit" in the *Great Learning* and concluded it to be the idea of Buddhism and Taoism. This is because he did not know ancient language.

3. The term straightforwardness is the opposite of being bent. Its virtue is to extend one's righteousness without making unreasonable compromises to others. "To straighten the Way" means not twisting the Way. Wording that says, "In the Three Dynasties, the Way was kept straight and

the affairs were conducted accordingly," means doing things consistently in accordance with the Way. Jinsai celebrated the word for straightforwardness and called it the absence of falsehood. This is a bad trait of our people. In short, it leads to the folly in misunderstanding the phrase, "the father conceals for the son, and the son conceals for the father. This is central to straightforwardness." The Duke of Yeh considered "disclosing" as being straighforward. Here Confucius explained this with the word "to conceal." The uprightness of Shih Yü was not simply that he did not conceal but that he risked his life for upholding his conviction. "Support the straightforward and set aside the bent," is a metaphor for the way that the appointment of talented and straightforward individuals will exercise beneficial influence over those in lower ranks. Lumber that is straight is said to be good, and the crooked is not good. Thus the straightforward person is said to be a good person, and the crooked one is not a good person. We can say on this basis, therefore, that the virtue of Kao T'ao and I Yin are of the same order as Shih Yü's virtue.

Mencius's critique on the phrase, "Bend a small portion to serve the laws" means that one should not change one's belief for any reason. Even the benevolent person and the princely ruler whose way is grand and virtues broad do things that seem bent and blemished. Cases of this are Confucius's competitiveness when hunting, or his being tempted to serve the autocratic Yang Huo, and rebellious Pi Hsi and Kung-shan Pu-niu. Later Confucians in dogmatic fashion judged all things in accordance with Mencius's assertions. This is wrong. Generally, straightforwardness is a fine virtue, but it is one among many others. For example, Po Yü's effort to keep "concealed his thoughts within himself," is not necessarily straightforward. Hence the princely ruler avoids promoting one idea at the expense of 100 other things.

THE MEAN, NORMAL, HARMONY, BALANCED [*CHŪ, YŌ, WA, CHŪ*]: EIGHT DEFINITIONS

1. The mean refers to neither exceeding nor falling short of a goal. It is also used as a name for the Way. Or as a name of a virtue. Or a name for

one's inner nature. When it is said that Shun applied the center of things to the governance of people, and that T'ang sought to construct the center for the people, these refer to the name of the Way. The explications are to be found in *History*. Thus there is no center within the feelings of the people, only with the princely rulers. However, the principle of governance under Heaven is to avoid excess yet not be in want. Hence all human beings whether intelligent or foolish seek only the middle. This is so since human beings came into existence. The inner nature of every human being is different, however, and views vary according to different natures. Every human being has a different stance, and with each standpoint each view differs from one another. Hence there is no true mean, no stability. And for this reason the kingdom deteriorates.

Therefore the Ancient Kings constructed their mean as a stable norm. The people of the kingdom then came to rely on this to carry out their activities. Hence norm is sometimes read as the mean. The Sages alone possessed knowledge of the mean, while the populace in general did not. In general rites, music, virtues, righteousness, and the system of 100 items are all parts of the mean, they all constituted the norm. However, when the Ancient Kings established the mean, they had no intention of imposing it upon the people as an impartial and precise principle; nor did they expect scholars to rely on the norm to seek out such an impartial, precise, and detailed principle. Their intent was to bring peace and well being to the kingdom. Hence they created the mean and rendered it as the norm, and had the people in the land rely on it to live their lives. After that, the kingdom came to be unified without falling into disrepair. Thus what the Ancient Kings constructed was not lofty but within the reach of the people to study and to practice. The wise and intelligent have no difficulty realizing it; and the foolish and unintelligent manage also to realize it. This is what is meant by the mean. This may be likened to building a castle town. Built in the east, it would be inconvenient to the princes of the west. Built in the west it would be inconvenient to the princes of the east. When built midway, the distance to be traversed by all princes will be made fair. Even though the distances are not completely equal, since this is not entirely possible, still the distances will have been reduced, making it possible for the people to endeavor to reach the object. The mean or the center indicates, therefore, that the Way of the Ancient Kings is not distant from the populace. And it is this sense of the center that must be studied.

However, the intelligence of the Ancient Kings was grand, their virtues were supreme achievements, and their thoughts were profound. They did not propose easy solutions for the immediate future, but nourished this idea of the mean and bequeathed it as a stable norm for the distant and indefinite future. The Way as it came to be called, was broad and encompassing and distant from human feelings. It was subtle and not easily known. This is why it was difficult to gauge the Sages. Confucians of later times who were limited in intelligence and shallow in their thinking, showed keen interest only in articulating their arbitrary interpretations. Instead, they pursued their goals with words, and they were thus unable to rely on the Way of the Ancient Sages to realize the virtues in themselves and contribute toward the governance of the people. Instead, they pursued their goals with words. The two teachers Ch'eng and Chu sought with partiality and with excess to realize fully the mysterious and profound and Jinsai selected only the idea of the spontaneity of action as the mean which appeared to derive from the Way of the Ancient Kings. Both are lodged in the ailment of arbitrary interpretation.

2. Terms such as the mean and harmony are names for virtues. The mean refers to goals that are not exceedingly high and are realized every day. Filiality, brotherly affection, loyalty and trust are examples of this. In Confucius's time, rites and music did not prevail and the people rarely realized the virtue of the mean. Hence the Confucian School focused their scholarship on the mean. The idea of the mean was expressed in the analogy that to go great distances we must begin nearby, and to climb great heights, we must begin from below. Those who are called high and brilliant, subtle and fine, broad and great, are all guided by the mean. Thus Tzu Ssu said that we should all be "guided by the mean." However, even if one possesses the virtue of the mean, one is not adequate to be called a gentleman without studying the Way. Confucius therefore identified the mean with the lives of people. There are also such phrases

as "the mean of the little people" and "choosing the mean." In the era of the Warring States, there is the reference, "talent does not realize the mean." While these are ordinary and vulgar sayings and do not convey the true meaning, they nonetheless are ancient wordings. The ideograph for normal, the second half of the compound for the mean, is similar in use to the divine and normal in describing the virtue of music. When referenced to the heavenly and earthly gods, the ideograph divine is used; when used with reference to the people as a whole, the ideograph normal is used. The reference in *History* to "doing things as normal and holding the divine in reverence" is again the same. The achievement of the people is called normal. It is not about the unchanging meaning in things. The Sung Confucianists were benighted when it came to philology. They only concentrated on making subtle analysis and named it as being the way of sages. It is erroneous.

3. Mean and harmony are the virtues of rites and music. In the *Rites of Chou* it is said that the mean is taught with rites, and harmony is taught with music. The ideograph for harmony carries the meaning of harmonious order. In constructing rites, the Ancient Kings made it possible for the wise to practice with ease and the unwise to manage to learn and act according to them. This is the idea of the mean. In creating music they harmonized the eight tones and the five voices, as in blending together five different flavors, to nourish human virtues and to celebrate the harmonious forces in the natural world. Moreover, as music conforms to the joys of human passion, it guides people with balance and harmony and finally leads them to be in accord with the moral order. Thereby people can realize their wishes. This is harmony. In the *Rites of Chou* there are also the six virtues of music – filiality, friendship, sacredness, the normal, the mean, harmony. Music is also set to provide balance and harmony. When the eight tones and the five voices are in perfect harmony, there is neither excessiveness nor inadequacy. As the *Doctrine of the Mean* puts it, "While feelings of anger, pleasure, sorrow, or joy are not yet manifest, it is called the mean. When the previous feelings arise and are attuned to one another, this is called harmony." In phrases such as this, the mean and harmony are interrelated.

The so-called mean is the virtue that defines one's inner nature. One's given nature is not the same as that of the birds and beasts. While there are differences between the wise and the foolish, the gifted and those less so, all human beings possess the spirit of living together and providing mutual nourishment and support. And they also are able to arrange and regulate their lives. In addition, by following what one learns, one's inner nature moves between good and evil. It can be described as taking the central position that makes one move between the left and the right, the front and the back. Hence this position is called the mean. Comparable to this is the saying, "people are given life in the central balance between heaven and earth." The phrase "feelings of pleasure, anger, sorrow, or joy are not yet manifest" refers to when one is first born and still totally without intelligence. This is when a person clearly possesses the virtue of the mean, and is in close accord with the Way of the Ancient Kings. This is not to say that it is a virtue without leanings or inclinations and thus not any different from the Sages. Those who refer to the virtue of the mean as "the great foundation of the kingdom" mean by it simply that the Sages created the Way by relying on the fact that every human being possessed that virtue as an inner nature, and went on to carry out all the affairs of the land on this basis.

The saying "human feelings arise and are attuned to one another" means that the teaching of rites and music nourish human virtues so that the feelings of pleasure, anger, sorrow and joy realize their proper expression. Hence it refers to the fact that the Way of the Ancient Kings and the inner natures of human beings are in harmonious accord and not in conflict. It is therefore said in the *Doctrine of the Mean*, "Harmony is the ultimate norm of the Way under Heaven." That is, "the Way is in accordance with the inner natures of human beings." It is not the same as stating that harmony is the act of balancing pleasure, anger, sorrow, and joy in their various degrees. Sung Confucian scholars were not skilled in ancient language and did not know the Way of the ancients. Their interpretive glosses are all incorrect, and scholars must be wary of this.

4. The term harmony, which is listed among the six virtues in the *Rites of Chou*, is the name of a virtue. What this means is that when human

beings study to realize their virtues, they are aware of the distinctions between the six virtues. Liu Hsia-hui's use of harmony is similar to this. The reference is to actual harmony between different things and the avoidance of conflicts. Ssu K'ung was said to have the special talent of harmony because he took responsibility for irrigation and the 100 occupations in manufacturing. In manufacturing, one must abide by the inner characteristics of metals, woods, leather hides and 100 different items, and create utensils based on these differing materials. Hence, widely differing elements must be brought together in their natural state and then skillfully harmonized according to the inner nature of these disparate things. Without doing so, the tasks at hand cannot be fulfilled.

5. Phrases such as this one from *History* that say, "Hold to the mean with sincerity," refer to the son of Heaven as he carries out his affairs. In ancient times, seizing the mean was said to be the way of the ruling prince. Thus, when carrying out the affairs of the son of Heaven, the phrase, "holding to the mean" was used. Without such a reading, the language in the texts of Yao and Yü would not be understandable.

6. The comment by Mencius that "those who maintain the mean nourish those who do not" refers to outstanding inner qualities which the mean represents. It is a common use of the term.

7. Phrases from the *Doctrine of the Mean* such as "strike the mean with proper timing" indicates moving forward or backward according to the needs of the moment, and to adjust these according to the appropriate rites. This is similar to "doing what is correct at the right moment." The ideograph for the mean is read with a flat tone expressing therefore "to strike" and is different from the use of the ideographic compounds meaning harmony or the median.

8. The ideograph for "balance" stands for correctness. In *History* it is said, "The imperial ruler extends his balanced mind to the people below. The people respond with their inner characters." It further says, "Heaven assists the people below, and creates rulers and teachers." The intention of these words is that Heaven establishes princely rulers and teachers who serve as models for the people. The people in turn respond to these teachers, and thereby do not lose their inner stability. The terms "extend

below" are comparable in usage to the phrases from the *Book of Rites*: "to extend below from the ancestral shrines"; "to extend downward from the mountain rivers"; "to extend downward from the five shrines"; and, "the prince extends downward his virtue to the vast populace." Demonstrating their rectitude as though derived from Heaven as "Heaven's appointment" or "Heaven's officials," princes and teachers are taken as models for the people. This is based on reverence for the Way of Heaven. The Way of the ancients was thus. Elsewhere it is written, "Heaven induces the righteous inner mind from the people," a phrase completely opposite to, "Heaven consumes one's spirit." People who realize this suddenly and do good works, ask in amazement, is this the work of Heaven? Thus, it is said, "Heaven attracts one's rectitude." The saying, "Being drawn toward Confucius," means to choose the rectitude that is in Confucius. It also means the rectitude in the language of Confucius.

GOOD AND FINE [*ZEN, RYŌ*]: THREE DEFINITIONS

1. Good is the opposite of evil. This is used in a wide variety of ways. An example of it can be seen in Mencius. He says, "What human beings desire to do is called goodness." Even though this is not, properly speaking, the Way of the Ancient Kings, in general those actions that promote the interests of human beings and lead to saving the people are all called good. These are things the people as a whole desire. The Way of the Ancient Kings seeks the highest realization of the good. There is nothing under Heaven that can exceed this. Hence the term, "ultimate goodness" is used to celebrate the Way of the Ancient Kings. It is also used with reference to specific human beings. For example, "Only goodness is a treasure," or "In goodness, one gains fulfillment. Without it one meets failure," or, "those who are good are promoted to teach others of lesser ability." All these phrases refer to good persons. While these persons are not sages, they establish laws, reform systems, or seek to order the nation and provide peace and well being to the people. Here they are called "good persons."

2. Goodness is also used in tandem with beauty. Beauty refers to brilliance that deserves to be seen. Goodness refers to what is properly right-

eous. Phrases such as, "to fully realize beauty," and, "to fully realize righteousness" all refer to music. Previous explanations about this are wrong. "The Way of the Ancient Kings is to be called 'beauty,'" and Mencius's goodness, trust, beauty, greatness, sageliness, and sacredness all indicate overlapping meanings of these two terms.

3. The ideograph meaning fine is used to indicate the absence of flaws. It is used with reference to specific talents. Examples are fine minister, fine physicians, fine ability, fine horses, the three fine officials, and fine utensils. Chu Hsi interpreted fine as being at once "pliant" and "straight." He saw these terms along with "compassion and goodness" as ideographic compounds in the classics and forced this interpretation. If fine means being pliant and straight, then the ancients would surely have said so. Moreover, compounds such as "fine intelligence" and "fine ability" indicate the particular talent that is naturally granted to each individual. They do not refer to the four original feelings of empathy, restraint, generosity, and moral correctness. Mencius had already used these concepts to argue that the Way of the Ancient Kings was built in accordance with the inner nature of human beings. He further referred to the ideas of "fine intelligence" and "fine ability" simply to point out that each individual possessed different kinds of intelligence and ability, being responsive not only to the "four origins" just noted, but also to what is close to the inner personal resources of each individual. All his arguments were to emphasize that the Way was close to each individual. Wang Yang-ming did not grasp this, and thus constructed a disciplined method through which an individual would "realize goodness and knowledge" within himself. It is wrong to seek goodness and knowledge totally within the self.

*

Addenda from *Benmei II*

HEAVEN, MANDATE, EMPERORS [*TEN, MEI, TEI*]
SOME DEFINITIONS

1. Heaven does not require explanation. All human beings are aware of it. When we consider it, it is blue and vast and beyond measurement. Within it the sun, moon, stars, and comets move together, and wind, rain, cold and heat work their ways. It is the Heaven from which everything receives its mandate, and is the source of a hundred gods. It is the object of reverence beyond comparison, as there is nothing to surpass it. Hence from ancient times sagely emperors and brilliant kings all followed Heaven in ordering their kingdoms, and paid reverence to the Way of Heaven in the manner in which they carried out their policies and teachings. The Six Classics of the Sages all, without exception, begin with reverence for Heaven. That is the first principle upon which to enter the Way of the Sages. It is not until scholars grasp that idea that they can acquire the Way of the Sages and comment on it. However, scholars of later generations were infatuated with their own intelligence and with boastful pride they perceived themselves as superior beings and neglected the teachings of the Ancient Kings and Confucius, while speaking only in terms of their subjective leanings. As a result, they came to present the thesis that "Heaven is universal principle" and regarded universal principle as the first truth. The intent here was to say that the Way of the Sages could be explained entirely with this idea of universal principle. Based on this view, the phrase "Heaven is universal principle" was uttered as though this was to extend the utmost reverence to Heaven. However, since universal principle is sought from within the self, this idea is also expressed to mean that "the individual self knows Heaven". Is this anything but terrible disrespect? For when this thesis is taken to its extreme position, it can only lead, inevitably, to the conclusion that "The Way of Heaven is beyond knowing." Ch'eng Tzu thus says "Heaven and Earth have no spirit yet changes in things run their course". How can this be so.

In *Divination*, it says, "In the repetition of the basic forms, the spirit of Heaven and Earth can be seen." Is it not clearly evident that Heaven possesses a spirit. Hence it is said in *History*, "Heaven has no partisan views. Yet Heaven offers affection to those who extend reverence to it." It is furthermore said, "The Way of Heaven blesses the good and causes misfortune on the evil". In *Divination*, it is also said, "Heaven reduces gifts to those who are arrogant while increases them to those who are humble." Confucius remarked, "If you insult Heaven, there will not be anything left to be revered." Are these statements not based on the spirit of Heaven?

Jinsai criticized the views of Sung Confucians. However, his scholarship is at the same level as those of later generations. In his words, "When Heaven is seen as possessing spirit, the result is to accept the idea of Heaven's vengeance. This is the case with the Han Confucians. When seen as not possessing spirit, the conclusion is emptiness. The Sung Confucians are the latter." He has simply provided good mediation between the two. But is this position valid? That is, placing Heaven somewhere between possessing and not possessing spirit? This is an unreasonable view. The fact that Heaven and human beings are not of the same order of things is akin to humans not being the same as the birds and beasts. Thus when humans seek to relate their spirit to those of birds and beasts, this is, in fact, impossible to do. But it is unacceptable to say, therefore, that there is no spirit in birds and beasts. Truly, how can Heaven be akin to the spirit of humans. And therefore, Heaven cannot be perceived and measured. Hence the saying "In Heaven's mandate there is no normal course", "Heaven's mandate is not extended in the ordinary sense". The ancient Sages constantly held Heaven in esteem and reverence because it was beyond anything that could be fathomed by measurement.

The view of Han Confucians regarding Heaven's deliverance of punishment is comparable to a legacy from ancient times. However, to talk about solar eclipses and earthquakes as Heaven's vengeance is to gauge Heaven according to personal viewpoints. The view of Sung Confucians that "Heaven is universal principle" similarly uses subjective knowledge to assess Heaven. This is true also of Jinsai's view that "Truly Heaven is to be sought in the realm of the nonvisible. It is the principle of Heaven's effort-less process of saving the people." Effortless working is the spirit of Heaven. Why is it necessary to speak of it as universal principle. That thesis thus resulted in the naming of spirit as being either Heaven's pos-sessing or not possessing spirit. It is regrettable.

2. In the *Songs* is the saying, " How vast and continuous is Heaven's man-date." Originally it simply meant that Heaven's gift of the great mandate to Chou was said to be so deep and extensive that it was beyond sight and was also like irresistible flowing water. Tzu Ssu relied on the idea of "ceaselessness of realizing truthfulness" or "inevitability of truthful-ness" to explain the meaning of Heaven. This is an idea that Tzu Ssu artic-ulated on his own authority and is not to be found in ancient texts. Hence he drew on a poetic line containing the term "inevitability" to authenti-cate his view. But such was not the aim of the poem. The Sung Confucians did not realize this and without much thought used the term, "truthful-ness", to describe the basic essence of the Way of Heaven. They also held that things they saw directly were valid. As truthfulness is but one virtue of Heaven, how can it exhaust the meaning of Heaven.

3. Chu Hsi said : "Yin/yang is not the Way. The reason why yin/yang follows the course that it takes is the Way." Jinsai said: "Yin/yang is not the Way. The ceaseless movement between yin/yang is the Way". In the *Book of Divination*, it says, "The Way of Heaven presents itself as yin/yang". Why is yin/yang not the Way? The Sages established the term yin/yang as the Way. However, these two scholars sought to improve on and surpass the Sages. It is irresponsible. From my view point, the reason why yin/yang follows its course is still only yin/yang. Jinsai's "The ceaseless movement to and from of yin/yang" is also only yin/yang. Both Jinsai and Chu Hsi engaged in making fine and trivial distinctions and separated these. Hence the conclusion is that "yin/yang is not the Way". The Way is not a matter of fine and trivial distinction. It does not have a trunk and peripheral branches. It is single and embraces all. Hence, Tzu Ssu used truthfulness to discuss this. Moreover the phrase in the *Book of Divination*, "One Yin/one Yang together is called the Way" was used originally to expound on divination. Hence it is also said in that classic, "Closing the

door is termed with the divination sign for earth. Opening it is referred to as heaven. Closing and opening is called change. The infinite continuousness of this is called process." Is this not the language of divination? Moreover, how can the meaning of the Way of Heaven be exhausted with a single term. However, in ancient times the Way of Heaven was explained in terms of fortune for the good and ill fortune for the wicked. Things that could not be explained were accepted as such. The teachers above relied on themselves as possessors of sagely knowledge and expressed pride in knowing Heaven. Hence, with much joy they spoke of the exquisite and subtle principle, and uttered things that the ancient Sages had not said. Indeed the contrariness of their views to the Way was extreme.

4. Sung Confucians say the following : "Life and death and convergences and dispersions are governed by universal principle". This is said out of being confident about knowing Heaven. Jinsai said: "In the way of the natural order, there is life only and no death. There are convergences and no dispersions. Death is when a life ends. Dispersions come when convergences are complete. Yet in the way of natural order there is life only." This too is based on the self-confidence in knowing Heaven. In the end, the idea of "convergence and dispersion" leads, without fail, to the various cycles in the natural order. Those who say "life only" inevitably adopt the conclusion that "the universe today is the timeless, eternal, universe." These views present optimistically what the self perceives in the present to describe what the self does not see, and to seek to persuade people to believe in their faith. These all see themselves as sages. They do not have faith in the Ancient Sages. They do not revere Heaven.

Heaven is not something that can be known. Hence the Sages were deeply respectful of Heaven and spoke only of "knowing Heaven's calling." To say, "Heaven knows me!" and to admit that one cannot know Heaven directly is the basis of utmost reverence. With Tsu Ssu and Mencius the words "knowing Heaven" came to be used for the first time. However, they only spoke of Heaven's mandate to one's inner nature, and thus rendered truthfulness as the virtue of inner nature. This was all that they meant to say. Mencius, too, in a limited way spoke of knowing that

Heaven and goodness were in harmony. This was all he said. However, once he and Tzu Ssu used the words 'knowing Heaven', the venerable scholars of later times came to speak of Heaven with arrogant self confidence. This was surely not the intent of the Ancient Kings and Confucius when they spoke of revering Heaven. This was also the unfortunate spreading of corrupt practices by these two scholars who enjoyed polemical arguments. In *Divination*, there are lines that say "unifying Heaven" and "managing Heaven". These are statements that refer only to the emperors. "Address Heaven as the highest priority and not transgress it". "Be ahead of Heaven yet not violate Heaven. Be behind Heaven yet follow its time." These all embellish the virtue of the sages. Generally, gentleman scholars of later generations arrogantly dedicated themselves to become sages and did not know ancient language and were not able to read ancient texts. They all adopted distorted ideas based on their own personal views. Scholars must reflect on this.

5. The term mandate means Heaven's imperative to the individual self. This is sometimes referred to as that which one possesses at birth and which continues into the present. In the *Doctrine of the Mean*, "Heaven's mandate is called one's inner nature". This is said in terms of life at its beginning. In the *Book of History* it says, "The mandate is not extended continuously". This is said to indicate its continuing existence in the present. Jinsai drew on the words of Tzu Hsia and Mencius to say that one's mandate was not necessarily determined at birth. He did not understand. Tzu Hsia and Mencius meant Heaven stood for things that were beyond human intelligence and described those things that conveyed Heaven's will to us as being mandate. But in fact a mandate is an imperative from Heaven, so that Heaven and mandate should not be separated. For this reason Confucius said, "In my fifties I came to know Heaven's mandate" meaning that he came to understand Heaven and its mandate to him. Is this not truly the case? Moreover, Mencius's saying, "Even without invitation they will still come", means simply that poverty and lowliness are always uninvited guests. Confucius said, "Wealth and high status are things people desire. Without following the appropriate way one cannot maintain them. People despise poverty and lowly status. To realize these

without following the way, one cannot depart from them." The path to wealth and high status is through benevolence and to poverty and lowly status through the absence of benevolence. The gentleman carries out benevolence and realizes his mandate. Hence, it is said in *History*: "Pray for Heaven's eternal mandate"; and in *Divination*: "Achieve your mandate and realize your purpose". And further, "Clarify your place and carry out your mandate". Only the gentleman does not realize poverty and lowly status. Mencius said no more than this.

6. Jinsai said: "How should we understand the meaning of mandate? Simply to be at peace. What is being at peace? To not be in doubt. Basically it cannot be explained with the wording of voice, sight, smell and taste. It is also perfect and complete. By relying on one's mandate, one is calm and unshaken without any doubt and confusion. This is what is meant by being at peace. This is what is meant by knowing. It cannot be known through the senses." Ch'eng Tzu conveyed the following: "To know the meaning of mandate means knowing one possesses a mandate and to thus have faith in it." All of the preceding adds up to an extremely superficial reading of the ideograph to know. This is used to mean when encountering life and death, existence and nonexistence, poverty and wellbeing, fame and dishonor, one is calm and steady and free of uncertainty and doubt and unwavering within one's self. It is said then that one knows one's mandate. The so-called knowing one's mandate and believing in it is understood as one need not be a gentleman to know one's mandate. Jinsai was satisfied with this language. However, from my point of view, how is this any different from the view of Ch'eng Tzu. The difference is only in the exaggeration and not of the words themselves. Further, Confucius's wording "Unless one knows one's mandate, one cannot be a gentleman" meant originally knowing that one must proceed according to the mandate that Heaven gives to the self. The reason why the Ancient Kings constructed the Way to establish peace and wellbeing among the people is that they knew Heaven's mandate to them. Hence, without knowing this, one cannot be a gentleman. The teachers of the Sung forgot that the Way of Ancient Kings was based on reverence to Heaven and on providing peace and well-being to the people. Instead,

they sought this entirely in the personal self and fell inadvertantly into the view of Chuang Tzu of sageliness within and kingliness without. From then on, although men of high talent have emerged, there has been only confusion and the absence of enlightened thinking. Even Jinsai with his intelligence and sensitivity falls similarly into that custom. Thus in the end his thinking is not very different from that of Zen Buddhism. It is truly unfortunate.

7. Confucius said: "In my fifties I knew Heaven's mandate". He meant he came to know Heaven's imperative to him to convey the Way of the Ancient Kings to later generations. Confucius also said: "Study from the lowly present and advance. Is it Heaven that knows me?" This is a comment about himself, of studying and advancing accordingly. Hence, by fully understanding himself, he was able to carry out Heaven's mandate to him to convey the Way. His comments elsewhere about the administrator of the town of I is again like this. Confucius studied the Way of the Ancient Kings and awaited Heaven's mandate. In his fifties he still had not attained court rank. Hence he came to realize that Heaven's mandate to him was not to carry out the Way in the world of practical affairs but to transfer its ideas to later generations. Were it not so why should he have waited until his fifties to know Heaven's mandate? Later Confucian scholars were unable to grasp the meaning of this, and vainly theorized about its spirit. Jinsai's explanation about mandate as "being free of doubt" and "being at peace" are examples of this. Indeed how can the spirit of the Sages be perceived. Moreover, Jinsai simply speaks from his personal vantage point about the imperturbability of the spirit. When the spirit is said to be thus, how can it convey the full meaning of the Sages. He is merely viewing the Sages from his personal feelings. Such a view is simply limited and pretentious, narrow and excessive.

8. The ideograph for emperor is also read as Heaven. Han Confucians spoke of it as exalted heavenly gods. This is the belief handed down as part of ancient custom. Sung Confucians said: "Heaven is principle. Emperor is the overall ruler." In this view, the overall ruler is rendered as universal principle, so that there is no cause to distinguish emperor and Heaven. It simply confuses our understanding. Therefore, Fu Hsi, Shen Nung, the

Yellow Emperor, Chuan Hsü and Emperor K'u of the most ancient epochs created the arts of hunting and fishing, farming and sericulture, weaving, architecture, transportation and writing that would not decline through the ages. The people utilized these skills daily, seeing them as the abiding way of human existence, and relied on them without questioning their origins. The light that was cast and the fresh dew that settled spread widely even to distant foreign lands, so that its virtue was received everywhere without exception. Even after ten-thousand generations, so long as there is humankind, it will persist indestructible. Their virtue is akin to the natural order itself in its breadth and continuity and is without comparison with other virtues.

Hence sages of later generations payed reverence to these rites and joined them with Heaven, which was rendered as identical with emperor and heavenly god. The names recorded as the five imperial rulers in *Rites* are these. When humans die, their physical bodies return to the soil and their spirit returns to Heaven. The godly spirit is impossible to gauge and cannot be separated or distinguished. Furthermore, the virtue of the five imperial rulers is akin to joining with Heaven through enshrinement and becoming inseparable from it. Thus in *Songs*, Heaven and emperor were referred to without distinction. The seven creators such as Yao and Shun and others already had enshrined this in their teachings and it has remained so for all the ages. And so the virtue of the five imperial heads is truly grand and should not be exalted simply as distant and dim. On the contrary, the Way of the Ancient Kings is firm and resolute and would not allow such to occur. The saying "Honor the ancestral beginnings by identifying the celestial origins" refers to the five imperial heads who are the supreme emperors. Han Confucianists interpreted supreme emperors to mean sacred Heavenly gods. Moreover, with regard to the five imperial rulers, they separated the divine nature of the five ethical practices and the imperial ruler. These are simply subjective interpretations. Generally in ancient times extending homage to the god of the earth was done with the rites of King Yü. In honoring ancestral founders, homage was extended by building a memorial stone and presenting offerings to one who represents the deceased. The same was true in paying reverence to

Heaven. The Way of the Ancient Kings joins together Heaven and humans. Hence it is said in *Rites*, "Joining humans with spirit and the divine is the ultimate realization of the teachings." The aim of practicing rites is to realize this. Further, where does the name of heavenly chief have its origin? If this were given the name of son of Heaven, and then named Heaven itself, this is incorrect because the Ancient Kings held such extreme reverence for Heaven. If it were adpoted from the name Heaven, this too would be wrong, for the Ancient Kings possessed the virtue of humility. When seen in this manner, the ideograph for emperor read as Heaven is joined to the five imperial rulers of ancient times. Indeed, this is indicative of the reverence that the Sages held for Heaven.

HUMAN NATURE, PASSION, TALENT [*SEI, JŌ, SAI*]: SOME DEFINITIONS

1. Human nature is the qualitative character in life. It corresponds to what Sung Confucians called material character. Sung Confucians distinguished between the basic and the material nature of human nature for scholarly reasons. Moreover, they misinterpreted Mencius's words that human nature is essentially equivalent to that of sages and the only difference between them is in the material character. As a result, Sung Confucians wished to become sages by transforming their material character. They argued that if human beings could possess only their basic innate nature and not the material character, they, too, would be sages. Why then should we study? Supposing human nature were material without the basic nature, then however hard one might study, the efforts would be in vain. Then why study? Sung Confucians hoped to encourage learning with their theory about the innate as against the material. However, as humans are already endowed with material character at birth, the so-called innate nature must belong to Heaven, not to humans. Moreover, universal principle cannot be restricted by anything even though it seems to be limited by material character. If we say that there is something that cannot be restricted, how can we differentiate human beings from birds and beasts? Thus, Sung Confucians further attempted

to make a distinction here by attributing the difference between a vital material energy and a stagnant one. We can see from this that the theory of innate nature is not tenable. What Sung Confucians taught is nothing but erroneous theory.

It is said in the *Book of History* that "human beings are endowed with the spirit that pervades all things." And in *Tso Chuan*, there is the saying that "humans are born receiving the mean of the natural order," In the *Book of Songs*, it is said that "Heaven produced the people and as the world of things pervade, laws come to exist as well. People firmly observe the way of the everyday and enjoy the virtues therein." Confucius interpreted these lines and said, "As there are things there are certainly laws. As the people adhere to these rules they enjoy their virtues." The *Book of Divination* states that "Seeking benefit and consistency is human nature and passion." In the notes of the same book, it is also stated that "What results in accomplishments is due to inner human nature." All these statements were made by the ancients to describe human nature. By understanding them together, the meaning of human nature becomes as clear as the light of day. It is said that spirit is opposite to the hard and fixed. This, however, is not comparable to the Sung Confucians' idea that although the human mind is not fixed, its workings are clearly visible. The mean is opposed to partiality. This, however, differs from the Sung Confucians' concept of being without partiality. These are all said with reference to the flexible movement in human nature. In other words, it can be comprehended in terms of things in the middle position, which is adjustable between the left and right, and the front and back. As there are things, people refer to some among them as beautiful. If things are seen as beautiful, people definitely wish to emulate them. It is human nature to do so. This is what is meant by the flexible and adaptive character of human nature. Confucius also stated that "The wise on high and the foolish below cannot be moved," meaning that except for the most wise and very foolish the human nature of most human beings move about well and with ease. Constancy refers to what cannot be changed. It means that human nature cannot be altered. The phrase "What leads to the realization of things is called human nature" means that what is accomplished by human beings differs according to their respectively different natures. Human nature is diverse – tough and gentle, volatile and stable, slow and quick, and active and static – all these are not to be altered as they are endowed at birth by Heaven. Nevertheless, as mentioned above, it is also a characteristic of human nature to be able to move flexibly. It becomes good when it follows the good, and it becomes bad when it follows the bad. The Sages, therefore, took into account the many different natures that are in human beings to establish teachings for people to study and practice. As people realize their virtues, they reveal distinctive differences on the basis of such diverse characteristics as tough and gentle, volatile and stable, slow and quick, and active and quiescent. Only the nature of the very foolish is said not to move. Thus there is a saying that "The people should be made to rely, as they cannot be made to know." The material character of human nature therefore cannot be altered and people cannot transform themselves to become sages. Thereby, it is said that the nine virtues of Yü and the six virtues of Chou differed in accordance with their respective human natures. Was this not truly so.

The teachings of the Ancient Kings, *Songs, History, Rites* and *Music,* are like the gentle breezes and sweet rains that nourish all living things and make them grow. Although living things differ in their inner characters, they all grow through nourishment. Bamboo grow into bamboo and trees into trees by receiving nourishment. So do grass into grass and crops into crops. When fully grown, they are utilized for building houses, making clothes, and producing food and drink. This is analogous to human beings who fully develop their talents through the teachings of the Ancient Kings, and with their separate talents render service as did the six ministers in the Kingdom of Chou and the nine ministers in the reigns of Yao and Shun. The phrase "one becomes good when one follows the good" means the full development of one's talent through nourishment based on the teachings of the Ancient Kings. This is like reaping a rich harvest of grain. The phrase "one becomes evil when one follows evil" refers to the failure to cultivate oneself with proper nourishment. This may be compared to a crop failure in a bad year. In other words, it is unnecessary for people to seek to transform their material character to to become a sage through learning. When Mencius says "Benevolence, righteousness, propriety, and wisdom are rooted in human mind" to explain the doctrine of goodness of human nature he does not mean that the people's inner qualities are all the same as those of the Sages. Kao Tzu's metaphorical depiction of human nature in terms of the willow tree is a splendid explanation. He also characterized it as being akin to swirling water, meaning that human nature constantly moves. Mencius, however, talked about it in exaggerated terms and distorted the meaning. As a result, Mencius constructed the idea that righteousness exists within the inner self to argue against Kao Tzu's view that it is external to the self. Mencius did so because of his great fondness for polemics and eventually caused the misunderstanding among Sung Confucians about human nature. His understanding of human nature as goodness and Hsün Tzu's of it being evil were both articulated to establish their distinctive schools. These two views emphasize only one specific aspect of humans while neglecting the others . Yang Tzu-yün's view that "good and evil are mixed" and Han Yü's view that "there are three specific levels in human nature" are not contrary to reason. Su Tzu-chan's "there is no good and evil as such" is an idea that echoes the views of Buddhism. It is Ou-yang Hsiu's observation that "The inner nature of human beings ought not to be thought of as preceding sageliness" that is indeed insightful.

Jinsai, in his interpretation of Mencius's doctine of the innate goodness of human nature, remarked that "though inner human nature differs in a thousand ways, its very nature is to recognize the good as good and the evil as evil. In this sense, human nature is one regardless of past or present, or being a sage or a fool." Jinsai eloquently expounded Mencius's doctrine. Nevertheless, although one may be able to distinguish good from evil, how can one necessarily translate this into action. He will surely say, "Although I am fond of beautiful women like the lustful Prince Ch'ao of Sung, without the proper formal arrangements, what can I do to gain from this?" If one can believe in the Way of the Ancient Kings, one will endevour to enhance his goodness upon hearing of the goodness of humankind, and, similarly, upon hearing of human evil, will endeavor to improve himself. Yet, if one does not have faith in the Way, one will perform selfish acts after hearing of human goodness, and one will surrender to despair after told of human evil. Therefore, the words of Hsün Tzu and Mencius are not helpful. These are not the words of the Sages. The problem is that they sought through their own language to convince people unsure of themselves to believe in their views. Yet how could they convince people with their words which were the commencement of 1,000 polemics. The negative effect of such teachings is truly enormous. The scholars did not seek the true understanding of human nature in the teachings of the Ancient Kings, and they favored polemics only. How sad it is.

3. In the classic of *Music* it is said, "The stillness that is with human beings at birth is Heaven's nature." The Sung Confucians' doctrine of "innate nature" and "restoring one's innate nature" was based on this statement. Shih Liang-wang and Jinsai said that these were the ideas of Lao Tzu and not the words of the Confucian School. However, music is for bringing order to one's inner nature and passion. In the teachings of the Ancient Kings nothing surpasses it in nourishing the inner natures of human beings in order that they may realize their virtues. Moreover in the teachings there is no talk about righteousness and reason or reliance on dedicated reflection, but only about gradual and effortless reliance on the laws of the emperor. Thus, on the theory of inner nature and passion, there was reference only to songs and music. Goodness and spitefulness, sadness and happiness, are feelings that all human beings have. However, when their workings move in extreme directions and regularity is not achieved, then the spirit of balance and harmony is inevitably undermined, and the sense of stability is lost. For this reason it is difficult to realize virtue. Hence music was created and taught. One's inner nature is received from Heaven and is the so-called center. This refers to when one is just born and does not yet know goodness and spitefulness, sadness and happiness. It is the so-called moment when a "human is born and there is stillness." This does not suggest that one should seek to return to that moment of birth. Nor does it mean that one can realize that moment through quiet contemplation. Music simply can bring quietude to passionate motion and to ward off extremes. Hence it refers to that moment

before extremes have yet to come into motion. It does not mean to exercise control over effectiveness by relying on the great basic resource in that moment of latency found in the *Doctrine of the Mean*. Simply put, humans receive their inner nature from the center of Heaven and earth. Hence the Ancient Kings constructed the Way by conforming to the inner nature of human beings. Confucians of later times did not understand ancient language. They did not understand ancient texts. They did not understand the method contained in the teachings of the Ancient Kings. They thus spoke hastily of inner nature as fundamental and innate virtue, and dedicated themselves to explain its content in terms of righteousness and reason. The result of this was the narrow position of the Sung Confucian scholars. Wang Yang-ming and Jinsai referred to the interpretations of the Sung Confucians and read the ancient texts and criticized them as not being true to the words of the Confucian School. In general they said that inner nature could not be separated from study. Hence the ancients often spoke of inner nature in terms of a child at birth. But this was the extent of it. Why prize especially that moment of childbirth? Such comments as Mencius's, "An adult does not lose the spirit of the newborn child" also served as the basis of the Sung Confucian theory about restoring origin. They simply did not realize that the term for adult, or great human, in the ancient texts refers only to the Great Sage.

4. The rendering of benevolence, righteousness, rites, and wisdom as inner nature began with the Confucian scholars of the Han and was completed by those of the Sung. The connection is the theory of the five relationships. However, it is said by Mencius as well "That which the prince understands to be inner nature rests on benevolence, righteousness, rites, and wisdom, which are not rooted in one's spirit." And again, "Taste, color, sound, smell, and sensation are what make up inner nature. As there is Heaven's calling in it the gentleman did not see this as inner nature. There is benevolence between father and child, righteousness between ruler and subject, rites between guest and host, wisdom as in the worthy person, and Heaven's Way for the Sages." These are all mandates. Following this is the inner nature of humans. The gentleman did not call it a mandate. These explain the main idea.

Jinsai argued diligently that benevolence, righteousness, propriety, and wisdom were not the same as inner nature and reverted to Mencius's view that inner nature was based on the spirit of these terms but that they were not inner nature itself. However, that theory allowed for a dispute over inner and outer and the establishment of separate schools. In reviewing Mencius's disputes with Kao Tzu over this, the words spilled over as from a spring, and debates flowed beyond one's choosing and did not cease until they drowned and silenced the views of others. This is surely the attitude that he took without realizing his responsibility for the scholarly disaster of the Sung Confucians of later generations. Benevolence and wisdom are virtues. Rites and righteousness are constructions of the Ancient Kings. Mencius too simply spoke of the Ancient Kings as being led by the nature of human beings to construct the Way and Virtue. Jinsai rendered benevolence, righteousness, propriety and wisdom as being equivalences of virtue. This is of course erroneous.

5. Passion refers to those feelings that express themselves without reflection, such as those of kindness, hatred, sadness, and joyfulness. These differ according to each person's inner character. The seven sensate feelings according to the handbook for physicians are those of "happiness, anger, sadness, reflectiveness, antipathy, astonishment, and fear." These are connected with the five visceral organs. Confucians speak of them as "happiness, anger, sadness, apprehension, love, wickedness, desire," or again as the four elements of "happiness, anger, sadness, and joy." These all refer to both extremes of like and dislike. Generally the distinction between feeling and passion is that feeling is an extension of reflection while passion is outside the reaches of reflection. Of the seven items, those that are not connected with inner human nature are referred to as feelings; and those that are so connected, are called passion. On the whole, the inner nature of humans is all about desire which can be tolerated when it enters the area of reflection. When things are not within the reaches of reflection, they fall within the sphere of desire that is inner nature. Thus, one's feelings can be muted or embellished, while the same cannot be said for passion. This explains the distinction between feelings and passion. Having stated that the inner nature of

extreme criminals and yet was still brimming with anger". In viewing these words of his, do they not indeed lead us to his view on passion. Passion is something that does not extend into reflective reason. It does not contain reason as in the teachings of music or the ethic of responsibility. And thus, music is relied on to bring order to inner nature and passion. This is the method in the teachings of the Ancient Kings. The scholars in the school of universal principle simply do not know this. Ch'eng Tzu said that "by restraining passion one thereby strikes the mean" – indeed, are these words not accurate. However, he does not know how to restrain passion. It is in fact erroneous to seek one's concrete aims on the basis of passion.

7. Talent means the same thing as the basic materials in humans. This human possession of basic materials can be likened to the make-up of wood. Wood can be shaped into poles or as pillars and beams. Likewise, human beings, by responding to the inner nature that is distinct to themselves, can seek to do what they can do well. This is defined as the material nature in the self. Mencius's comment that "talent cannot be blamed" or that "Heaven endows talent" and again, "They are unable to realize their talent," all refer to the inner nature of humans. Jinsai correctly noted that "ability is located in one's inner nature." As an example, Chuan Hsü's untalented son is said to be unworthy, that he is without use. It is said that he lacks ability. References such as to the Duke of Chou's "many different talents and achievements" and P'en Ch'eng-K'uo's "possessing less talent" are used to illustrate this. In later times, the term for talent was simply said to mean ability.

PRINCIPLE, MATTER, HUMAN DESIRE [*RI*, *KI*, *JINYOKU*]: FIVE DEFINITIONS

1. Principle is universally present in all affairs and things. When we calculate things with our minds, we try to determine how things will definitely be or not be. This is to rely on principle. In general, when people wish to do good, they do so in accordance with a principle that is deemed good; and similarly when evil deeds are done, these are in accord with a

principle that is deemed evil. Acts are committed as the mind is conscious of these principles. Principle, therefore, does not have an inherently fixed norm. It is pervasive. And yet people tend to view it in accordance with their distinctive inner nature. For example, jellied sweets are known to be what they are. Yet, Po I saw them as a source for "nourishing the elderly"; while the thief Tao Chih emphasized their utility in making certain that doors can be opened quietly. There is only one way to explain this. Each person determines what should be observed, and excludes what is not necessary. Thus, they observe the same object in different ways. Unless principle is carefully examined, it cannot be said to be integrative of things. But how can the principle of the entire kingdom be completely examined. Only the Sages can fully realize their own natures and nourish those of other human beings and of creatures and things, and bring together the virtues of Heaven and earth. Only the Sages, in short, are capable of investigating the principle in things, and grasping their norms as they relate to propriety and righteousness. Thus the phrase in the *Book of Changes* "the exhaustive study of principle" refers to the Sages alone. It is not within the reach of ordinary men to study it. For this reason, the Way of the Ancient Kings and Confucius did not exclude principle but did not teach it, and placed emphasis instead on righteousness. When the righteousness of the Ancient Kings is examined and its reason understood thereby, its principles will be apparent to all as stable norms upon which to act. Being visible to all, principle need not be described in detail.

Followers of Lao Tzu and Chuang Tzu spoke with great emotion about principle. This is because they prized nature and sought to destroy the Way of the Ancient Kings. Mencius who similarly enjoyed polemics claimed of the Ancient Kings and Confucius things they had not said, and used these to influence people around him. Thus he said, "Principle and righteousness are like one to my way of thinking, just as meats that have been fattened on greens and grain are in harmony with my taste in food. Mencius, however, mentioned righteousness along with principle because the teachings of Confucius were still influential in his day. Scholars of Sung coming 1,000 years later, were insistent on presenting their willful views, and, seeking to become sages quickly, they failed to establish a reliable foundation. They were not familiar with ancient language and did not have a correct understanding of the Way. Being satisfied with Mencius alone, who is easy to read, they sought the Way primarily through their own minds and then could not but rely on the idea of principle in doing so. Their emphasis on the idea of universal principle came as an inevitable conclusion.

Principle is in all things. Hence principle is fine and subtle. In reflecting on the Sung Confucian scholars , I think that they thought that by combining the fine and subtle, the result would be something vast. This cannot be. When a small amount of weight is added the error in the combined total can be quite great. Similarly, from a short length, the added total may show great error. This is because ordinary people see things only as they are close to them as compared with the Sages who possessed the grand frame of things. From a broad view, no minute details were excluded. This is why the Sages are without peers. If people too should follow the teachings of the Sages and grasp the grand frame of things, they will see clearly the little things at hand. While something may be lost here or there, great harm will not result because the large framework remains intact. What then is this grand frame of things. It is rites and righteousness. These refer to the norms established by the Sages. The Sung Confucians placed high value on principle that led them in the end to not revere the Sages as their teachers and instead advanced the idea of principle as being from within themselves. This explains their failings. Thus they said that even those who do not study can intuitively avoid acting in ways that are contrary to principle. Their view that only gentlemen can distinguish between rites that are not rites and righteousness that is not righteous is due to their lack of learning.

Those who mimic the ideas of Sung Confucians in today's world remain adamant and continue to say, "Rites and righteousness were of course established by the Sages. But we must first know the principle upon which the Sages did this or we will simply follow blindly rites and righteousness , thus practicing rites in ways that are not proper and righteousness that is not righteous." This is merely the reasoning behind the Sung

Confucians' insistence on exhausting the meaning of principle. They are truly unaware of how they struggle to overcome and surpass the Sages. They fail miserably to assess their own weaknesses. They do not follow the teachings of Sages and seek instead to fathom the minds of the Sages, which is truly impossible to do.

The teachings of the Sages are in *Songs*, *History*, *Rites* and *Music*. If one studies these and quietly stores them within, the principle upon which they based rites and righteousness will become apparent. However, while the intelligence of someone might suffice to do this, it might not be so in another. It is not something that can be forcibly imposed. For those who might not comprehend, Confucius thus said, "The people should rely on them. They cannot be taught to understand them." Even the Sages were aware that not everyone would understand them. Thus, those who wish to make students understand principle first and then carry out practices accordingly, are asking that each of these students become sages. Why is it necessary to utilize the sages in this way? The flaw in the exhaustive study of principle, therefore, is that it leads to the abandonment of the Sages themselves.

Jinsai commented, "The Way means practice. It is an active term. Principle refers to existing. It is a term without life. The Sages viewed the Way as concrete, and thus they explained principle as active. Lao Tzu viewed the Way as empty. His explanation of principle is thus inactive." Jinsai also said: "The Way was originally an active term because it referred to the mystery of continuous life and change. Principle basically is inactive. Its ideographs refer to the regularity of form and design in jewels. Thus, principle can describe the regularity in events and things. But it is not adequate for describing the mystery of continuous life and change". These are the words of a deranged person speaking in a dream. As the Way was established by the Sages, how can it be referred to as their having "viewed the Way"? Why contrast it with Lao Tzu? The Way was constructed to bring peace to the people. It cannot be explained by the idea of the continuous process of life and change. The ideograph for principle that refers to border and design was invented by Ts'ang Chieh for the convenience of aiding his memory. It need not be adhered to. Moroever, the

Way is based on the image of the road. Why refer to it as either active or inactive? The basic idea is that the Way is meant to be practiced, and principle is meant to be seen. Lao Tzu and Chuang Tzu and the Sung Confucians were all primarily concerned with things they see. Therefore, they only delight in speaking of principle. If the theory of principle can be advanced in terms of active and inactive, then Lao Tzu and Chuang Tzu can also be made to speak of the Way and virtue. How can this make sense? In other words, principle cannot be dismissed. Should one follow the teachings of the Sages and rely on rites and righteousness as norms, then why should he view principle as an ailment? Jinsai is simply like one who burned himself with hot soup and blew on cold salad. Scholars should reflect on this.

2. The term for the category of matter was not spoken in ancient times. However, it was used in formal arguments. In the *Book of Changes* are the words, "The positive element in matter stores itself in a dormant state"; or in *Rites*, "The vibrant virtue of Heaven and earth is matter" or again the reference to "the dignity in matter." The reference to principle and matter as opposites began with the Sung Confucians. Their idea was that in the yin/yang process of change, things move forward and disappear and allow others to come and continue onward. This is matter. However, while things come and go, there is something in the process that is timeless and unchanging. This is principle. That which comes to life and then perishes is called matter; and that which does not perish is termed principle. This view is like Lao Tzu's comparison between the fine and the coarse, or the Buddhist theory of phenomena and pneumena. The so-called "timeless and unchanging" is simply the virtue of constancy among the four virtues in *Changes*. As there are three other virtues, namely of origination, universality, and beneficialness, how can constancy alone exhaust the Way of Heaven. Thus, those who prize the Way know that it pervades everything, the fine and the coarse, the main trunk and the tributary branches. It is unnecessary to create a theory about the distinction between principle and matter. It is a theory that leads to the view that Heaven and earth is the accumulation of matter, and hence that the sun and the moon, earth and rocks, people and things, and

grasses and trees are all made up of matter. Yet, the so-called matter is not an ancient word. Phrases such as Jinsai's "throughout Heaven and earth there is only the single energetic matter" do not express the feeling of reverence that the Sages held for Heaven. Hence the gentleman does not take this position.

3. It is said in the *Book of Changes*, "What is above form is called the Way. Things with form are instruments." The Sung Confucians' theory of principle and matter that rests on this reference, regards the Way as principle and instruments as matter. This can only be called a truly enormous mistake. The so-called instruments in *Changes* are references to functional tools. Hence the following lines: "Carts are instruments for a prince"; or, "Those who create instruments value their shapes"; "None is greater than the Sages in providing things and putting them to use, and in producing instruments to benefit the kingdom"; "The falcon is a bird, the bow with arrows is an instrument, and humans use this instrument to shoot the arrow. Gentlemen carry instruments and time their acts"; "Instruments are known according to their shapes." None of the above refers to the category of matter. References such as "Fu Hsi invented nets to prevent the captured from escaping, and Shen Nung invented plows to accumulate benefits" indicate the meaning in *Changes* that forms are chosen and instruments created. Instrument is used only in this way.

The term "above form" or the metaphysical refers to instruments that have not yet been given shape. It speaks to there being only the way of divination. Only after they have been given shapes do instruments come into existence. These are all mainly references to the creation of instruments. It is thus said "Transforming through direction is called change; pushing forward and carrying things out is called interaction; raising forth to benefit the people of the entire kingdom is called achievement." All these are references that celebrate divination, and terms such as the way, instruments, change, interaction, and achievement, are all related to divination. In the previous section are also the following lines, "Closing the door is rendered with an ideograph meaning earth, and opening the door with one that signifies heaven. The movement back and forth is called change. Moving while tending toward one and then the other is called interaction. The visible acquire shapes. Those things with shapes that gain form are called instruments. The control and use of these instruments is through rules. Making them useful to the people as a whole is called divine." In such passages, the Way and instruments are not set apart as opposites. This is clearly the case. Sung Confucians thus committed a tremendous error. Jinsai's comments, "Generating wind is the way of a fan; and items such as paper and wood are instruments" reveal that he too does not understand the sentences about the "metaphysical and physical nature of form." They are all mistaken in their views because they did not seek the meanings in the language itself.

To study divination is originally to contemplate everything in a comprehensive manner. Only after that can divination serve practical ends. However, to consider everything in a broad manner without first knowing the meaning of language will be the source of committing errors. When people see the ideograph for "way" they tend to say it means "the Way of the Sages" and "the Way of Heaven." The phrase "yin/yang is the Way" is a case in point. These reveal a complete lack of knowledge. To say, "closing and opening refer to change and the constant movement without end is the process in things," refers to nothing other than the interaction of yin and yang. Putting these sentences together, the so-called way here refers to change and process. They are simply about divination. The references to the so-called instruments refer to the rites and music by the Ancient Kings, which gentlemen study to realize their talents and virtues or further, govern the kingdom and bring peace to the people. The establishment of rites and music is also thought of as the creation of instruments. However, if first the meanings of change and process are not clarified as part of the Way, the Way itself cannot be carried out. Hence the real significance of the phrase "above shape and with shape." It is not about the unfolding of things in nature. To study divination, it is necessary to view all things in comprehensive manner. The various sentences contain different meanings and they should not be confused. Thus, the way of divination, and the Way of Heaven and the Way of the Ancient Kings, each indicate distinct things. As knowledge of ancient language declined in later ages, the concept of principle came to occupy a destroy Heaven's principle and allows human desire to become bound-less. This produces in turn the mind of disobedience, fraud, licentious-ness and disorder. And becaue of this, the strong dominate the weak, the many attack the few, the intelligent deceive the foolish, the brave are cruel to the timid, the ill are left not ministered to, the elderly, the young and orphaned, and the homeless are left untended. This is the road to great disaster.

The previous argument explains why the Ancient Kings created rites and music with which to govern the people. Hence the arguments about human desire being the "desire within one's nature," and about the human spirit of likes and dislikes, are only with reference to rites and music regulating the senses of desire and bringing likes and dislikes into proper balance. From the outset, there was no purpose "to eradicate human desire." The term "Heaven's principle" was used to distinguish human beings from the animal world. It was thus called the "nature of Heaven." It is completely different from the explanations of the Sung Confucians. The phrase "the quietude at childbirth" refers to the moment when likes and dislikes are still only latent. This is not to glorify being an infant. The moment of quietude is completely unlike the Sung Confucians' reference to it as the "imperturbable stillness." As the moment when likes and dislikes are latent, it contrasts with the dynamic influx of pref-erences as one advances in age. Only music regulates inner human nature and passion. Music is thus, also, discussed in terms of likes and dis-likes, movement and quietude. In *Rites* and *Music* are the phrases, "Music is produced from within and hence it is calm" and "Rites are constructed without and hence they are visually patterned." These all explain why the Ancient Kings created rites and music. They tell us why it is unneccessary to speak of Heaven's principle and human desire as basic elements in the exercise of moral discipline.

It was Ch'eng Tzu who first rendered Heaven's principle and human desire as basic to moral discipline. Ch'eng Tzu was intimately familiar with the ideas of Shao Yung and admired his high intelligence. It appears that Ch'eng Tzu was impressed with Shao Yung's method of "doubling numbers" and secretly used this approach to give order to the Way of the

Sages. Shao Yung's learning is based on numbers and relates to the practice of divination. Divination is used to give meaning to matters lacking certainty and to clarify subtle nuances. It is reasonable therefore to separate things that we see in the natural order into dual entities. Ch'eng Tzu's approach to knowledge was to emphasize the observation of things as being of primary importance. Confounded by the profound and complex nature of the Way of the Ancient Kings, Ch'eng Tzu borrowed Shao Yung's divination method of doubling numbers and divided the Way into binary parts. As supporting evidence, he took from *Rites* the terms "Heaven's principle" and "human desire"and embellished them. Often used by Confucians in later times, these terms do not retain the original meaning in *Rites*. The Sung Confucian emphasis on these concepts as basic to moral discipline is not at all in keeping with the teachings of the Ancient Kings and Confucius where human virtues are carefully nourished, so that evil is turned into good. There are no binary opposites. Sung Confucian scholarship held the observation of things as being of primary importance in seeking knowledge. Their tendency to see all things in terms of dual parts led to the inevitable consequence. Thus while the aim of this scholarship was to challenge the ideas of Buddhism, it reinforced the dualistic ideas of underlying reality and the secular reality of passion and, also, the competing ideas of the universe of enlightenment and the social world of confusion. It is truly lamentable.

Keizairoku Shūi
Addendum to "On the political economy"

*

DAZAI SHUNDAI

ON FOOD AND MONEY

Question: It is a well-known fact of recent times that large and small daimyo alike are impoverished and lack financial resources. They are said to borrow from between 10 and 50 or 60 percent of their retainers' stipends. If this proves to be inadequate, the people of the domain are prevailed upon to produce the necessary funds to save the day. As this is often still insufficient, they borrow on an annual basis from the large merchant houses of Edo, Kyoto, and Osaka. Often failing to repay what has been borrowed, the interest on the loans accumulates several times. Some years ago during the Kanbun and Enpō eras [c. 1661–1681], Kumazawa Banzan estimated that the volume of cash borrowed by daimyo was about 200 times the total of the available money in all of Japan. Today, some seventy years later, the amount borrowed is a 1,000 times more. Should the daimyo seek to redeem their debts where would this cash, which exists in name only, come from? Given this predicament, all that can be done is to spend the time of day devising ways to face the emergency at hand. There are some retainers of daimyo who excel at this and have put their considerable minds to formulate specific plans. For various reasons, however, they have not been able to realize their aims.

The translation is from Rai Tsutomu ed., *Nihon shisōshi taikei 37: Sorai Gakuha* (Tokyo: Iwanami Shoten, 1972), pp. 45–56. An earlier version of this translation appeared in Select Papers (9:93) of the Center for East Asian Studies at the University of Chicago. Shundai completed his work on political economy in 1730.

Perhaps they acted too hastily. Perhaps by contesting the views of higher ministers, they were accused of misconduct and had their plans withdrawn. They may have angered the unenlightened and were defeated while carrying out their plans. They may have incited riots among the people. Perhaps they were simply unable to get their plans underway due to the continued extravagance of the daimyo. Or, perhaps, the daimyo himself is to be blamed for acting wrongly and failing to entrust the matters to his retainers. Any one of these can wreck a project, and having even the talent of Kuang Chung, or the faithfulness of Pi Kan and Wu Tzu-hsü will be of little use. On occasion, a retainer looks into the future and submits a carefully-worked out plan to encounter the emergency that is not quite yet at hand, but as things seem to be going well for the moment, the daimyo and his ministers fail to respond to the proposal. When the emergency does arise, a shrewd individual appears, proposing commercial schemes, deceiving money lenders, borrowing money and grain, and somehow coming up with a temporary solution. Such a retainer is then honored for his achievement by the daimyo and his ministers, and immediately given awards, an increase in stipend, and an advancement in status. We are reminded of the ancient fable about the householder who would not heed the warning that the firewood in his house, being piled too closely to the stove pipe, should be moved elsewhere and the stove pipe bent away. One evening, a fire did, of course, break out. The householder then rushed about the neighborhood for help, and, overjoyed that the fire was extinguished with this help, he hosted a feast of fine meats and wines to thank his neighbors. Had he listened to the advice to begin with and shifted the firewood and turned the stove pipe, there would have been neither a fire nor the expense of the feast. Not having profited from the advice of others and thus causing a fire, he then deigned to honor those who extinguished it for him. Similarly, failing to grasp the fundamentals, and indifferent to proper planning, tens of thousands in cash are borrowed to overcome sudden crises. But only the needs of the immediate moment are met. Falling short of comprehending the total context, only the needs of the immediate moment are met – much, as the saying goes, like splashing water over molten lava. When the crisis is over, the level of poverty is worse than before. Kumazawa Banzan was surely looking forward into our time when he observed that the domains were edging slowly toward disaster. Whatever the plan, nothing seems to work any more. Is there, then, a strategy that might still be found to save the current situation?

Response : In general, the technique of managing the economy is akin to a physician administering to an illness. The fundamental approach to curing an ailment is to seek out its basic source, although in an emergency the observable symptoms are directly treated. The same is true of the economy. The construction of a political system is central to any comprehensive form of rule. Without a political system, the customs of society are torn asunder and the needs of the country are not attended to. Under such circumstances, crises cannot be resolved. The reconstruction of the basic system of government in the entire country, however, cannot be achieved through the efforts of a single domain. The entire structure of government must be reorganized if there is to be effective management of the economy. Despite this fact, it would be foolish for a domain to ignore the specific things that might be done for its economy and to allow it to drift steadily toward disaster. Comparable to the physician who ministers to the ailment at hand in an emergency, the pressing disorders within the economy today must be diagnosed and treated.

In ancient Japan, gold and silver were scarce and cash was not minted. Throughout society the use of gold and silver was rare. The needs for cash, too, were satisfied by importing it from other countries. Beginning in the early 1600s the supply of gold and silver increased enormously, and from about 1636 the minting of cash coins also increased. Large transactions were now carried out with gold and silver, and small ones, with cash coins. From this period on, people from throughout the land, regardless of status, began to flock to Edo. The tradition was established whereby all travelling expenses were paid for with money. Even those who did not travel came to behave in this way, relying less on grain and cloth, and more on gold and silver, and believing that wherever one lived, whether it be in the mountains or in the flatlands, the needs of grain and cloth could easily be met as long as one possessed gold and silver. Thus it is that we find ourselves in today's world of money.

Grain is viewed simply in terms of its adequacy for morning and evening meals. And fabric is similarly seen only in its relation to clothing needs. Beyond these considerations, everything is money. Large and small expenses are all paid for from one moment to the next so that the people of today value money 100 times more than in ancient times. Indeed, though one may have adequate food and clothing today, one will find it difficult to make his way in society if short on money. Not only is this true for poor commoners, but also for the aristocracy, including the daimyo. Like merchants, therefore, stipended retainers and daimyo all tend to satisfy their needs with money and thus devise ways to acquire it. This may well be the most urgent task of the day. The best way to earn money is to trade. In one of the domains in the country, trade has been relied on to meet expenses since ancient times. The daimyo of Tsushima governs a small domain, having a rice yield for stipends of barely 20,000 *koku*. However, by buying commodities such as ginseng roots at an inexpensive rate from Korea, controlling these goods within the domain, and selling them at high prices, he has more financial resources to spare than another daimyo with a rice income of 200,000 *koku*. The daimyo of Matsumae rules a domain of 7,000 *koku* of rice. However, he controls the products within the domain as well as goods purchased from the Ainu, and then he sells them at favorable prices. The level of wealth he possesses is thus beyond the reach of other daimyo who may be worth 50,000 *koku* of rice. The daimyo of Tsuwano of Sekishū receives rice income of 40,000 *koku*. By controlling the manufacturing and sale of writing paper, however, his wealth is comparable to 150,000 *koku* of rice. The daimyo of Hamada, also from that same region, learned from Tsuwano and manufactured his own writing paper, so that his wealth grew from 50,000 *koku* of rice to equal the value of 100,000 *koku*. Satsuma is an enormous domain to begin with. But by regulating the import and sale of goods from the Ryūkyū Islands, its wealth exceeds other domains within our seas. Large number of goods are also shipped from China through the Ryūkyūs to Satsuma, and thence to other parts of the country. Tsushima, Satsuma, and Matsumae are examples of domains that have a monopoly on the import and sale of goods from foreign lands so that other daimyo may not be able to emulate them. Others such as Tsuwano and Hamada acquire great wealth by maintaining a monopoly over goods manufactured in their domains, and then selling them through a single outlet. The daimyo of Niimiya, who is also the chief minister for the domain of Kishū, receives a rice income of 30,000 *koku*. By controlling the produce of mountains and seas of Kumano, however, his wealth is comparable to 100,000 *koku*. Strategies can be devised based on the economic practices of these domains, since it must be concluded that every domain, regardless of its relative size, produces something. It may be that some domains will have more specialist produce than others. Where such produce is low, the people of the domain ought to be taught and supervised so that by relying on the natural advantages of the land they will plant, besides the usual grains, anything that might be useful for trade, whether these be trees or grasses, to maximize agricultural production. Moreover, the people should be taught appropriate manufacturing skills so that during moments of leisure when agricultural labor is not called for, they will produce other goods that are useful to human beings, and which will be traded with other domains to contribute to the maintenance of the domainal economy. Such is the technique of enriching the domains.

The domains as a rule calculate their taxes on rice production. Besides this, however, produce harvested in the mountains and the seas, and manufactured goods such as hemp, silk, thread, cotton, wicker baskets, mats, nets, and umbrellas, all sold directly by the people themselves, should also be treated as taxable commodities. The taxable amount may vary from between one-twentieth or one-thirtieth to about one-fiftieth or one-hundredth of the value of the commodity itself. It is also to be paid in cash. In customary language this is called a miscellaneous tax. What remains after the tax is paid is said to be privately owned [*watakushi mono*], and the income derived from trading these goods is entirely personal. This is consistent with ancient law. Many of our domains today, however, do not levy such a tax. The reason seems to be the following. In olden days, farmer-warriors fulfilled their duty by collecting from among commoners a proper allotment of fighting men and horses. The tax on rice, therefore, was merely one part out of ten. A rice field with a yield of 100 *koku*, for example, would be taxed the equivalent of 10 *koku* of unhulled rice. Since the required number of men and horses need not be maintained on a continuous basis, the one-tenth tax on rice sufficed to meet domainal expenses. Since the warrior class is now separated from the peasantry, it is necessary for men and horses to be maintained on a regular basis where the daimyo resides. The tax on rice production is therefore usually about four parts out of ten. Out of a harvest of 100 *koku*, 40 unhulled *koku* are taken. Since the portion of rice production taken as tax is so large, additional taxes on other commodities would cause much suffering among the people. In many places, therefore, these taxes are not levied. Due to the inadequacy of financial resources, however, some domains in recent years have imposed special commodity taxes that did not exist traditionally. The people reacted against them, and in many instances rioted. Much prudence is, indeed, called for.

It would seem in the light of today's economy that the daimyo should purchase with cash the various agricultural and manufactured goods of the domain, and sell them in turn to whoever wishes to buy them then and there. The remaining goods should then be transported by boat or horseback to Edo, Kyoto, and Osaka. When the people, on their own, ship and sell their goods elsewhere, they invariably face transportation costs. A boat will have a shipping charge, and there will be a carrying charge for horseback. Selling goods elsewhere involves a reliance on merchant agents. There will be brokers. There will be meal expenses while spending nights at the agent's home. When the sales are transacted, a commission will be levied by the dealer. There will be workers' fees and offerings to the merchant's protective shrine. And when all is done, there will be some thank-you money for the agent. There are all sorts of fees of this kind involved so that when the various expenses are withdrawn, the remaining income from the sales for the people would not be large. Furthermore, merchants from other domains buy domainal products and sell them to other dealers. There are travel expenses for these merchants going to and from the domain. Should they spend several days where the goods are being produced, there will be meal expenses, in addition to the cost of transportation by boat and horse. These expenses are subtracted from the sales. These merchants invariably buy goods at the lowest possible price and sell them to make the most profit. Since the original producers do not themselves travel to sell their own products, they agree to inexpensive rates, and though they are unburdened by labor and other costs, they still do not make much profit. Now then, the daimyo should apply his cash funds towards buying all the produce of the domain, and carefully measure the advantage of selling them either to a merchant or to an agent. Although the price may be somewhat unfavorable, because the goods would be collected in a central location and transported to large cities such as Osaka to be stored and sold when the market is favorable, the profits that accrue would be much greater than that of goods sold by individuals within the domain. These individuals do not have the workers to transport their goods nor, as mentioned, do they have the funds to cover transportation charges. Since they would welcome the greater profits rather than sell on their own to merchants, they ought not to conceal any of their products and deliver all that they have.

However, should corrupt officials purchase the goods of the people at a price lower than what the people could fetch by selling it on their own, there will be much displeasure among them and they will conceal and surreptitiously sell their products themselves. As there will be laws forbidding such sales, many will be found guilty and the people will rebel. It is generally the feeling among the populace that while taxes on rice to support the daimyo's fixed needs for stipends are reasonable, additional taxes on manufactured goods are not. Thus, they are forced to choose between enduring the hardship of delivering up taxable goods, or sending on inferior goods as tax and selling their better produce to merchants elsewhere. Officials who uncover such practices will seek out the offenders, bringing on additional misery. Failings of this sort emerge when special taxes are placed on domainal products. In our degenerate times, corrupt officials are arrogant in their treatment of the gentle commoners and produce a number of such evils. Were the daimyo to offer their own cash to buy all the produce of the domain and turn it into higher profits happens that, unfortunately, the remaining son passes away, turns out to be incompetent, or becomes physically ill. The daimyo in question then seeks, usually without success, to retrieve the son of his who is being raised by a relative, or seeks to adopt a son from kin or from an unrelated family, thereby maintaining the continuity of the house. The daimyo of Takeda is an example of this in recent times. Considering all besides the eldest son to be an excessive burden, he sent his other sons away to be raised elsewhere. This is an evil practice. Some justification may be found for poverty-stricken retainers or commoners to do so, but it ought not to be practiced among daimyo. What ought to be done about second and third sons so that the course of conduct mentioned above is ended?

Response: This practice can be solved easily. In common parlance, the eldest son of the daimyo is called the "heir apparent" [*seishi*]. In ancient times, he was also called "crown prince" [*taishi*], although this term was not used until later times. The second sons and the ones following are termed "young nobles" [*kōshi*].The heir apparent will succeed the ruling prince. Young nobles are all simply "retainers" [*shin*]. This is obviously true of sons of concubines, but of legitimate wives as well. From the moment of birth they are retainers. They are called young nobles only because they are the children of the ruling prince. The offspring of young nobles are referred to as "noble grandsons" [*kōson*]. These descendants are given new family names, which means the formation of a separate house, or as we say today, acquiring a "surname" [*myōji*]. In ancient times, lords generally possessed only a single family name and did not branch out with new surnames. The lord of Ch'i had only the family name of Chiang; Yu, that of Chi; Sung, that of Tzu; and Ch'en, Kuei. A family name connects descendants in a common lineage. Minamoto, Taira, Fujiwara, and Tachibana are examples of this in Japan. Branch surnames were introduced to clarify the family genealogy as descendents separated and spread outward. In Japan, these would be families such as Niita, Ashikaga, Miura, and Hojo. The reason the branch surnames were given long ago to domainal lords and their offspring who were noble descendants, was that the number of young nobles and their offspring proliferated enormously, causing confusion, and so new names were granted to

From an early age onwards they will be instructed in the ways of the proper behavior of a subject, and in the avoidance of extravagance. As they advance, they should observe with unswerving vigor the rules governing vassal-to-lord relations. At twenty, they should be granted a stipend and formally counted among the ranks of the retainers. Their stipends should not be large. Ordinarily, daimyo possessing between 10,000 and 30,000 *koku* of rice income should grant about 200 *koku* to each of his young nobles; from 40–50,000 up to 80–90,000 *koku*, the allotment should be 300 *koku* each; above 100,000 *koku*, about 500 *koku* each; above 200,000 *koku*, about 1000 *koku* each; above 300,000 *koku*, about 1,500 *koku* each; and above 500,000 *koku*, about 2,000 *koku* each. Each daimyo, regardless of the size of his income, should gauge the relative wealth of his domain and not be bound by the above as if they were fixed rules.

To summarize a little further, young nobles rank below high stewards [*taibu*]. They are not assigned formal posts and, therefore, should not be entrusted with political responsibilities. They may be used as high-ranking envoys making ritual calls on the Bakufu. In military matters as well, they should be subordinated to the high stewards. Should a member of this group possess outstanding talent, he might be assigned, according to his special ability, to an official position. If he is endowed with moral virtue, he may also be promoted to the position of high steward and entrusted with political duties. Among the large domains, many young nobles and noble grandsons are advanced as retainers into the ranks of high stewards, and assigned political duties. On rare occasions, however, some of them are raised to the levels of middle and upper retainers, and given administrative posts. This is a good thing. A person such as this may rise up, perhaps, even become the ruling prince himself. Even if these nobles continued over some time as retainers or as administrators, should the lord not have a legitimate successor, one of these might then be allowed to succeed the lord. They might also succeed to the house of a kin who does not have an heir. As remarked above about these families, a young noble obviously should inherit the stipend granted to the noble as a retainer. And then, from one generation to the next, a son should continue to inherit that stipend. Should there not be a legitimate heir, an illegitimate son may be selected. If such a succession, unfortunately, is still unavailable, an appropriate candidate should be sought from a related house in another area. If even then an heir cannot be found, the house should be done away with, by which is meant destroying it. The house should not continue by adopting sons of unrelated noble families. This is in accordance with ancient law. It is because, in defiance of ancient law, heirs are adopted from unrelated noble families to maintain the continuity of the house that the number of noble grandson families has proliferated, and with it, the amount of stipends needed has also increased, causing the decline of the governing house.

It is a common practice today for a daimyo above seventeen who does not yet have an heir to designate a successor in the event of an unexpected emergency while out on his travels. This is commonly referred to as "provisional adoption." If young nobles were not sent out of the domain and raised entirely within it, such provisional adoptions outside the house would be unnecessary. If this were practiced, the ancestral domain would also be protected from outside usurpation. Now, if it is the misfortune of the daimyo not to have a son and also to lack young nobles and noble grandsons, the blood line of the house is then broken as an act of Heaven. Being enraged by it means nothing. If daimyo plan on making young nobles and noble grandson retainers, this should also be stated before such children are born, and then raised accordingly from birth. A lack of resolve about this ancient rule will result in children being raised at the first as princes and later being precipitously demoted, invariably causing much resentment. The decline and fall of a domain will have begun. Young nobles and noble grandsons are thus best handled according to ancient law. Given the social mores of our day, it will prove to be impossible to raise children bearing the title of "son of the lord," even if the stipends mentioned earlier were to be increased fivefold.

Index

*